Get to know *our* ships
...up close and personal

SAULT STE. MARIE

Home to the famous Soo Locks and situated near Lake Superior lighthouses, Tahquamenon Falls, and thrilling casino action, Sault Ste. Marie is the perfect place for your Northern Michigan adventure!

World-class museums, spectacular natural sights and the down-home hospitality of the Upper Peninsula are yours for the taking in Sault Ste. Marie.

Great Lakes Shipwreck Museum & Whitefish Point Lighthouse
(906) 635-1742
www.shipwreckmuseum.com

Soo Locks Boat Tours and Dinner Cruises
1-800-432-6301
www.soolocks.com

Kewadin Casino
1-800-539-2346
www.kewadin.com

Tahquamenon Falls
(906) 492-3415
One of the largest waterfalls east of the Mississippi River

Museum Ship Valley Camp & Tower of History
1-888-744-7867
www.saulthistoricsites.com

Below: The *Edgar B. Speer* is upbound off Rotary Island, Sault Ste. Marie, Michigan

Sault Ste Marie
PURE MICHIGAN℠

Choose from over 1200 hotel rooms and reserve yours online at
www.saultstemarie.com
1-800-647-2858

1

2

Contents

ISBN: 978-1-891849-20-6 © 2015
*No part of this book may be
published, broadcast, rewritten or
redistributed without permission.*

Marine Publishing Co. Inc.
317 S. Division St. #8
Ann Arbor, MI 48104
1-855-KYS-SHIP (855-597-7447)
roger@knowyourships.com
KnowYourShips.com

Researchers: Matt Miner,
Wade P. Streeter, John Vournakis
and George Wharton
Crew: Kathryn O'Gould, Nancy
Kuharevicz, Audrey LeLievre, Neil
Schultheiss, William Soleau

Editor/Publisher: Roger LeLievre
Founder: Tom Manse

COVER: Alpena, oldest operating steamer on the lakes, at Duluth. (Glenn Blaszkiewicz)
THIS PAGE: Cuyahoga unloading at Alpena, Mich. (Chanda McClain)
BACK COVER: Algoma Montrealais, St. Marys River. (Roger LeLievre)

Passages

A look at the shipping scene since our last edition

Algoma Quebecois being cut up at the Marine Recycling Corp. yard at Port Colborne, Ont., in early 2014. (Jeff Cameron)

First, there was ice ...

By any measure, the winter of 2013-14 was the most brutal in decades. The U.S. Coast Guard started breaking ice on Dec. 6, 2013, the earliest date ever. Iron ore shipments slipped 20 percent in December and then plunged 37 percent in January.

Ice conditions were even worse in March. Vessels were stuck for days all around the lakes. The first convoy headed downbound to Gary, Ind., should have taken 62 hours to make the run but ended up taking 11 days. It took the *Stewart J. Cort* 30 days to deliver its first cargo. *American Spirit, Edgar B. Speer, Presque Isle* and *CSL Assiniboine* were among vessels that incurred serious ice damage.

There was little relief in April. The U.S. and Canadian coast guards, the latter augmented by the East Coast icebreakers *Pierre Radisson, Martha L. Black* and *Des Grosilliers*, had to convoy vessels across Lake Superior until May 2. It wasn't until April 13 that a vessel was able to enter Marquette Harbor and load ore. As April came to an end, the lakes iron ore trade totaled just 6.2 million tons, a decrease of 43 percent compared to the same point in 2013. Even at the end of June, iron ore cargoes were still down by 17 percent. Several lakers that had not been scheduled to operate in 2014 – *John J. Boland, Adam E. Cornelius, Algoma Progress* and *Algoma Montrealais* – were reactivated to help narrow the gap in iron ore, coal, grain and other cargoes.

The good news? All that snow and ice led to an impressive rebounding of Great Lakes water levels during 2014.

Canadian Coast Guard's Pierre Radisson to the rescue on Lake Erie. (Paul Beesley)

Herbert C. Jackson, Paul R. Tregurtha, James R. Barker and Radcliffe R. Latimer beset on the upper St. Marys River. (Paul Beesley)

USCG Mackinaw cutting a track for Stewart J. Cort. *(Paul Beesley)*

American Integrity and Indiana Harbor. *(Sean Vary)*

USCG Biscayne Bay breaks a track for Arthur M. Anderson. *(John Rice)*

U.S. COAST GUARD

104

Erika Kobasic breaking ice at Escanaba, Mich. The ore dock is in the background *(John Rice)*

More boats were scrapped ...

As 2015 began, we said farewell to the last steam-powered lake vessel sailing under the Canadian flag, Algoma Central Corp.'s 1962-built *Algoma Montrealais* (see below). Reactivated due to demand in 2014, she sailed much of the season and then laid up for the last time at Montreal. An overseas scrap tow will likely take place in 2015. ... Algoma Central Corp. also retired its *Algoma Transfer* and *Algoma Progress*. The former – a hybrid of several vessels, one dating back to the days of World War II – arrived at Port Colborne, Ont., to be scrapped in the spring, while the latter, a self-unloader built in 1968, made her final port there in late December 2014. ... A little less clear-cut is the fate of the former American Steamship Co. steamer *American Fortitude* (ex-*Ernest T. Weir* and *Courtney Burton*). The vessel was sold for scrap in 2014 ... maybe (see Page 12).

THE LAST STEAMER

Once there were hundreds. Now there are no steam-powered vessels left sailing under the Canadian flag. The retirement of the classic laker *Algoma Montrealais* at the end of the 2014 shipping season marked the end of an era. The vessel was built in 1962 for the Papachristidis Co. Ltd. as *Montrealais*, and passed to Upper Lakes Shipping Ltd. in 1972. By 2011, she was at work for the Algoma Central Corp. as *Algoma Montrealais*. Her last season found her as busy as always, carrying ore, grain and cement up and down the lakes and St. Lawrence Seaway.

Above, damaged in a 1980 collision. Below, painted in Upper Lakes Shipping colors. (Roger LeLievre Collection)

Algoma Montrealais Inbound at Duluth, Minn., for the final time on Dec. 1, 2014. (Glenn Blaszkiewicz)

American Fortitude began sailing in 1952 as Ernest T. Weir. (Peter B. Worden Collection)

FAREWELL TO THE FORTITUDE

The 1953-built steamer *American Fortitude* reached the end of the line in 2014, when she was sold for scrap to a Brownsville, Texas, firm. She was christened *Ernest T. Weir* (2) for the National Steel Corporation, and sailed on their behalf until 1978, when she was purchased by the Columbia Transportation Div., Oglebay Norton Co., as a replacement for the lost *Edmund Fitzgerald*. Rechristened *Courtney Burton*, she sailed under that name until the Oglebay Norton fleet was bought in 2006 by the American Steamship Co. She was renamed *American Fortitude*, although (other than the stack) she was never painted in their colors. The vessel was laid up in Toledo, Ohio, in late 2008, and never ran again. Towed as far as Montreal for scrap in late 2014, the Brownsville deal fell through and the tow returned to the lakes for winter layup at Oswego, N.Y. *American Fortitude* will probably end up at a Great Lakes scrapyard in 2015.

Scrap tow in Lake Erie on Nov. 26, 2014. (Graham Grattan)

American Fortitude on the St. Marys River, July 1, 2006. (Roger LeLievre)

Plans have been abandoned to turn the 1904-built J.B. Ford into a marine museum. She will likely be scrapped instead. (Roger LeLievre, 1978)

2 MORE ALGOMAS GONE

Algoma Progress and *Algoma Transfer* were declared surplus tonnage and sent to the boneyard by the Algoma Central Corp. last season. The *Algoma Progress'* story is pretty straightforward – she was built as a self-unloader in 1968 as *Canadian Progress* for Upper Lake Shipping Ltd., and was renamed *Algoma Progress* in 2011 after a fleet merger with Algoma. The *Algoma Transfer's* history is a little more complicated, since the forward end and cargo section came from one vessel, the 1943-built *J.H. Hillman Jr.* (later *Crispin Oglebay*-2) and the aft section was added on from the *Cabot* (later *Canadian Explorer*). She was a unique hybrid, a Great Lakes workhorse with a career that included time spent as a cargo transfer vessel at Hamilton, Ont., named, appropriately, *Hamilton Transfer*.

Algoma Progress in the Welland Canal on the way to the scrapper, Dec. 30, 2014. (Ted Wilush)

SWL 757 KG

Transitions, lay-ups ...

The 1906-built *St. Marys Challenger* made the change from a powered steamer to a barge in early 2014, much to the dismay of maritime history fans. ... The saltwater tanker *Algoma Hansa* came under the Canadian flag in 2014 as a replacement for the aging *Algoeast* (ex-*Texaco Brave* and *Imperial St. Lawrence*). ...*American Victory* and *Edward L. Ryerson* continue in long-term lay-up at Superior, Wis. ... *American Valor* and *Sarah Spencer* are laid up at Toledo, Ohio. The barge *McKee Sons* is now inactive at Muskegon, Mich. ... A new life awaits the 1902-vintage steamer *Columbia*, being refurbished at Toledo, Ohio, by New York's S.S. Columbia Project. The group hopes to restore the former Detroit River passenger vessel to operation on the East Coast.

Algoeast in 2001. *(Jeff Cameron)*

Barge St. Marys Challenger inbound at Grand Haven Jan. 11, 2015, assisted by the tug Meredith Ashton. *(Sam Hankinson)*

Tug Capt. Keith tows Columbia to Toledo for drydocking. (Wade P. Streeter)

Fleets greet new members ...

More new, high-efficiency Canadian-flagged vessels came to the Great Lakes from China-based shipyards in 2014. First was Algoma Central Corp.'s *Algoma Harvester*, christened at Hamilton, Ont., last July 17. At the beginning of 2015, *CWB Marquis* and *CSL St.-Laurent* arrived. They will begin service on the lakes and seaway in 2015, as will *CWB Strongfield* and *CSL Welland*. The CWB boats are owned by the Canadian Wheat Board and operated by Algoma Central Corp. The CSL vessels belong to Montreal-based Canada Steamship Lines. ... One to watch out for in mid-2015 is the rebuilt saltwater tanker *Lalandia Swan*, being converted in China to a Great Lakes/St. Lawrence Seaway self-unloader for Canada's Lower Lakes Towing. Her new name, *Manitoulin*, has been carried by many Great Lakes vessels in the past.

Algoma Harvester loading her first cargo, at Superior, Wis. (Gene Onchulenko)

Crewmembers watch the Algoma Harvester christening at Hamilton, Ont. (Ted Wilush)

Algoma Harvester arriving at Hamilton, Ont., on her maiden voyage, July, 16, 2014. (Ted Wilush)

CSL Welland arrives at Montreal, Que., on Jan. 2, 2015. (René Beauchamp)

CWB Marquis, en route to the Great Lakes from a Chinese shipyard, taking on fuel at Davao City, Philippines, on Nov. 11, 2014. *(Dennis VandenEyenden)*

CSL WELLAND

Extraordinary Equinox ...

When *'Know Your Ships'* was offered the chance to check out Canada's new *Algoma Equinox*, we jumped at the opportunity. The first in a series of eight technologically advanced ships Algoma is building in China as part of a $400 million fleet renewal program, the vessel represents the next step in the evolution of Great Lakes and Seaway shipping on the Canadian side of the lakes.

Algoma Equinox on the St. Marys River in 2014.

During our visit, the *Equinox* loaded 29,600 tons of Canadian wheat at one of the seemingly endless elevators that dot the waterfront at Thunder Bay, Ont., beneath the looming presence of one of the area's most striking natural features, Mount McKay. The cargo would be unloaded at Baie Comeau, Que., on the eastern end of the St. Lawrence Seaway, six days hence.

Her stats are impressive. *Algoma Equinox* is 45 percent more efficient than older members of the fleet. It also operates with a closed-loop, exhaust gas scrubbing system that eliminates 97 percent of all sulfur oxide emissions coming from the stack. Exhaust and heat become water vapor. Solids and chemicals in the exhaust are collected, stored in a tank and disposed of ashore. Since this is the first application of an IMO-approved integrated scrubber on a Great Lakes/St. Lawrence Seaway vessel, technicians from the manufacturer were continuing to tweak the system as *KYS* rode along.

For this trip, Capt. Seann O'Donoughue was relief master, filling in for regular skipper Capt. Ross Armstrong. Charlene Coady was first mate. Chief engineer was Francois Tremblay, and Yohan Laberge was second engineer. Chief cook was Cheryl Hobley, and second cook / baker was Abderrahmane Bouaraba.

"We've got an energetic group of people, and everybody is learning the new ship together and working as a team to learn the handling, ballasting, the new technology and where everything is stowed," said O'Donoughue. "The ship was built to international standards. We have to 'Canadianize' it –make it specific to our Great Lakes trade. Just getting used to certain things – spotting the ship for the locks, handling the ship in the rivers, the higher speed – it's a challenge."

The ship has an efficient design, with no sense that corners were cut in order to save money. There's even some wood trim in the hallways and in the pilothouse. Being a new boat, there's a conscious effort to keep her clean, and the sight of a crewman with a feather duster or a wax mop is common. *Algoma Equinox* rides smoothly compared to other diesel-driven lakers, with noticeably less vibration and significantly less noise. ➡

Each member of the crew has a private cabin and washroom, with a bed, desk and wardrobe. Everyone has satellite TV and broadband Internet. There are two rec rooms and an exercise room. Among the *Algoma Equinox*'s most striking features are the wraparound, floor-to-ceiling windows on the bridge that provide unparalleled visibility.

"It really feels like a starship bridge," agreed O'Donoughue. "Your field of view is so wide, and you can see exactly what the ship is doing. Even though we have a high degree of electronics, shiphandling on the Great Lakes is a highly visual and hands-on thing. We have to be able to see, feel, and anticipate what the ship is doing. We've got three stations for navigating the vessel on the bridge … the design is set up to a global standard with everything at your fingertips."

Capt. Seann O'Donoughue (center), flanked by mates Ian D'Mello and Charlene Coady.

The Equinox-class vessels were designed in Finland, the main engine is from Germany's Wärtsilä, the steering gear was manufactured by Rolls-Royce and the bridge systems are by Sperry and a host of other familiar names. The crew is from Canada and speaks French as well as English. Although her parts may have been assembled in China, at Nantong Mingde Heavy Industries, the vessel has a distinct international feel.

O'Donoughue said he understands the sentiment of people who wish the vessel had

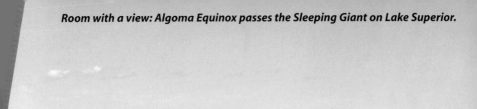

Room with a view: Algoma Equinox passes the Sleeping Giant on Lake Superior.

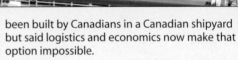

been built by Canadians in a Canadian shipyard but said logistics and economics now make that option impossible.

"I know we would like to have built the ship here, but there really is no yard that can do it," he said. "And there are no experienced workers now in the labor force that you'd need in Canada. The best, most economical way to build a ship is to go to a yard that's used to building ships.

"We went to a designer, Delta Marine, that knows ships and designs them for all aspects of the marine industry and said, 'We need a specialized ship for the Great Lakes to handle a specific way and to have specific dimensions and details, including environmental requirements, the space for ballast water equipment and new emission standards. The ship had to be fuel efficient and still be a Great Lakes ship and a good carrier.' They had to work out a design to have a high-speed, fuel-efficient hull and a longevity of 40 years. A lot of work went into designing it. I think they built a nice ship.

"Once the ship was designed, it went out to tender to all the different yards. The company had an eye to how many ships it would need to replace the fleet and to the future."

He said fleet renewal just makes sense. Algoma's efforts are being mirrored by Canada Steamship Lines, which has also welcomed several new vessels to the fleet the past few years with more to come, as has Montreal-based Fednav. "Marine transportation is here to stay. It is much more fuel-efficient and environmentally friendly," he observed. ➲

Top: The center of three control locations on the bridge. Bottom: Top view of an engine.

Loading wheat at Thunder Bay, Ont.

O'Donoughue started his sailing career in 1984 at age of 16 on the brigantine *Playfair*. He's one of those guys who can take a demanding job – conning a ship through a busy harbor for example – and make it look easy. He enjoys lighthearted banter, he laughs easily and is quick with a joke, and there's a good-natured camaraderie evident among the 18 crewmembers, many of whom tend to be on the younger side.

"I found my love for sailing and the Great Lakes with the tall ships. I spent my first five years sailing the summers in high school …I've been with Algoma since 1989," he recalled. "I'm originally from Montreal, I spent summers along the St. Lawrence Seaway as a kid, which is where I spawned my passion for the ships."

O'Donoughue, 46, is active in the International Shipmasters' Association and is the group's past president. He's passionate about his current role as chairman of the ISMA scholarship fund that helps aspiring mariners attend the Great Lakes Maritime Academy at Traverse City, Mich., and Georgian College in Owen Sound, Ont., as well as offering hawsepipe scholarships to those who choose to advance through the ranks instead of attending the academies.

He takes every opportunity aboard ship to pass on his skills to the up-and-comers.

Arriving at Thunder Bay under the watchful presence of Mount McKay.

"We get the young guys, teach the new crew. That's part of the job," he said. "Most of our captains have been trained to be teachers. A lot of guys are retiring, there are going to be lots of job openings in the Great Lakes fleet in the next 10-20 years."

For O'Donoughue – who left for China last fall to take command of the third vessel of the Equinox series, the *CWB Marquis,* and bring her back to the Great Lakes – sailing was the right choice.

"When I was a kid I thought ships were big and cool, and I still think that. I love it," he said. – *Story, photos by Roger LeLievre*

Algoma Equinox is the first in a series of eight Equinox-class vessels being built at Nantong Mingde shipyard for the Algoma Central Corp. She was followed in 2014 by Algoma Harvester and CWB Marquis. More will be arriving in 2015.

Top: Chief Cook Cheryl Hobley and second cook / baker Abderrahmane Bouaraba. Below: A light moment between Capt. O'Donoughue and Chief Engineer Francois Tremblay.

AAA CLASS – Vessel design popular on the Great Lakes in the early 1950s. *Arthur M. Anderson* is one example.

AFT – Toward the back, or stern, of a ship.

AHEAD – Forward.

AMIDSHIPS – The middle point of a vessel, referring to either length or width.

ARTICULATED TUG/BARGE (ATB) – Tug-barge combination. The two vessels are mechanically linked in one axis but with the tug free to move, or articulate, on another axis.

BACKHAUL – The practice of carrying a revenue-producing cargo (rather than ballast) on a return trip from hauling a primary cargo.

BARGE – Vessel with no engine, either pushed or pulled by a tug.

BEAM – The width of a vessel measured at the widest point.

BILGE – Lowest part of a hold or compartment, generally where the rounded side of a ship curves from the keel to the vertical sides.

BOW – Front of a vessel.

BOW THRUSTER – Propeller mounted transversely in a vessel's bow under the water line to assist in moving sideways. A stern thruster may also be installed.

BRIDGE – The platform above the main deck from which a ship is steered/navigated. Also: PILOTHOUSE or WHEELHOUSE.

BULKHEAD – Wall or partition that separates rooms, holds or tanks within a ship's hull.

BULWARK – The part of the ship that extends fore and aft above the main deck to form a rail.

DATUM – Level of water in a given area, determined by an average over time.

DEADWEIGHT TONNAGE – The actual carrying capacity of a vessel, equal to the difference between the light displacement tonnage and the heavy displacement tonnage, expressed in long tons (2,240 pounds or 1,016.1 kilograms).

DECK SPRINKLERS: The reason for water spraying on a vessel's deck is to help cool the upper part of a boat and prevent hogging (bending due to temperature differences above and below the waterline). With decks exposed to the sun all day the surface can get very hot. The hull of the boat under water stays cooler. Hogging can affect cargo capacity and the depth to which a boat can load.

DISPLACEMENT TONNAGE – The actual weight of the vessel and everything aboard her, measured in long tons. The displacement is equal to the weight of the water displaced by the vessel. Displacement tonnage may be qualified as light, indicating the weight of the vessel without cargo, fuel and stores, or heavy, indicating the weight of the vessel loaded with cargo, fuel and stores.

DRAFT – The depth of water a ship needs to float. Also, the distance from keel to water line.

FIT OUT – The process of preparing a vessel for service after a period of inactivity.

FIVE-YEAR INSPECTION – U.S. Coast Guard survey, conducted in a drydock every five years, of a vessel's hull, machinery and other components.

FLATBACK – Lakes slang for a non-self-unloader.

FOOTER – Lakes slang for 1,000-foot vessel.

FOREPEAK – The space below the forecastle.

FORWARD – Toward the front, or bow, of a ship.

FREEBOARD – The distance from the water line to the main deck.

GEARLESS VESSEL – One that is not a self-unloader.

GROSS TONNAGE – The internal space of a vessel, measured in units of 100 cubic feet (2.83 cubic meters) = a gross ton.

HATCH – An opening in the deck through which cargo is lowered or raised. A hatch is closed by securing a hatch cover over it.

IMO # – Unique number issued by International Maritime Organization, or IMO, to ships for identification. Not all vessels have an IMO number.

INTEGRATED TUG/BARGE (ITB) – Tug-barge combination in which the tug is rigidly mated to the barge. *Presque Isle* is one example.

IRON DECKHAND – Mechanical device that runs on rails on a vessel's main deck and is used to remove and replace hatch covers.

JONES ACT – A U.S. cabotage law that mandates that cargoes moved between American ports be carried by U.S.-flagged, U.S.-built and U.S.-crewed vessels.

KEEL – A ship's steel backbone. It runs along the lowest part of the hull.

LAID UP or **LAY-UP** – Out of service.

MARITIME CLASS – Style of lake vessel built during World War II as part of the nation's war effort. *Mississagi* is one example.

NET REGISTERED TONNAGE – The internal capacity of a vessel available for carrying cargo. It does not include the space occupied by boilers, engines, shaft alleys, chain lockers or officers' and crew's quarters. Net registered tonnage is usually referred to as registered tonnage or net tonnage and is used to calculate taxes, tolls and port charges.

RIVER CLASS SELF-UNLOADER – Group of vessels built in the 1970s to service smaller ports and negotiate narrow rivers such as Cleveland's Cuyahoga. *Manitowoc* is one example.

SELF-UNLOADER – Vessel able to discharge its own cargo using a system of conveyor belts and a movable boom.

STEM – The extreme forward end of the bow.

STEMWINDER – Vessel with all cabins aft (also sternwinder).

STERN – The back of the ship.

STRAIGHT-DECKER – Non-self-unloading vessel.

TACONITE – Processed, pelletized iron ore. Easy to load and unload, this is the primary type of ore shipped on the Great Lakes and St. Lawrence Seaway. Also known as pellets (see below).

TRACTOR TUG – Highly maneuverable tug propelled by either a Z-drive or cycloidal system rather than the traditional screw propeller.

TURKEY TRAIL – Route from North Channel (above Manitoulin Island) into the St. Marys River, named for the many courses which zigzag through the area's islands, shoals and ports.

Fleet Listings

Baie St. Paul and Cedarglen meet in the St. Marys River. (Roger LeLievre)

BAIE ST. PAUL

TRILLIUM CLASS

1CH1

CEDARGLEN

Listed after each vessel in order are: Type of Vessel, Year Built, Type of Engine, Maximum Cargo Capacity (at midsummer draft in long tons) or Gross Tonnage*, Overall Length, Breadth and Depth (from the top of the keel to the top of the upper deck beam) or Draft*. Only vessels over 30 feet long are included. The figures given are as accurate as possible and are given for informational purposes only. Vessels and owners are listed alphabetically as per American Bureau of Shipping and Lloyd's Register of Shipping format. Builder yard and location, as well as other pertinent information, are listed for major vessels; former names of vessels and years of operation under the former names appear in parentheses. A number in brackets following a vessel's name indicates how many vessels, including the one listed, have carried that name.

KEY TO TYPE OF VESSEL

2B ....Brigantine	DS...Spud Barge	PF ....Passenger Ferry
2S ....2-Masted Schooner	DV..Drilling Vessel	PK.......................Package Freighter
3S ....3-Masted Schooner	DW ....Scow	PV ....Patrol Vessel
4S ....4-Masted Schooner	ES ....Excursion Ship	RR........................Roll On/Roll Off
AC...............................Auto Carrier	EV ....Environmental Response	RT ....Refueling Tanker
AT ....Articulated Tug	FB ....Fireboat	RV..........................Research Vessel
ATB ....Articulated Tug/Barge	FD........................Floating Dry Dock	SB ....Supply Boat
BC................................Bulk Carrier	GC ....General Cargo	SC ....Sand Carrier
BK....................Bulk Carrier/Tanker	GL......................................Gate Lifter	SR ....Search & Rescue
BT................................Buoy Tender	GU ....Grain Self-Unloader	SU........................... Self-Unloader
CA ....Catamaran	HL..........Heavy Lift Vessel	SV ....Survey Vessel
CC ....Cement Carrier	IB ....Ice Breaker	TB ....Tugboat
CF ....Car Ferry	IT ....Integrated Tug	TF ....Train Ferry
CO ....Container Vessel	ITB................Integrated Tug/Barge	TK .... Tanker
CS ....Crane Ship	MB ....Mailboat	TS ....Tall Ship
DB ....Deck Barge	MU ....Museum Vessel	TT ....Tractor Tugboat
DH..............................Hopper Barge	PA ....Passenger Vessel	TV.............................. Training Vessel
DR...Dredge	PB .... Pilot Boat	TW .... Towboat

KEY TO PROPULSION

B...Barge	R.....................Steam – Triple Exp. Compound Engine
D...Diesel	S............................ Steam – Skinner "Uniflow" Engine
DE.. Diesel Electric	T..Steam – Turbine Engine
Q ....Steam – Quad Exp. Compound Engine	W ....Sailing Vessel (Wind)

Fleet Name Vessel Name	IMO #	Vessel Type	Year Built	Engine Type	Cargo Cap. or Gross*	Overall Length	Breadth	Depth
A-1 **ABACO MARINE TOWING LLC, CLAYTON, NY**								
Bowditch		TB	1954	D	76*	65' 00"	22' 00"	8' 04"
Built: Missouri Valley Steel, Inc., Leavenworth, KS (Oriskany, Hot Dog)								
Carina		TB	1954	D	64*	61' 05"	17' 09"	8' 03"
Built: Higgins Inc., New Orleans, LA (Charles R. Higgins, Augusta Withington)								
A-2 **ALGOMA CENTRAL CORP., ST. CATHARINES, ON.** *(algonet.com)*								
Algolake	7423093	SU	1977	D	32,807	730' 00"	75' 00"	46' 06"
Built: Collingwood Shipyards, Collingwood, ON								
Algoma Conveyor	9619268	SU	2015	D	36,800	740' 00"	78' 00"	48' 03
Built: Nantong Mingde Heavy Industry Co., Ltd., Nantong City, China								
Algoma Discovery	8505848	BC	1987	D	34,380	729' 09"	75' 09"	48' 05"
Built: 3 Maj Brodogradiliste d.d., Rijeka, Croatia (Malinska '87-'97, Daviken '97-'08)								
Algoma Enterprise	7726677	SU	1979	D	33,854	730' 00"	75' 11"	46' 07"
Built: Port Weller Dry Docks, Port Weller, ON (Canadian Enterprise '79-'11)								
Algoma Equinox	9613927	BC	2013	D	39,400	740' 00"	78' 00"	48' 03
Built: Nantong Mingde Heavy Industry Co., Ltd., Nantong City, China								
Algoma Guardian	8505850	BC	1987	D	34,380	729' 09"	75' 09"	48' 05"
Built: 3 Maj Brodogradiliste d.d., Rijeka, Croatia (Omisalj '87-'97, Goviken '97-'08)								
Algoma Harvester	9613939	BC	2014	D	39,400	740' 00"	78' 00"	48' 03
Built: Nantong Mingde Heavy Industry Co., Ltd., Nantong City, China								
Algoma Mariner	9587893	SU	2011	D	37,399	740' 00"	77' 11"	49' 03
Built: Chengxi Shipyard Co. Ltd., Jiangyin City, China (Laid down as Canadian Mariner {2})								

Algoma Navigator 6707961 SU 1967 D 30,324 729' 00" 75' 10" 40' 06"
Built: J. Readhead & Sons, South Shields, England; converted from a saltwater bulk carrier in '80; converted to a self-unloader in '97; both conversions by Port Weller Dry Docks, St. Catharines, ON (Demeterton '67-'75, St. Lawrence Navigator '75-'80, Canadian Navigator '80-'81)

Algoma Niagara 9619311 SU 2015 D 36,800 740' 00" 78' 00" 48' 03
Built: Nantong Mingde Heavy Industry Co., Ltd., Nantong City, China

Algoma Olympic 7432783 SU 1976 D 33,859 730' 00" 75' 00" 46' 06"
Built: Port Weller Dry Docks, Port Weller, ON (Canadian Olympic '76-'11)

Algoma Sault 9619294 SU 2015 D 36,800 740' 00" 78' 00" 48' 03
Built: Nantong Mingde Heavy Industry Co., Ltd., Nantong City, China

Algoma Spirit 8504882 BC 1986 D 34,380 729' 00" 75' 09" 48' 05"
Built: 3 Maj Brodogradiliste d.d., Rijeka, Croatia (Petka '86-'00, Sandviken '00-'08)

Algoma Transport {2} 7711737 SU 1979 D 32,678 730' 00" 75' 11" 46' 07"
Built: Port Weller Dry Docks, Port Weller, ON (Canadian Transport '79-'11)

Algomarine 6816607 SU 1968 D 26,755 730' 00" 75' 00" 39' 08"
Built: Davie Shipbuilding Co., Lauzon, QC; converted to a self-unloader by Port Weller Dry Docks, St. Catharines, ON, in '89 (Lake Manitoba '68-'87)

Algorail {2} 6805531 SU 1968 D 23,810 640' 05" 72' 00" 40' 00"
Built: Collingwood Shipyards, Collingwood, ON

Algosoo {2} 7343619 SU 1974 D 30,284 730' 00" 75' 00" 44' 06"
Built: Collingwood Shipyards, Collingwood, ON; last Great Lakes vessel built with cabins at the bow

Algosteel {2} 6613299 SU 1966 D 26,949 730' 00" 75' 00" 39' 08"
Built: Davie Shipbuilding Co., Lauzon, QC; converted to a self-unloader by Port Weller Dry Docks, St. Catharines, ON, in '89 (A. S. Glossbrenner '66-'87, Algogulf {1} '87-'90)

Algoway {2} 7221251 SU 1972 D 23,812 646' 06" 72' 00" 40' 00"
Built: Collingwood Shipyards, Collingwood, ON

Algowood 7910216 SU 1981 D 32,253 740' 00" 75' 11" 46' 06"
Built: Collingwood Shipyards, Collingwood, ON; lengthened 10' in '00 at Port Weller Dry Docks, St. Catharines, ON

Capt. Henry Jackman 8006323 SU 1981 D 30,590 730' 00" 75' 11" 42' 00"
Built: Collingwood Shipyards, Collingwood, ON; converted to a self-unloader by Port Weller Dry Docks, St. Catharines, ON, in '96 (Lake Wabush '81-'87)

John B. Aird 8002432 SU 1983 D 31,000 730' 00" 75' 10" 46' 06"
Built: Collingwood Shipyards, Collingwood, ON

John D. Leitch 6714586 SU 1967 D 34,127 730' 00" 77' 11" 45' 00"
Built: Port Weller Dry Docks, Port Weller, ON; rebuilt with new mid-body, widened 3' by the builders in '02 (Canadian Century '67-'02)

Peter R. Cresswell 8016641 SU 1982 D 30,590 730' 00" 75' 11" 42' 00"
Built: Collingwood Shipyards, Collingwood, ON; converted to a self-unloader by Port Weller Dry Docks, St. Catharines, ON, in '98 (Algowest '82-'01)

Radcliffe R. Latimer 7711725 SU 1978 D 36,668 740' 00" 77' 11" 49' 03"
Built: Collingwood Shipyards, Collingwood, ON; rebuilt with a new forebody at Chengxi Shipyard Co. Ltd., Jiangyin City, China, in '09 (Algobay '78-'94, Atlantic Trader '94-'97, Algobay '97-'12)

Tim S. Dool 6800919 BC 1967 D 31,054 730' 00" 77' 11" 39' 08"
Built: Saint John Shipbuilding & Drydock Co., Saint John, NB; widened by 3' at Port Weller Dry Docks, St. Catharines, ON, in '96 (Senneville '67-'94, Algoville '94-'08)

Hull 161 (yet to be named) 9619270 SU 2015 D 36,800 740' 00" 78' 00" 48' 03
Built: Nantong Mingde Heavy Industry Co., Ltd., Nantong City, China

A-3 **ALGOMA TANKERS LTD., ST. CATHARINES, ON – DIVISION OF ALGOMA CENTRAL CORP.**

Algocanada 9378591 TK 2008 D 11,453 426' 01" 65' 00" 32' 08"
Built: Eregli Shipyard, Zonguldak, Turkey

Algoma Dartmouth 9327516 RT 2007 D 3,512 296' 11" 47' 11" 24' 11"
Built: Turkter Shipyard, Tuzla, Turkey; vessel is engaged in bunkering operations at Halifax, NS (Clipper Bardolino '07-'08, Samistal Due '08-'09)

Algoma Hansa 9127186 TK 1998 D 16,775 472' 07" 75' 06" 40' 08"
Built: Alabama Shipyard Inc., Mobile, AL (Amalienborg '98-'98)

Algonova {2} 9378589 TK 2008 D 11,453 426' 01" 65' 00" 32' 08"
Built: Eregli Shipyard, Zonguldak, Turkey (Eregli 04 '07-'08)

Algosar {2} 7634288 TK 1978 D 12,000 434' 06" 65' 00" 29' 04"
Built: Levingston Shipbuilding Co., Orange, TX (Gemini '78-'05)

Algoscotia 9273222 TK 2004 D 19,160 488' 03" 78' 00" 42' 00"
Built: Jiangnan Shipyard (Group) Co. Ltd., Shangahi, China

Algosea 9127198 TK 1998 D 17,258 472' 07" 75' 04" 40'08"
Built: Alabama Shipyard Inc., Mobile, AL (Aggersborg '98-'05)

Michipicoten off Marquette, Mich., at sunrise. (Rod Burdick)

A-4 OWNED BY CWB (CANADIAN WHEAT BOARD), OPERATED BY ALGOMA CENTRAL CORP. *(cwb.ca)*

CWB Marquis	9613953	BC	2014	D	39,400	740' 00"	78' 00"	48' 03

Built: Nantong Mingde Heavy Industry Co., Ltd., Nantong City, China

CWB Strongfield	9613941	BC	2014	D	39,400	740' 00"	78' 00"	48' 03

Built: Nantong Mingde Heavy Industry Co., Ltd., Nantong City, China

A-5 ALPENA SHIPWRECK TOURS, ALPENA, MI *(alpenashipwrecktours.com)*

Lady Michigan		ES	2010	D	90*	65' 00"	19' 00"	11' 00"

A-6 AMERICAN STEAMSHIP CO., WILLIAMSVILLE, NY *(americansteamship.com)*

Adam E. Cornelius {4}	7326245	SU	1973	D	29,200	680' 00"	78' 00"	42' 00"

Built: American Shipbuilding Co., Toledo, OH; (Roger M. Kyes '73-'89)

American Century	7923196	SU	1981	D	80,900	1,000' 00"	105' 00"	56' 00"

Built: Bay Shipbuilding Co., Sturgeon Bay, WI (Columbia Star '81-'06)

American Courage	7634226	SU	1979	D	24,300	636' 00"	68' 00"	40' 00"

Built: Bay Shipbuilding Co., Sturgeon Bay, WI (Fred R. White Jr. '79-'06)

American Integrity	7514696	SU	1978	D	80,900	1,000' 00"	105' 00"	56' 00"

Built: Bay Shipbuilding Co., Sturgeon Bay, WI (Lewis Wilson Foy '78-'91, Oglebay Norton '91-'06)

American Mariner	7812567	SU	1980	D	37,300	730' 00"	78' 00"	42' 00"

Built: Bay Shipbuilding Co., Sturgeon Bay, WI (Laid down as Chicago {3})

American Spirit	7423392	SU	1978	D	62,400	1,004' 00"	105' 00"	50' 00"

Built: American Shipbuilding Co., Lorain, OH (George A. Stinson '78-'04)

American Valor	5024738	SU	1953	T	26,200	767' 00"	70' 00"	36' 00"

Built: American Shipbuilding Co., Lorain, OH; lengthened 120' by Fraser Shipyard, Superior, WI, in '74; converted to a self-unloader in '82; entered long-term lay-up Nov. 13, 2008, at Toledo, OH (Armco '53-'06)

American Victory	5234395	SU	1942	T	26,700	730' 00"	75' 00"	39' 03"

Built: Bethlehem Shipbuilding and Drydock Co., Sparrows Point, MD; converted from saltwater tanker to a Great Lakes bulk carrier by Maryland Shipbuilding in '61; converted to a self-unloader by Bay Shipbuilding Co., Sturgeon Bay, WI, in '82; entered long-term lay-up Nov. 12, 2008, at Superior, WI (Laid down as Marquette, USS Neshanic [AO-71] '42-'47, Gulfoil '47-'61, Pioneer Challenger '61-'62, Middletown '62-'06)

Buffalo {3}	7620653	SU	1978	D	24,300	634' 10"	68' 00"	40' 00"

Built: Bay Shipbuilding Co., Sturgeon Bay, WI

Burns Harbor {2}	7514713	SU	1980	D	80,900	1,000' 00"	105' 00"	56' 00"

Built: Bay Shipbuilding Co., Sturgeon Bay, WI

H. Lee White {2}	7366362	SU	1974	D	35,400	704' 00"	78' 00"	45' 00"

Built: Bay Shipbuilding Co., Sturgeon Bay, WI

Indiana Harbor	7514701	SU	1979	D	80,900	1,000' 00"	105' 00"	56' 00"

Built: Bay Shipbuilding Co., Sturgeon Bay, WI

John J. Boland {4}	7318901	SU	1973	D	34,000	680' 00"	78' 00"	45' 00"

Built: Bay Shipbuilding Co., Sturgeon Bay, WI (Charles E. Wilson '73-'00)

Sam Laud	7390210	SU	1975	D	24,300	634' 10"	68' 00"	40' 00"

Built: Bay Shipbuilding Co., Sturgeon Bay, WI

St. Clair {3}	7403990	SU	1976	D	44,800	770' 00"	92' 00"	52' 00"

Built: Bay Shipbuilding Co., Sturgeon Bay, WI

Walter J. McCarthy Jr.	7514684	SU	1977	D	80,500	1,000' 00"	105' 00"	56' 00"

Built: Bay Shipbuilding Co., Sturgeon Bay, WI (Belle River '77-'90)

OWNED BY SEAJON LLC, FORT LAUDERDALE, FL; OPERATED BY AMERICAN STEAMSHIP CO.

Ken Boothe Sr.		ATB	2011	D	1,179*	135' 04"	50' 00"	26' 00"

Built: Donjon Shipbuilding & Repair, Erie, PA; paired with the self-unloading barge Lakes Contender

Lakes Contender		SU	2012	B	33,892	740' 04"	78' 00"	45' 00"

Built: Donjon Shipbuilding & Repair, Erie, PA

A-7 AMHERSTBURG FERRY CO. INC, AMHERSTBURG, ON

The Columbia V		PA/CF	1946	D	46*	65' 00"	28' 10"	8' 06"

Built: Champion Auto Ferries, Algonac, MI (Crystal O, St. Clair Flats)

The Ste. Claire V		PA/CF	1997	D	82*	86' 06"	32' 00"	6' 00"

Built: Les Ateliers Maurice Bourbonnais Ltée, Gatineau, QC (Courtney O., M. Bourbonnais)

A-8 ANDRIE INC., MUSKEGON, MI *(andrietg.com)*

A-390		TK	1982	B	2,346*	310' 00"	60' 00"	17' 00"

Built: St. Louis Shipbuilding & Steel Co., St. Louis, MO (Canonie 40 '82-'92)

A-397		TK	1962	B	2,928*	270' 00"	60' 01"	22' 05"

Built: Dravo Corp., Pittsburgh, PA (Auntie Mame '62-'91, Iron Mike '91-'93)

A-410		TK	1955	B	3,793*	335' 00"	54' 00"	17' 00"

Built: Ingalls Shipbuilding Corp., Birmingham, AL (Methane '55-'63, B-6400 '63-'71, Kelly '71-'86, Canonie 50 '86-'93)

Barbara Andrie — 5097187 — TB — 1940 — D — 298* — 122'00" — 29'07" — 16'00"
Built: Pennsylvania Shipyards Inc., Beaumont, TX (Edmond J. Moran '40–'76)
Endeavour — — TK — 2009 — B — 7,232* — 360'00" — 60'00" — 24'00"
Built: Jeffboat LLC, Jeffersonville, IN
Karen Andrie {2} — 6520454 — TB — 1965 — D — 516* — 120'00" — 31'06" — 16'00"
Built: Gulfport Shipbuilding, Port Arthur, TX (Sarah Hays '65–'93)
Rebecca Lynn — 6511374 — TB — 1964 — D — 433* — 112'07" — 31'06" — 16'00"
Built: Gulfport Shipbuilding, Port Arthur, TX (Kathrine Clewis '64–'96)

ANDRIE SPECIALIZED, NORTON SHORES, MI (andriejackup.com)
Meredith Ashton — 8951487 — TB — 1981 — D — 127* — 68'08" — 26'01" — 9'04"
Built: Service Marine Group Inc., Amelia, LA (The Rock, Specialist, Alpha)
Robert W. Purcell — — TB — 1943 — D — 29* — 45'02" — 12'10" — 7'08"
Built: Sturgeon Bay Shipbuilding, Sturgeon Bay, WI

OPERATED BY ANDRIE INC. FOR OCCIDENTAL CHEMICAL CORP., MUSKEGON, MI
Spartan — 7047461 — AT — 1969 — D — 190* — 121'01" — 32'01" — 10'09"
Built: Burton Shipyard, Port Arthur, TX; paired with barge Spartan II
(Lead Horse '69–'73, Gulf Challenger '73–'80, Challenger {2} '80–'93, Mark Hannah '93–'10)
Spartan II — — TK — 1980 — B — 8,050 — 407'01" — 60'00" — 21'00"
Built: Sturgeon Bay Shipbuilding Co., Sturgeon Bay, WI (Hannah 6301 '80–'10)

A-9 APOSTLE ISLANDS CRUISES INC., BAYFIELD, WI (apostleisland.com)
Ashland Bayfield Express — — PA — 1995 — D — 13* — 49'00" — 18'05" — 5'00"
Island Princess {2} — — ES — 1973 — D — 63* — 65'07" — 20'05" — 7'03"

A-10 ARCELORMITTAL MINES CANADA INC., MONTREAL, QC (arcelormittal.com/minescanada)
Brochu — 7305899 — TT — 1973 — — 390* — 98'11" — 36'00" — 12'04"
Built: Star Shipyards Ltd., New Westminster, BC
Vachon — 7305904 — TT — 1973 — D — 390* — 98'11" — 36'00" — 12'04"
Built: Star Shipyards Ltd., New Westminster, BC

A-11 ARGEE BOAT CRUISES LTD., PENETANGUISHENE, ON (georgianbaycruises.com)
Georgian Queen — — ES — 1918 — D — 249* — 119'00" — 36'00" — 16'06"
Built: Port Arthur Shipbuilding, Port Arthur, ON (Victoria '18–'18, Murray Stewart '18–'48, David Richard '48–'79)

A-12 ARNOLD TRANSIT CO., MACKINAC ISLAND, MI (arnoldline.com)
Algomah — — PF/PK — 1961 — D — 81* — 93'00" — 29'08" — 5'02"
Built: Paasch Marine Services Inc., Erie, PA
Beaver — — CF — 1952 — D — 84* — 64'09" — 30'02" — 6'05"
Built: Lock City Machine/Marine, Sault Ste. Marie, MI
Chippewa {6} — — PF/PK — 1962 — D — 81* — 93'00" — 29'08" — 5'02"
Built: Paasch Marine Services Inc., Erie, PA
Corsair — — CF — 1955 — D — 98* — 94'06" — 33'01" — 8'01"
Built: Blount Marine Corp., Warren, RI
Huron {5} — — PF/PK — 1955 — D — 99* — 91'06" — 25'00" — 7'00"
Built: Paasch Marine Services Inc., Erie, PA
Island Express — — PF/CA — 1988 — D — 90* — 82'07" — 28'06" — 8'04"
Built: Gladding-Hearn Shipbuilding, Somerset, MA
Isle Royale Queen III — — PA — 1959 — D — 88* — 74'03" — 18'04" — 6'05"
Built: T.D. Vinette Co., Escanaba, MI (Isle Royale Queen II)
Mackinac Express — — PF/CA — 1987 — D — 90* — 82'07" — 28'04" — 8'04"
Built: Gladding-Hearn Shipbuilding, Somerset, MA
Mackinac Islander — — CF — 1947 — D — 99* — 84'00" — 30'00" — 8'02"
Built: Sturgeon Bay Shipbuilding, Sturgeon Bay, WI (Drummond Islander '47–'02)
Ottawa {2} — — PF/PK — 1959 — D — 81* — 93'00" — 29'08" — 5'02"
Built: Paasch Marine Services Inc., Erie, PA
Straits Express — — PF/CA — 1995 — D — 99* — 101'00" — 28'08" — 10'00"
Built: Marinette Marine Corp., Marinette, WI
Straits of Mackinac II — — PF/PK — 1969 — D — 89* — 89'11" — 27'00" — 8'08"
Built: Blount Marine Corp., Warren, RI

A-13 ASI GROUP LTD., ST. CATHARINES, ON (asi-group.com)
ASI Clipper — — SV — 1939 — D — 64* — 70'00" — 23'00" — 6'06"
Built: Port Colborne Iron Works, Port Colborne, ON (Stanley Clipper '39–'94, Nadro Clipper '94–'08)

Grain-laden Tecumseh in the Poe Lock at Sault Ste. Marie, Mich. (Mike Mishler)

Great Republic upbound below Detroit, Mich. (Wade P. Streeter)

A-14	**ATLAS MARINE SERVICES LLC, FISH CREEK, WI**						
	Atlas	PA	1992	D	12*	30' 04"	11' 05"	5' 04"
	Northern Lighter	GC	1973	D	5*	36' 00"	9' 09"	1' 06"
B-1	**B & L TUG SERVICE, THESSALON, ON**						
	C. West Pete	TB	1958	D	29*	65' 00"	17' 05"	6' 00"
	Built: Erieau Shipbuilding & Drydock Co. Ltd., Erieau, ON						
B-2	**BABCOCK MARINE & SHORELINE SERVICES, SARNIA, ON**						
	Lime Island	TB	1953	D	24*	42' 08"	12' 00"	6' 00"
	Built: Knudsen Brothers Shipbuilding & Dry Dock, Superior, WI (E.C. Knudsen, Wells Larsen)						
B-3	**BASIC MARINE INC., ESCANABA, MI** *(basicmarine.com)*						
	BMI-192	DB	2009	B	1219*	220' 02"	55' 00"	12' 00"
	BMI-FDD-1	FD	1981		301*	160' 02"	65' 00"	8 08"

Danicia	8991774	TB	1943	DE	240*	110' 02"	26' 04"	14' 08"

Danicia   8991774   TB   1943   DE   240*   110' 02"   26' 04"   14' 08"
Built: Ira S. Bushey and Sons Inc., Brooklyn, NY; inactive at Escanaba, MI
(USCGC Chinook [WYT / WYTM-96] '44-'86, Tracie B '86-'98)

Erika Kobasic   TB   1939   DE   226*   110' 00"   25' 01"   14' 03"
Built: Gulfport Shipbuilding, Port Arthur, TX (USCGC Arundel [WYT / WYTM-90] '39-'84, Karen Andrie '84-'90)

Escort   TB   1969   D   26*   50' 00"   14' 00"   6' 03"
Built: Jakobson Shipyard, Oyster Bay, NY

Greenstone   TK   1977   B   114*   81' 00"   24' 00"   7' 09"

Krystal   TB   1954   D   23*   45' 02"   12' 08"   6' 00"
Built: Roamer Boat Co., Holland, MI (ST-2168 '54-'62, Thunder Bay '62-'02)

Nickelena   TB   1973   D   240*   109' 00"   30' 07"   15' 08"
Built: Marinette Marine Corp., Marinette, WI (USS Chetek [YTB-827] '73-'96, Chetek '96-'00, Koziol '00-'08)

Baie Comeau arrives at Duluth, Minn.,
on Jan. 5, 2015. (Glenn Blaszkiewicz)

B-4   **BAY CITY BOAT LINES LLC, BAY CITY, MI** *(baycityboatlines.com)*

Islander	ES	1946	D	39*	53' 04"	19' 09"	5' 04"
Princess Wenonah	ES	1954	D	96*	64' 09"	31' 00"	7' 03"

Built: Sturgeon Bay Shipbuilding Co., Sturgeon Bay, WI (William M. Miller '54-'98)

B-5   **BAYSAIL, BAY CITY, MI** *(baysailbaycity.org)*

Appledore IV	2S/ES	1989	W/D	48*	85' 00"	18' 08"	8' 08"

Built: Treworgy Yachts, Palm Coast, FL

Appledore V	2S/ES	1992	W/D	34*	65' 00"	14' 00"	8' 06"

Built: Treworgy Yachts, Palm Coast, FL (Westwind, Appledore)

B-6   **BEAUSOLEIL FIRST NATION TRANSPORTATION, CHRISTIAN ISLAND, ON** *(chimnissing.ca)*

Indian Maiden	PA/CF	1987	D	91.5*	73' 06"	23' 00"	8' 00"

Built: Duratug Shipyard & Fabricating Ltd., Port Dover, ON

Sandy Graham	PA/CF	1957	D	212*	125' 07"	39' 09"	8' 00"

Built: Barbour Boat Works Inc., New Bern, NC

B-7   **BEAVER ISLAND BOAT CO., CHARLEVOIX, MI** *(bibco.com)*

Beaver Islander	PF/CF	1963	D	95*	96' 03"	27' 02"	8' 03"

Built: Sturgeon Bay Shipbuilding, Sturgeon Bay, WI

Emerald Isle {2}	PF/CF	1997	D	95*	130' 00"	38' 00"	12' 00"

Built: Washburn & Doughty Associates Inc., East Boothbay, ME

B-8   **BLOUNT SMALL SHIP ADVENTURES, WARREN, RI, USA** *(blountsmallshipadventures.com)*

Grande Caribe	8978631	PA	1997	D	97*	182' 07"	39' 01"	9' 10"
Grande Mariner	8978643	PA	1998	D	97*	182' 07"	39' 01"	9' 10"
Niagara Prince	8978629	PA	1994	D	99*	174' 00"	40' 00"	9' 00"

B-9   **BLUE HERON CO. LTD., TOBERMORY, ON** *(blueheronco.com)*

Blue Heron V	ES	1983	D	24*	54' 06"	17' 05"	7' 02"
Flowerpot	ES	1978	D	39*	47' 02"	15' 08"	5' 06"
Flowerpot Express	ES	2011	D	59*	49' 07"	16' 05"	1' 25"
Great Blue Heron	ES	1994	D	112*	79' 00"	22' 00"	6' 05"

B-10   **BLUEWATER FERRY CO., SOMBRA, ON** *(bluewaterferry.com)*

Daldean	CF	1951	D	145*	75' 00"	35' 00"	7' 00"

Built: Erieau Shipbuilding & Drydock Co. Ltd., Erieau, ON

Ontamich	CF	1939	D	55*	65' 00"	28' 10"	8' 06"

Built: Champion Auto Ferries, Harsens Island, MI (Harsens Island '39-'73)

B-11   **BRIGANTINE INC., KINGSTON, ONT.** *(brigantine.ca)*

St. Lawrence II	TV	1954	W/D	34*	72' 00"	15' 00"	8' 06"

B-12   **BUCHANAN LUMBER SALES LTD., THUNDER BAY, ON**

W. N. Twolan	5384360	TB	1962	D	299*	106' 00"	29' 05"	15' 00"

Built: George T. Davie & Sons, Lauzon, QC

B-13   **BUFFALO DEPARTMENT OF PUBLIC WORKS, BUFFALO, NY**

Edward M. Cotter	FB	1900	D	208*	118' 00"	24' 00"	11' 06"

Built: Crescent Shipbuilding, Elizabeth, NJ (W. S. Grattan 1900-'53, Firefighter '53-'54)

B-14   **BUFFALO SAILING ADVENTURES INC., AMHERST, NY** *(spiritofbuffalo.com)*

Spirit of Buffalo	2S/ES	1992	D/W	34*	73' 00"	15' 06"	7' 02"

B-15   **BUSCH MARINE INC., CARROLLTON, MI**

BMT 3	DB	1965	B	280*	120' 01"	36' 01"	7' 06"
Edwin C. Busch	TB	1935	D	18*	42' 06"	11' 11"	5' 00"

Built: Manitowoc Shipbuilding Co., Manitowoc, WI (Paul L. Luedtke '35-'02, Joanne '02-'09)

Gregory J. Busch	5156725	TB	1919	D	299*	151' 00"	27' 06"	14' 07"

Built: Whitney Bros. Co., Superior, WI (Humaconna '19-'77)

STC 2004	TK	1963	B	1,230*	250' 00"	50' 00"	12' 00"

C-1   **CALUMET RIVER FLEETING INC., CHICAGO, IL** *(calumetriverfleeting.com)*

Aiden William	TB	1954	D	120*	82' 00"	23' 06"	9' 09"

Built: Defoe Shipbuilding Co., Bay City, MI (John A. McGuire '54-'87, William Hoey {1} '87-'94, Margaret Ann '94-'08, Steven Selvick '08-'14)

Audrie S	TW	1956	D	268*	102' 00"	28' 00"	8' 00"

Built: Calumet Shipyard & Drydock Co., Chicago, IL (Cindy Jo '56-'66, Katherine L. '66-'93, Daryl C. Hannah '93-'12)

John M. Selvick	8993370	TB	1898	D	256*	118' 00"	24' 03"	16' 00"

Built: Chicago Shipbuilding Co., Chicago, IL (Illinois {1} 1898-'41, John Roen III '41-'74)

John Marshall	7223261	TB	1972	D	199*	111' 00"	35' 00"	15' 05"

Built: Main Iron Works, Houma, LA (Miss Lynn '72-'78, Newpark Sunburst '78-'83, Atlantic Tempest '83-'92, Catherine Turecamo '92-'14)

Kimberly Selvick		TW	1975	D	93*	57' 07"	28' 00"	10' 00"

Built: Grafton Boat Co., Grafton, IL (Scout '75-'02)

Nathan S		TB	1951	D	144*	84' 01"	23' 06"	9'06"

Built: Ira S. Bushey & Sons Inc., Brooklyn, NY (Huntington '51-'05, Spartacus '05-'06, Huntington '06-'08)

Niki S		TW	1971	D	39*	42' 00"	18' 00"	6' 00"

Built: Scully Bros. Boat Builders, Morgan City, LA (Miss Josie '71-'79, Matador VI '79-'08)

Terry D		TB	1954	D	76*	66' 00"	19' 00"	9' 00"

(Sanita '54-'77, Soo Chief '77-'81, Susan M. Selvick '81-'96, Nathan S. '96-'02, John M. Perry '02-'08, Zuccolo '08-'12, Carla Selvick '12-'14)

C-2 CANADA STEAMSHIP LINES INC., MONTREAL, QC – DIVISION OF THE CSL GROUP INC. *(cslships.com)*

Atlantic Erie	8016639	SU	1985	D	37,411	736' 07"	75' 10"	50' 00"

Built: Collingwood Shipyards, Collingwood, ON (Hon. Paul Martin '85-'88)

Atlantic Huron {2}	8025680	SU	1984	D	34,860	736' 07"	77' 11"	46' 04"

Built: Collingwood Shipyards, Collingwood, ON; converted to a self-unloader in '89 and widened 3' in '03 at Port Weller Dry Docks, St. Catharines, ON (Prairie Harvest '84-'89, Atlantic Huron {2} '89-'94, Melvin H. Baker II {2} '94-'97)

Baie Comeau {3}	9639892	SU	2013	D	37,690	739' 10"	77' 11"	48' 05"

Built: Chengxi Shipyard Co. Ltd., Jiangyin City, China

Baie St. Paul {2}	9601027	SU	2012	D	37,690	739' 10"	77' 11"	48' 05"

Built: Chengxi Shipyard Co. Ltd., Jiangyin City, China

Birchglen {2}	8119273	BC	1983	D	33,824	730' 01"	75' 09"	48' 00"

(Canada Marquis '83-'91, Federal Richelieu '91-'91, Federal MacKenzie '91-'01, MacKenzie '01-'02)

Cedarglen {2}	5103974	BC	1959	D	29,518	730' 00"	75' 09"	40' 04"

*Built: Schlieker-Werft, Hamburg, Germany; rebuilt, lengthened with a new forebody at Davie Shipbuilding Co., Lauzon, QC, in '77 (**Stern section:** Ems Ore '59-'76, **Fore section:** Montcliffe Hall '76-'88, Cartierdoc '88-'02)*

CSL Assiniboine	7413218	SU	1977	D	36,768	739' 10"	78' 00"	48' 05"

Built: Davie Shipbuilding Co., Lauzon, QC; rebuilt with a new forebody at Port Weller Dry Docks, St. Catharines, ON, in '05 (Jean Parisien '77-'05)

CSL Laurentien	7423108	SU	1977	D	37,795	739' 10"	78' 00"	48' 05"

*Built: Collingwood Shipyards, Collingwood, ON; rebuilt with new forebody in '01 at Port Weller Dry Docks, St. Catharines, ON (**Stern section:** Louis R. Desmarais '77-'01)*

CSL Niagara	7128423	SU	1972	D	37,694	739' 10"	78' 00"	48' 05"

*Built: Collingwood Shipyards, Collingwood, ON; rebuilt with a new forebody in '99 at Port Weller Dry Docks, St. Catharines, ON (**Stern section:** J. W. McGiffin '72-'99)*

CSL St-Laurent	9665281	BC	2014	D	35,529	739' 10"	77' 11"	48' 05"

Built: Yangfan Shipbuilding Co. Ltd., Zhoushan City, China

CSL Tadoussac	6918716	SU	1969	D	30,051	730' 00"	77' 11"	41' 11"

Built: Collingwood Shipyards, Collingwood, ON; rebuilt with new mid-body, widened 3' at Port Weller Dry Docks, St. Catharines, ON, in '01 (Tadoussac {2} '69-'01)

CSL Welland	9665279	BC	2014	D	35,529	739' 10"	77' 11"	48' 05"

Built: Yangfan Shipbuilding Co. Ltd., Zhoushan City, China

Frontenac {5}	6804848	SU	1968	D	26,822	729' 07"	75' 00"	39' 08"

Built: Davie Shipbuilding Co., Lauzon, QC; converted to a self-unloader by Collingwood Shipyards, Collingwood, ON, in '73

Mapleglen {3}	7910163	BC	1981	D	35,067	729' 11"	75' 10"	47' 01"

Built: Cockerill Yards N.V., Hoboken, Belgium (Federal Maas {1} '81-'95, Lake Michigan '95-'09)

Oakglen {3}	7901148	BC	1980	D	35,067	729' 11"	75' 10"	47' 01"

Built: Boelwerf Vlaanderen Shipbuilding N.V., Temse, Belgium (Federal Danube '80-'95, Lake Ontario '95-'09)

Pineglen {2}	8409331	BC	1985	D	33,197	736' 07"	75' 11"	42' 00"

Built: Collingwood Shipyards, Collingwood, ON (Paterson '85-'02)

Rt. Hon. Paul J. Martin	7324405	SU	1973	D	37,694	739' 07"	77' 11"	48' 04"

*Built: Collingwood Shipyards, Collingwood, ON; rebuilt with a new forebody in '00 at Port Weller Dry Docks, St. Catharines, ON (**Stern section:** H. M. Griffith '73-'00)*

Salarium	7902233	SU	1980	D	35,123	730' 00"	75' 11"	46' 06"

Built: Collingwood Shipyards, Collingwood, ON (Nanticoke '80-'09)

Spruceglen {2}	8119261	BC	1983	D	33,824	730' 01"	75' 09"	48' 00"

Built: Govan Shipyards, Glasgow, Scotland (Selkirk Settler '83-'91, Federal St. Louis '91-'91, Federal Fraser {2} '91-01, Fraser '01-'02)

Thunder Bay {2}	9601039	SU	2013	D	37,690	739' 10"	77' 11"	48' 05"
Built: Chengxi Shipyard Co. Ltd., Jiangyin City, China									
Whitefish Bay {2}	9639880	SU	2013	D	37,690	739' 10"	77' 11"	48' 05"
Built: Chengxi Shipyard Co. Ltd., Jiangyin City, China									

C-3 CANADIAN COAST GUARD (FISHERIES AND OCEANS CANADA), OTTAWA, ON *(www.ccg-gcc.gc.ca)*
  CENTRAL AND ARCTIC REGION, MONTREAL, QC

Cape Chaillon, Cape Commodore, Cape Discovery, Cape Dundas, Cape Hearne,								
Cape Providence, Cape Rescue	SR	2004	D	34*	47' 09"	14' 00"	4' 05"
Cape Lambton, Cape Mercy,								
Thunder Cape	SR	2000	D	34*	47' 09"	14' 00"	4' 05"
Cape Storm	SR	1999	D	34*	47' 09"	14' 00"	4' 05"
Caribou Isle	BT	1985	D	92*	75' 06"	19' 08"	7' 04"
Built: Breton Industrial & Marine Ltd., Port Hawkesbury, NS								
Constable Carrière 9586069	PV	2012	D	253*	141' 07"	22' 09"	9' 09"
Built: Irving Shipbuilding Inc., Halifax, NS								
Caporal Kaeble V 9586045	PV	2012	D	253*	141' 07"	22' 09"	9' 09"
Built: Irving Shipbuilding Inc., Halifax, NS								
Corporal Teather C.V. 9586057	PV	2012	D	253*	141' 07"	22' 09"	9' 09"
Built: Irving Shipbuilding Inc., Halifax, NS								
Cove Isle	BT	1980	D	80*	65' 07"	19' 08"	7' 04"
Built: Canadian Dredge & Dock Co. Ltd., Kingston, ON								
Griffon 7022887	IB	1970	D	2,212*	234' 00"	49' 00"	21' 06"
Built: Davie Shipbuilding Co., Lauzon, QC								
Gull Isle	BT	1980	D	80*	65' 07"	19' 08"	7' 04"
Built: Canadian Dredge & Dock Co. Ltd., Kingston, ON								
Kelso	RV	2009	D	63*	57' 07"	17' 01"	4' 09"
Limnos 6804903	RV	1968	D	489*	147' 00"	32' 00"	12' 00"
Built: Port Weller Dry Docks, St. Catharines, ON								
Private Robertson VC 9586033	PV	2012	D	253*	141' 07"	22' 09"	9' 09"
Built: Irving Shipbuilding Inc., Halifax, NS								
Samuel Risley 8322442	IB	1985	D	1,988*	228' 09"	47' 01"	21' 09"
Built: Vito Steel Boat & Barge Construction Ltd., Delta, BC								

  QUEBEC REGION, QUÉBEC, QC *(Vessels over 100' only have been listed)*

Amundsen 7510846	IB	1978	D	5,910*	295' 09"	63' 09"	31' 04"
Built: Burrard Dry Dock Co., North Vancouver, BC *(Sir John Franklin '78-'03)*								
Des Groseilliers 8006385	IB	1983	D	5,910*	322' 07"	64' 00"	35' 06"
Built: Port Weller Dry Docks, St. Catharines, ON								
F. C. G. Smith 8322686	SV	1985	D	439*	114' 02"	45' 11"	11' 02"
Built: Georgetown Shipyard, Georgetown, PEI								
Martha L. Black 8320432	IB	1986	D	3,818*	272' 04"	53' 02"	25' 02"
Built: Versatile Pacific Shipyards, Victoria, BC								
Pierre Radisson 7510834	IB	1978	D	5,910*	322' 00"	62' 10"	35' 06"
Built: Burrard Dry Dock Co., North Vancouver, BC								
Tracy 6725432	BT	1968	D	837*	181' 01"	38' 00"	16' 00"
Built: Port Weller Dry Docks, St. Catharines, ON								

C-4 CAUSLEY MARINE CONTRACTING LLC, BAY CITY, MI

Jill Marie	TB	1891	D	24*	60' 00"	12' 06"	6' 00"
Built: Cleveland Shipbuilding Co., Cleveland, OH *(Cisco 1891-'52, Capama-S '52-'07)*								

C-5 CEMBA MOTOR SHIPS LTD., PELEE ISLAND, ON

Cemba	TK	1960	D	17*	50' 00"	15' 06"	7' 06"

C-6 CENTRAL MARINE LOGISTICS INC., GRIFFITH, IN *(centralmarinelogistics.com)*

Edward L. Ryerson 5097606	BC	1960	T	27,500	730' 00"	75' 00"	39' 00"
Built: Manitowoc Shipbuilding Co., Manitowoc, WI; in lay-up at Superior, WI, since May 2009								
Joseph L. Block 7502320	SU	1976	D	37,200	728' 00"	78' 00"	45' 00"
Built: Bay Shipbuilding Co., Sturgeon Bay, WI								
Wilfred Sykes 5389554	SU	1949	T	21,500	678' 00"	70' 00"	37' 00"
Built: American Shipbuilding Co., Lorain, OH; converted to a self-unloader by Fraser Shipyards, Superior, WI, in '75								

C-7 CHAMPION MARINE INC., ALGONAC, MI

Champion	CF	1941	D	69*	65' 00"	25' 09"	5' 08"
Middle Channel	CF	1997	D	81*	79' 00"	30' 00"	6' 05"

Vessel Name	IMO	Type	Year		Tonnage	Length	Beam	Depth
North Channel		CF	1967	D	67*	75'00"	30'04"	6'01"
South Channel		CF	1973	D	94*	79'00"	30'03"	6'01"

C-8   CHARITY ISLAND TRANSPORT INC., AU GRES, MI (charityisland.net)

Vessel Name	IMO	Type	Year		Tonnage	Length	Beam	Depth
North Star		PA	1949	D	14*	50'05"	14'06"	3'06"
Shirley Ann		PA	2007	D	11*	45'00"	14'00"	3'05"

C-9   CHARLEVOIX COUNTY TRANSPORTATION AUTHORITY, CHARLEVOIX, MI

Vessel Name	IMO	Type	Year		Tonnage	Length	Beam	Depth
Charlevoix {1}		CF	1926	D	43*	47'00"	30'00"	3'08"

C-10   CHICAGO DEPARTMENT OF WATER MANAGEMENT, CHICAGO, IL

Vessel Name	IMO	Type	Year		Tonnage	Length	Beam	Depth
James J. Versluis		TB	1957	D	126*	83'00"	22'00"	11'02"

Built: Sturgeon Bay Shipbuilding Co., Sturgeon Bay, WI

C-11   CHICAGO FIRE DEPARTMENT, CHICAGO, IL

Vessel Name	IMO	Type	Year		Tonnage	Length	Beam	Depth
Christopher Wheatley		FB	2011	D	300*	90'00"	25'00"	12'02"

Built: Hike Metal Products Ltd., Wheatley, ON

Vessel Name	IMO	Type	Year		Tonnage	Length	Beam	Depth
Victor L. Schlaeger		FB	1949	D	350*	92'06"	24'00"	11'00"

C-12   CHICAGO'S FIRST LADY CRUISES, CHICAGO, IL (cruisechicago.com)

Vessel Name	IMO	Type	Year		Tonnage	Length	Beam	Depth
Chicago's Classic Lady		ES	2014	D	93*	98'00"	32'00"	6'02"
Chicago's First Lady		ES	1991	D	62*	96'00"	22'00"	9'00"
Chicago's Leading Lady		ES	2011	D	92*	92'07"	32'00"	6'09"
Chicago's Little Lady		ES	1999	D	70*	69'02"	22'08"	7'00"

C-13   CHICAGO FROM THE LAKE LTD., CHICAGO, IL (chicagoline.com)

Vessel Name	IMO	Type	Year		Tonnage	Length	Beam	Depth
Ft. Dearborn		ES	1985	D	72*	64'10"	22'00"	7'03"
Innisfree		ES	1980	D	35*	61'09"	15'06"	5'07"
Marquette {6}		ES	1957	D	39*	50'07"	15'00"	5'05"

C-14   CITY OF TORONTO, TORONTO, ON (toronto.ca/parks)

Vessel Name	IMO	Type	Year		Tonnage	Length	Beam	Depth
Ned Hanlan II		TB	1966	D	22*	41'06"	14'01"	5'05"

Built: Erieau Shipbuilding & Drydock Co. Ltd., Erieau, ON

Vessel Name	IMO	Type	Year		Tonnage	Length	Beam	Depth
Ongiara	6410374	PA/CF	1963	D	180*	78'00"	12'04"	9'09"

Built: Russel Brothers Ltd., Owen Sound, ON

Vessel Name	IMO	Type	Year		Tonnage	Length	Beam	Depth
Sam McBride		PF	1939	D	387*	129'00"	34'11"	6'00"

Built: Toronto Dry Dock Co. Ltd., Toronto, ON

Vessel Name	IMO	Type	Year		Tonnage	Length	Beam	Depth
Thomas Rennie		PF	1951	D	387*	129'00"	32'11"	6'00"

Built: Toronto Dry Dock Co. Ltd., Toronto, ON

Vessel Name	IMO	Type	Year		Tonnage	Length	Beam	Depth
Trillium		PF	1910	R	564*	150'00"	30'00"	8'04"

Built: Poulson Iron Works, Toronto, ON; last sidewheel-propelled vessel on the Great Lakes

Vessel Name	IMO	Type	Year		Tonnage	Length	Beam	Depth
William Inglis		PF	1935	D	238*	99'00"	24'10"	6'00"

Built: John Inglis Co. Ltd., Toronto, ON (Shamrock {2} '35-'37)

C-15   CJC CRUISES INC., GRAND LEDGE, MI (detroitprincess.com)

Vessel Name	IMO	Type	Year		Tonnage	Length	Beam	Depth
Detroit Princess		PA	1993	D	1,430*	222'00"	62'00"	11'01"

Built: LEEVAC Shipyards Inc., Jennings, LA (Players Riverboat Casino II '93-'04)

C-16   CLEARWATER MARINE LLC, HOLLAND, MI (clearwatermarinellc.com)

Vessel Name	IMO	Type	Year		Tonnage	Length	Beam	Depth
G.W. Falcon		TB	1936	D	22*	49'07"	13'08"	6'02"

Built: Fred E. Alford, South Haven, MI (J.W. Walsh, Anna Marie)

C-17   CLEVELAND FIRE DEPARTMENT, CLEVELAND, OH

Vessel Name	IMO	Type	Year		Tonnage	Length	Beam	Depth
Anthony J. Celebrezze		FB	1961	D	42*	66'00"	17'00"	5'00"

Built: Paasch Marine Services Inc., Erie, PA

C-18   CLUB CANAMAC CRUISES, TORONTO, ON (canamac.com)

Vessel Name	IMO	Type	Year		Tonnage	Length	Beam	Depth
Stella Borealis		ES	1989	D	356*	118'00"	26'00"	7'00"

C-19   COLUMBIA YACHT CLUB, CHICAGO, IL (columbiayachtclub.com)

Vessel Name	IMO	Type	Year		Tonnage	Length	Beam	Depth
Abegweit		CF	1947	D	6,694*	372'06"	61'00"	24'09"

Built: Marine Industries Ltd., Sorel, QC; former CN Marine Inc. vessel last operated in 1981; in use as a private, floating clubhouse in Chicago, IL (Abegweit '47- '81, Abby '81- '97)

C-20   CONSTRUCTION POLARIS INC., L'ANCIENNE-LORETTE, QC (constructionpolaris.com)

Vessel Name	IMO	Type	Year		Tonnage	Length	Beam	Depth
Point Viking	5118840	TB	1962	D	207*	98'05"	27'10"	13'05"

Built: Davie Shipbuilding Co., Lauzon, QC (Foundation Viking '62-'75)

C-21   COOPER MARINE LTD., SELKIRK, ON

Vessel Name	IMO	Type	Year		Tonnage	Length	Beam	Depth
J.W. Cooper		PB	1984	D	25*	48'00"	14'07"	5'00"

Alpena discharges a cargo of storage cement into J.A.W. Iglehart at Superior, Wis. (Mike Sipper)

Juleen I		PB	1972	D	23*	46' 00"	14' 01"	4' 05"
Mrs. C.		PB	1991	D	26*	50' 00"	14' 05"	4' 05"
Stacey Dawn		TB	1993	D	14*	35' 09"	17' 04"	3' 05"
Wilson T. Cooper		DB	2009	D	58*	56' 08"	23' 06"	5' 08"

C-22 CORPORATION OF THE TOWNSHIP OF FRONTENAC ISLANDS, WOLFE ISLAND, ON

Howe Islander		CF	1946	D	13*	53' 00"	12' 00"	3' 00"

Built: Canadian Dredge & Dock Co. Ltd., Kingston, ON

Simcoe Islander		PF	1964	D	24*	47' 09"	18' 00"	3' 06"

Built: Canadian Dredge & Dock Co. Ltd., Kingston, ON

C-23 CROISIÈRES AML INC., QUÉBEC, QC *(croisieresaml.com)*

AML Levant	9056404	ES	1991	D	380*	112' 07"	29' 0"	10' 02"

Built: Goelette Marie Clarisse Inc., LaBaleine, QC (Famille Dufour)

AML Suriot		ES	2002	D	171*	82' 00"	27' 00"	6' 00"

Built: RTM Construction, Petite Rivière-St-François, QC (Le Coudrier de l'Isle '02-'14)

AML Zephyr		ES	1992	D	171*	82' 00"	27' 00"	6' 00"

Built: Katamarine International, Paspebiac, QC (Le Coudrier de l'Anse '92-'14)

Cavalier Maxim		ES	1962	D	752*	191' 02"	42' 00"	11' 07"

Built: John I. Thornycroft & Co., Wollston, Southampton, England (Osborne Castle '62-'78,
Le Gobelet D' Argent '78-'88, Gobelet D' Argent '88-'89, Le Maxim '89-'93)

Grand Fleuve		ES	1987	D	499*	145' 00"	30' 00"	5' 06"

Built: Kanter Yacht Co., St. Thomas, ON

Louis Jolliet	5212749	ES	1938	R	2,436*	170' 01"	70' 00"	17' 00"

Built: Davie Shipbuilding Co., Lauzon, QC

C-24 CRUISE TORONTO INC., TORONTO ON *(cruisetoronto.com)*

Obsession III		ES	1967	D	160*	66' 00"	25' 00"	6' 01"

Built: Halter Marine, New Orleans, LA (Mystique)

C-25 CTMA GROUP (NAVIGATION MADELEINE INC.), CAP-AUX-MEULES, QC *(ctma.ca)*

C.T.M.A. Vacancier	7310260	PA/RR	1973	D	11,481*	388' 04"	70' 02"	43' 06"

Built: J.J. Sietas KG Schiffswerft, Hamburg, Germany (Aurella '80-'82, Saint Patrick II '82-'98,
Egnatia II '98-'00, Ville de Sete '00-'01, City of Cork '01-'02)

C.T.M.A. Voyageur	7222229	PA/RR	1972	D	4,526*	327' 09"	52' 06"	31' 07"

Built: Trosvik Versted A/S, Brevik, Norway (Anderida '72-'81, Truck Trader '81-'84, Sealink '84-'86, Mirela '86-'86)

D-1 DAN MINOR & SONS INC., PORT COLBORNE, ON

Andrea Marie I		TB	1986	D	87*	75' 02"	24' 07"	7' 03"

Built: Ralph Hurley, Port Burwell, ON

Jeanette M.		TB	1981	D	31*	70' 00"	20 01"	6' 00"

Built: Hike Metal Products, Wheatley, ON

Susan Michelle		TB	1995	D	89*	79' 10"	20' 11"	6' 02"

Built: Vic Powell Welding Ltd., Dunnville, ON

Welland		TB	1954	D	94*	86' 00"	20' 00"	8' 00"

Built: Russel-Hipwell Engines, Owen Sound, ON

D-2 DEAN CONSTRUCTION CO. LTD., BELLE RIVER, ON *(deanconstructioncompany.com)*

Americo Dean		TB		D	15*	45' 00"	15' 00"	5' 00"
Annie M. Dean		TB	1981	D	58*	50' 00"	19' 00"	5' 00"
Bobby Bowes		TB	1944	D	11*	37' 04"	10' 02"	3' 06"
Canadian Jubilee		DR	1978	B	896*	149' 09"	56' 01"	11' 01"
Neptune III		TB	1939	D	23*	53' 10"	15' 06"	5' 00"

D-3 DEAN MARINE & EXCAVATING INC., MOUNT CLEMENS, MI *(deanmarineandexcavating.com)*

Andrew J.		TB	1950	D	25*	47' 00"	15' 07"	8' 00"
Kimberly Anne		TB	1965	D	65*	55' 02"	18' 08"	8' 00"

Built: Main Iron Works, Houma, LA (Lady Lisa, Lucy, Mrs. Alma)

Marissa Rose		TB	1987	D	19*	41' 13"	14' 00"	5' 00"

D-4 DETROIT CITY FIRE DEPARTMENT, DETROIT, MI

Curtis Randolph		FB	1979	D	85*	77' 10"	21' 06"	9' 03"

Built: Peterson Builders Inc., Sturgeon Bay, WI

D-5 DEWEY LEASING LLC, ROCHESTER, NY

Ronald J. Dahlke		TB	1903	D	58*	63' 04"	17' 06"	9' 00"

Built: Johnston Bros., Ferrysburg, MI (Bonita '03-'14, Chicago Harbor No. 4 '14-'60, Eddie B. '60-'69,
Seneca Queen '69-'70, Ludington '70-'96, Seneca Queen '96-'04)

D-6 **DIAMOND JACK'S RIVER TOURS, DETROIT, MI** *(diamondjack.com)*

Diamond Belle	ES	1958	D	93*	93' 06"	25' 00"	7' 00"

Built: Hans Hansen Welding Co., Toledo, OH (Mackinac Islander {2} '58-'90, Sir Richard '90-'91)

Diamond Jack	ES	1955	D	82*	72' 00"	25' 00"	7' 03"

Built: Christy Corp., Sturgeon Bay, WI (Emerald Isle {1} '55-'91)

Diamond Queen	ES	1956	D	94*	92' 00"	25' 00"	7' 02"

Built: Marinette Marine Corp., Marinette, WI (Mohawk '56-'96)

D-7 **DISCOVERY WORLD AT PIER WISCONSIN, MILWAUKEE, WI** *(discoveryworld.org)*

Denis Sullivan	TV/ES	2000	W/D	99*	138' 00"	22' 08"	10' 06"

Built: Wisconsin Lake Schooner, Milwaukee, WI

D-8 **DUC D' ORLEANS CRUISE BOAT, CORUNNA, ON** *(ducdorleans.com)*

Duc d' Orleans II	ES	1987	D	120*	71' 03	23' 02"	7' 07"

Built: Blount Marine Corp., Warren, RI (Spirit of Newport '87-'06)

D-9 **DUNDEE ENERGY LTD., TORONTO, ON** *(eurogascorp.com)*
Vessels are engaged in oil and gas exploration on Lake Erie

Dr. Bob	DV	1973	B	1,022*	160' 01"	54' 01"	11' 01"

Built: Cenac Shipyard Co. Inc., Houma, LA (Mr. Chris '73-'03)

J.R. Rouble	DV	1958	D	562*	123' 06"	49' 08"	16' 00"

Built: American Marine Machinery Co., Nashville, TN (Mr. Neil)

Miss Libby	DV	1972	B	924*	160' 01"	54' 01"	11' 01"

Built: Service Machine & Shipbuilding Corp., Morgan City, LA

Sarah No. 1	TB	1969	D	43*	72' 01"	17' 03"	6' 08"
Timesaver II	DB	1964	B	510*	91' 08"	70' 08"	9' 01"

D-10 **DUROCHER MARINE, DIV. OF KOKOSING CONSTRUCTION CO., CHEBOYGAN, MI** *(kokosing.biz)*

Champion {3}	TB	1974	D	125*	75' 00"	23' 05"	9' 05"

Built: Service Machine & Shipbuilding Co., Amelia, LA

General {2}	TB	1954	D	119*	71' 00"	19' 06"	10' 00"

Built: Missouri Valley Bridge & Iron Works, Leavenworth, KS (U. S. Army ST-1999 '54-'61, USCOE Au Sable '61-'84, Challenger {3} '84-'87)

Joe Van	TB	1955	D	32*	57' 09"	15' 00"	7' 00"

Built: W.J. Hingston, Buffalo, NY

Nancy Anne	TB	1969	D	73*	60' 00"	20' 00"	8' 00"

Built: Houma Shipbuilding Co., Houma, LA

Ray Durocher	TB	1943	D	20*	45' 06"	12' 05"	7' 06"
Valerie B.	TB	1981	D	101*	65' 00"	25' 06"	10' 00"

Built: Rayco Shipbuilders & Repairers, Bourg, LA (Mr. Joshua, Michael Van)

E-1 **EASTERN UPPER PENINSULA TRANSPORTATION AUTH., SAULT STE. MARIE, MI** *(www.eupta.net)*

Drummond Islander III	CF	1989	D	96*	108' 00"	37' 00"	7' 02"

Built: Moss Point Marine Inc., Escatawpa, MS

Drummond Islander IV	CF	2000	D	97*	148' 00"	40' 00"	12' 00"

Built: Basic Marine Inc., Escanaba, MI

Neebish Islander II	CF	1946	D	90*	89' 00"	25' 09"	5' 08"

Built: Lock City Machine/Marine, Sault Ste. Marie, MI (Sugar Islander '46-'95)

Sugar Islander II	CF	1995	D	90*	114' 00"	40' 00"	10' 00"

Built: Basic Marine Inc., Escanaba, MI

E-2 **ECOMARIS, MONTREAL, QC** *(ecomaris.org)*

Roter Sand	TV/2S	1999	W/D	28*	65' 02"	17' 07"	8' 03"

E-3 **EMPRESS OF CANADA ENTERPRISES LTD., TORONTO, ON** *(empressofcanada.com)*

Empress of Canada	ES	1980	D	399*	116' 00"	28' 00"	6' 06"

Built: Hike Metal Products, Wheatley, ON (Island Queen V {2} '80-'89)

E-4 **ENTERPRISE MARISSA INC., QUEBEC, QC**

Cap Brulé	TB		D	12*	39' 09"	10' 00"	2' 00"
Cape Crow	TB	1951	D	14*	37' 08"	10' 05"	5' 00"
Soulanges	TB	1905	D	72*	77' 00"	17' 00"	8' 00"

Built: Cie Pontbriand Ltée., Sorel, QC (Dandy '05-'39)

E-5 **ERICSON MARINE FREIGHT INC., BAYFIELD, WI**

Outer Island	PK	1942	D	173*	112' 00"	32' 00"	8' 06"

(LCT 203 '42-'46, Pluswood '46-'53)

E-6   **ERIE ISLANDS PETROLEUM INC., PUT-IN-BAY, OH** *(putinbayfuels.com)*

Cantankerus		TK	1955	D	43*	56' 00"	14' 00"	6' 06"

Built: Marinette Marine Corp., Marinette, WI

E-7   **ERIE SAND AND GRAVEL CO., ERIE, PA** *(eriesandandgravel.com)*

J. S. St. John	5202524	SC	1945	D	415*	174' 00"	31' 09"	15' 00"

Built: Smith Shipyards & Engineering Corp., Pensacola, FL (USS YO-178 '45-'51, Lake Edward '51-'67)

E-8   **ESSROC CANADA INC., MISSISSAUGA, ON** *(essroc.com)*
       VESSELS MANAGED BY ALGOMA CENTRAL CORP.

Metis	5233585	CC	1956	B	5,800	331' 00"	43' 09"	26' 00"

Built: Davie Shipbuilding Co., Lauzon, QC; lengthened 72', deepened 3'06" in '59 and converted to a self-unloading cement barge in '91 by Kingston Shipbuilding & Dry Dock Co., Kingston, ON

Stephen B. Roman	6514900	CC	1965	D	7,600	488' 09"	56' 00"	35' 06"

Built: Davie Shipbuilding Co., Lauzon, QC; converted to a self-unloading cement carrier by Collingwood Shipyards, Collingwood, ON, in '83 (Fort William '65-'83)

E-9   **EVERETTE J. GAYTON, OAK PARK, MI**

Titan		TB	1940	D	31*	56' 03"	15' 08"	7' 00"

F-1   **FINCANTERI MARINE GROUP LLC., STURGEON BAY, WI** *(bayshipbuildingcompany.com)*

Bayship		TB	1943	D	19*	45' 00"	12' 04"	5' 03"

Built: Sturgeon Bay Shipbuilding Co., Sturgeon Bay, WI (Sturshipco)

F-2   **FITZ SUSTAINABLE FORESTRY MANAGEMENT LTD., MANITOWANING, ON**

Wyn Cooper		TB	1973	D	25*	48' 00"	13' 00"	4' 00"

F-3   **FOXY LADY CRUISES, GREEN BAY, WI** *(foxyladycruises.com)*

Foxy Lady II		ES	2003	D	61*	73' 05"	20' 00"	5' 05"

     (Marco Island Princess)

F-4   **FRASER SHIPYARDS INC., SUPERIOR, WI** *(frasershipyards.com)*

FSY II		TB	2013	D	32*	45' 00"	13' 00"	6' 05"
FSY III		TB	1959	D	30*	47' 04"	13' 00"	6' 06"

     (Susan A. Fraser '59-'78, Maxine Thompson)

FSY IV		TB	1956	D	24*	43' 00"	12' 00"	5' 06"

     (Wally Kendzora)

G-1   **GAELIC TUGBOAT CO., DETROIT, MI** *(gaelictugboat.com)*

Marysville		TK	1973	B	1,136*	200' 00"	50' 00"	12' 06"

     (N.M.S. No. 102 '73-'81)

Patricia Hoey {2}		TB	1949	D	146*	88' 06"	25' 06"	11' 00"

Built: Alexander Shipyard Inc., New Orleans, LA (Propeller '49-'82, Bantry Bay '82-'91)

Shannon	8971669	TB	1944	D	145*	101' 00"	25' 08"	13' 00"

Built: Consolidated Shipbuilding Corp., Morris Heights, NY (USS Connewango [YT / YTB / YTM-388] '44-'77)

William Hoey	5029946	TB	1951	D	149*	88' 06"	25' 06"	11' 00"

Built: Alexander Shipyard Inc., New Orleans, LA (Atlas '51-'84, Susan Hoey {1} '84-'85, Atlas '85-'87, Carolyn Hoey '87-'13)

G-2   **GAFCO CORP., GROSSE POINTE FARMS, MI**

Linnhurst		TB	1930	D	11*	37' 05"	10' 05"	4' 08"

Built: Great Lakes Engineering Works, Ecorse, MI (G.L.E. WKS, Toledoan, Grosse Ile)

G-3   **GALCON MARINE LTD., TORONTO, ON** *(galconmarine.com)*

Barney Drake		TB	1954	D	10*	31' 02"	9 05"	3' 04"

Built: Toronto Dry Dock Co. Ltd., Toronto ON (T.T.&S. No. 9)

Kenteau		TB	1937	D	15*	54' 07"	16' 04"	4' 02"

Built: George Gamble, Port Dover, ON

Patricia D		TB	1958	D	12*	38' 08"	12' 00"	3' 08"

Built: Toronto Drydock Co. Ltd., Toronto, ON (Big Chief III)

Pitts Carillon		DB	1959	B	260*	91' 08"	39' 00"	8' 01"

Built: Walter Young Machinery & Equipment Ltd., Waubaushine, ON (Omar D.S. 34 '59-'80)

Pitts No. 3		DB	1961	B	107*	78' 02"	32' 00"	5' 05"

Built: Thomas Storey Engineers Ltd., Stockport, England

G-4   **GALLAGHER MARINE CONSTRUCTION CO. INC., ESCANABA, MI**

Bee Jay		TB	1939	D	19*	45' 00"	13' 00"	7' 00"

GANANOQUE BOAT LINE LTD., GANANOQUE, ON *(ganboatline.com)*

Thousand Islander	7227346	ES	1972	D	200*	96' 11"	22' 01"	5' 05"
Thousand Islander II	7329936	ES	1973	D	200*	99' 00"	22' 01"	5' 00"
Thousand Islander III	8744963	ES	1975	D	376*	118' 00"	28' 00"	6' 00"
Thousand Islander IV	7947984	ES	1976	D	347*	110' 09"	28' 04"	10' 08"
Thousand Islander V	8745187	ES	1979	D	246*	88' 00"	24' 00"	5' 00"

G-6 GANNON UNIVERSITY, ERIE, PA *(gannon.edu)*

Environaut		RV	1950	D	18*	48' 00"	13' 00"	4' 05"

G-7 GEO. GRADEL CO., TOLEDO, OH *(geogradelco.com)*

Crow		DB	1955	B	416*	110' 00"	42' 00"	9' 06"
John Francis		TB	1965	D	99*	75' 00"	22' 00"	9' 00"

Built: Bollinger Shipbuilding Inc., Lockport, LA (Dad '65-'98, Creole Eagle '98-'03)

Mighty Jake		TB	1969	D	15*	36' 00"	12' 03"	7' 03"
Mighty Jessie		TB	1954	D	57*	61' 02"	18' 00"	7' 03"
Mighty Jimmy		TB	1945	D	34*	56' 00"	15' 10"	6' 05"
Mighty John III		TB	1962	D	24*	45' 00"	15' 00"	5' 10"

(Niagara Queen '62-'99)

Moby Dick		DB	1952	B	835	121' 00"	33' 02"	10' 06"
Pioneerland		TB	1943	D	53*	58' 00"	16' 08"	8' 00"
Prairieland		TB	1955	D	35*	49' 02"	15' 02"	6' 00"
Timberland		TB	1946	D	20*	41' 03"	13' 01"	7' 00"

G-8 GOODTIME CRUISE LINE INC., CLEVELAND, OH *(goodtimeiii.com)*

Goodtime III		ES	1990	D	95*	161' 00"	40' 00"	11' 00"

Built: LEEVAC Shipyards Inc., Jennings, LA

G-9 GRAND PORTAGE / ISLE ROYALE TRANSPORTATION LINE, WHITE BEAR LAKE, MN *(isleroyaleboats.com)*

Sea Hunter III		ES	1985	D	47*	65' 00"	16 00"	7' 05"
Voyageur II		ES	1970	D	40*	63' 00"	18' 00"	5' 00"

GRAND RIVER NAVIGATION CO. – SEE LOWER LAKES TRANSPORTATION CO. – Fleet L-15

G-10 GRAND VALLEY STATE UNIVERSITY, ANNIS WATER RESOURCES, MUSKEGON, MI *(gvsu.edu/wri)*

D. J. Angus		RV	1986	D	16*	45' 00"	14' 00"	4' 00"
W. G. Jackson		RV	1996	D	80*	64' 10"	20' 00"	5' 00"

G-11 GRAVEL & LAKE SERVICES LTD., THUNDER BAY, ON

George N. Carleton		TB	1943	D	97*	82' 00"	21' 00"	11' 00"

Built: Russel Brothers Ltd., Owen Sound, ON (HMCS Glenlea [W-25] '43-'45, Bansaga '45-'64)

Peninsula		TB	1944	D	261*	111' 00"	27' 00"	13' 00"

Built: Montreal Drydock Ltd., Montreal, QC (HMCS Norton [W-31] '44-'45, W.A.C. 1 '45-'46)

Robert John		TB	1945	D	98*	82' 00"	20' 01"	11' 00"

Built: Canadian Dredge & Dock Co., Kingston, ON (HMCS Gleneagle [W-40] '45-'46, Bansturdy '46-'65)

Wolf River		BC	1956	D	5,880	349' 02"	43' 07"	25' 04"

Built: Port Weller Dry Docks, Port Weller, ON; last operated in 1998; laid up at Thunder Bay, ON
(Tecumseh {2} '56-'67, New York News {3} '67-'86, Stella Desgagnés '86-'93, Beam Beginner '93-'95)

G-12 GREAT LAKES DOCK & MATERIALS LLC, MUSKEGON, MI *(greatlakesdock.com)*

Duluth		TB	1954	D	87*	70' 01"	19' 05"	9' 08"

Built: Missouri Valley Bridge & Iron Works, Leavenworth, KS (U. S. Army ST-2015 '54-'62)

Fischer Hayden		TB	1967	D	64*	54' 00"	22' 01"	7' 01"

Built: Main Iron Works Inc., Houma, LA (Gloria G. Cheramie, Joyce P. Crosby)

Sarah B.		TB	1953	D	23*	45' 00"	13' 00"	7' 00"

Built: Nashville Bridge Co., Nashville, TN (ST-2161 '53-'63, Tawas Bay '63-'03)

William C. Gaynor	8423818	TB	1956	D	187*	94' 00"	27' 00"	11' 09"

Built: Defoe Shipbuilding Co., Bay City, MI (William C. Gaynor '56-'88, Captain Barnaby '88-'02)

G-13 GREAT LAKES ENVIRONMENTAL RESEARCH LABORATORY, ANN ARBOR, MI *(glerl.noaa.gov)*

Huron Explorer		RV	1979	D	15*	41' 00"	14' 08"	4' 08"
Laurentian		RV	1974	D	129*	80' 00"	21' 06"	11' 00"
Shenehon		SV	1953	D	90*	65' 00"	17' 00"	6' 00"

G-14 GREAT LAKES FLEET INC., DULUTH, MN (KEY LAKES INC., MANAGER)

Arthur M. Anderson	5025691	SU	1952	T	25,300	767' 00"	70' 00"	36' 00"

Built: American Shipbuilding Co., Lorain, OH; lengthened 120' in '75 and converted to a self-unloader in
'82 at Fraser Shipyards, Superior, WI

Vessel Name	IMO/Hull #	Type	Year	Engine	Capacity/Tonnage	Length	Breadth	Depth
Cason J. Callaway	5065392	SU	1952	T	25,300	767' 00"	70' 00"	36' 00"

Built: Great Lakes Engineering Works, River Rouge, MI; lengthened 120' in '74 and converted to a self-unloader in '82 at Fraser Shipyards, Superior, WI

Edgar B. Speer	7625952	SU	1980	D	73,700	1,004' 00"	105' 00"	56' 00"

Built: American Shipbuilding Co., Lorain, OH

Edwin H. Gott	7606061	SU	1979	D	74,100	1,004' 00"	105' 00"	56' 00"

Built: Bay Shipbuilding Co., Sturgeon Bay, WI; converted from shuttle self-unloader to deck-mounted self-unloader at Bay Shipbuilding, Sturgeon Bay, WI, in '96

Great Republic	7914236	SU	1981	D	25,600	634' 10"	68' 00"	39' 07"

Built: Bay Shipbuilding Co., Sturgeon Bay, WI (American Republic '81-'11)

John G. Munson {2}	5173670	SU	1952	T	25,550	768' 03"	72' 00"	36' 00"

Built: Manitowoc Shipbuilding Co., Manitowoc, WI; lengthened 102' in '76 at Fraser Shipyards, Superior, WI

Philip R. Clarke	5277062	SU	1952	T	25,300	767' 00"	70' 00"	36' 00"

Built: American Shipbuilding Co., Lorain, OH; lengthened 120' in '74 and converted to a self-unloader in '82 at Fraser Shipyards, Superior, WI

Presque Isle {2}	7303877	IT	1973	D	1,578*	153' 03"	54' 00"	31' 03"

Built: Halter Marine, New Orleans, LA; paired with the self-unloading barge Presque Isle

Presque Isle {2}		SU	1973	B	57,500	974' 06"	104' 07"	46' 06"

Built: Erie Marine Inc., Erie, PA

[ITB Presque Isle OA dimensions together]						1,000' 00"	104' 07"	46' 06"
Roger Blough	7222138	SU	1972	D	43,900	858' 00"	105' 00"	41' 06"

Built: American Shipbuilding Co., Lorain, OH

G-15 THE GREAT LAKES GROUP, CLEVELAND, OH (thegreatlakesgroup.com)

THE GREAT LAKES TOWING CO., CLEVELAND, OH – DIVISION OF THE GREAT LAKES GROUP

Vessel Name	Hull #	Type	Year	Engine	Tonnage	Length	Breadth	Depth
Arizona		TB	1931	D	98*	74' 08"	19' 09"	11' 06"
Arkansas {2}		TB	1909	D	97*	74' 08"	19' 09"	11' 06"
(Yale '09-'48)								
California		TB	1926	DE	97*	74' 08"	19' 09"	11' 06"
Colorado		TB	1928	D	98*	78' 08"	20' 00"	12' 04"
Favorite		FD	1983			90' 00"	50' 00"	5' 00"
Florida		TB	1926	D	99*	71' 00"	20' 02"	11' 02"
(Florida '26-'83, Pinellas '83-'84)								
Idaho		TB	1931	DE	98*	78' 08"	20' 00"	12' 04"
Illinois {2}		TB	1914	D	98*	71' 00"	20' 00"	12' 05"
Indiana		TB	1911	DE	97*	74' 08"	19' 09"	11' 06"
Iowa		TB	1915	D	97*	74' 08"	19' 09"	11' 06"
Kansas		TB	1927	D	97*	74' 08"	19' 09"	11' 06"
Kentucky {2}		TB	1929	D	98*	78' 08"	20' 00"	12' 04"
Louisiana		TB	1917	D	97*	74' 08"	19' 09"	11' 06"
Maine {1}		TB	1921	D	96*	71' 00"	20' 01"	11' 02"
(Maine {1} '21-'82, Saipan '82-'83, Hillsboro '83-'84)								
Massachusetts		TB	1928	D	98*	78' 08"	20' 00"	12' 04"
Milwaukee		DB	1924	B	1,095	172' 00"	40' 00"	11' 06"
Minnesota {1}		TB	1911	D	98*	78' 08"	20' 00"	12' 04"
Mississippi		TB	1916	DE	97*	74' 08"	19' 09"	11' 06"
Missouri {2}		TB	1927	D	149*	88' 04"	24' 06"	12' 03"
(Rogers City {1} '27-'56, Dolomite {1} '56-'81, Chippewa {7} '81-'90)								
Nebraska		TB	1929	D	98*	78' 08"	20' 00"	12' 05"
New Jersey		TB	1924	D	98*	78' 08"	20' 00"	12' 04"
(New Jersey '24-'52, Petco-21 '52-'53)								
New York		TB	1913	D	98*	78' 08"	20' 00"	12' 04"
North Carolina {2}		TB	1952	DE	145*	87' 09"	24' 01"	10' 07"
(Limestone '52-'83, Wicklow '83-'90)								
North Dakota		TB	1910	D	97*	74' 08"	19' 09"	11' 06"
(John M. Truby '10-'38)								
Ohio {3}	6507440	TB	1903	D	194*	101' 02"	26' 00"	13' 07"
Built: Great Lakes Towing Co., Chicago, IL (M.F.D. No. 15 '03-'52, Laurence C. Turner '52-'73)								
Oklahoma		TB	1913	DE	97*	74' 08"	19' 09"	11' 06"
(T. C. Lutz {2} '13-'34)								
Pennsylvania {3}		TB	1911	D	98*	78' 08"	20' 00"	12' 04"
Rhode Island		TB	1930	D	98*	78' 08"	20' 00"	12' 04"
South Carolina		TB	1925	D	102*	79' 06"	21' 01"	11' 03"
(Welcome {2} '25-'53, Joseph H. Callan '53-'72, South Carolina '72-'82, Tulagi '82-'83)								

Superior {3}		TB	1912	D	147*	82' 00"	22' 00"	10' 07"
(Richard Fitzgerald '12-'46)								
Texas		TB	1916	DE	97*	74' 08"	19' 09"	11' 06"
Vermont		TB	1914	D	98*	71' 00"	20' 00"	12' 05"
Virginia {2}		TB	1914	DE	97*	74' 08"	19' 09"	11' 06"
Washington {1}		TB	1925	DE	97*	74' 08"	19' 09"	11' 06"
Wisconsin {4}		TB	1897	D	105*	83' 00"	21' 02"	9' 06"
(America {3}, Midway)								
Wyoming		TB	1929	D	104*	78' 08"	20' 00"	12' 04"

G-16 GREAT LAKES MARITIME ACADEMY, TRAVERSE CITY, MI *(nmc.edu/maritime)*

Anchor Bay		TV	1953	D	23*	45' 00"	13' 00"	7' 00"
Built: Roamer Boat Co., Holland, MI (ST-2158 '53-'62)								
Northwestern {2}		TV	1969	D	12*	55' 00"	15' 00"	6' 06"
Built: Paasch Marine Services Inc., Erie, PA (USCOE North Central '69-'98)								
State of Michigan	8835451	TV	1985	D	1,914*	224' 00"	43' 00"	20' 00"
Built: Tacoma Boatbuilding Co., Tacoma, WA (USNS Persistent '85-'98, USCG Persistent '98-'02)								

G-17 GREAT LAKES OFFSHORE SERVICES INC., PORT DOVER, ON

H. H. Misner		TB	1946	D	28*	66' 09"	16' 04"	4' 05"
Built: George Gamble, Port Dover, ON								

G-18 GREAT LAKES SCHOONER CO., TORONTO, ON *(greatlakesschooner.com)*

Challenge		ES	1980	W/D	76*	96' 00"	16' 06"	8' 00"
Built: Kanter Yachts Co., Port Stanley, ON								
Kajama		ES	1930	W/D	263*	128' 09"	22' 09"	11' 08"
Built: Nobis Krug, Rensburg, Germany								

G-19 GREAT LAKES SCIENCE CENTER, ANN ARBOR, MI *(glsc.usgs.gov)*

Arcticus		RV	2014	D		77' 03"	26' 11"	11' 00"
Built: Burger Boat Co., Manitowoc, WI								
Kaho		RV	2011	D	55*	70' 02"	18' 00"	
Kiyi		RV	1999	D	290*	107' 00"	27' 00"	12' 02"
Muskie		RV	2011	D	55*	70' 02"	18' 00"	
Sturgeon		RV	1977	D	325*	100'00"	25' 05"	10' 00"

G-20 GREAT LAKES SHIPWRECK HISTORICAL SOCIETY, SAULT STE. MARIE, MI *(shipwreckmuseum.com)*

David Boyd		RV	1982	D	26*	47' 00"	17' 00"	3' 00"*

G-21 GROUPE DESGAGNÉS INC., QUÉBEC CITY, QC *(groupedesgagnes.com)*

OPERATED BY SUBSIDIARY TRANSPORT DESGAGNÉS

Amelia Desgagnés	7411167	GC	1976	D	7,349	355' 00"	49' 00"	30' 06"
Built: Collingwood Shipyards, Collingwood, ON (Soodoc {2} '76-'90)								
Anna Desgagnés	8600507	RR	1986	D	17,850	569' 03"	75' 07"	44' 11"
Built: Kvaerner Warnow Werft GmbH, Rostock, Germany; re-registered in the Bahamas in 2006								
(Truskavets '86-'96, Anna Desgagnés '96-'98, PCC Panama '98-'99)								
Camilla Desgagnés	8100595	GC	1982	D	6,889ww	436' 04"	67' 07"	46' 03"
Built: Kroeger Werft GmbH & Co. KG, Rendsburg, Germany (Camilla 1 '82-'04)								
Catherine Desgagnés	5133979	GC	1962	D	8,394	410' 03"	55' 06"	31' 00"
Built: Hall, Russel and Co., Aberdeen, Scotland (Gosforth '62-'72, Thorold {4} '72-'85)								
Claude A. Desgagnés	9488059	GC	2011	D	12,671	454' 05"	69' 11"	36' 01"
Built: Sanfu Ship Engineering, Taizhou Jiangsu, China (Elsborg '11-'12)								
Melissa Desgagnés	7356501	GC	1975	D	7,500	355' 00"	49' 00"	30' 06"
Built: Collingwood Shipyards, Collingwood, ON (Ontadoc {2} '75-'90)								
Rosaire A. Desgagnés	9363534	GC	2007	D	12,575	453' 00"	68' 11"	36' 01"
Built: Quingshan/Jiangdong/Jiangzhou Shipyards, Jiangzhou, China (Beluga Fortification '07-'07)								
Sedna Desgagnés	9402093	GC	2009	D	12,413	456' 00"	68' 11"	36' 01"
Built: Quingshan/Jiangdong/Jiangzhou Shipyards, Jiangzhou, China (Beluga Festivity '09-'09)								
Zélada Desgagnés	9402081	GC	2008	D	12,413	453' 00"	68' 11"	36' 01"
Built: Quingshan/Jiangdong/Jiangzhou Shipyards, Jiangzhou, China (Beluga Freedom '09-'09)								

THE FOLLOWING VESSELS CHARTERED TO PETRO-NAV INC., MONTREAL, QC, A SUBSIDIARY OF GROUPE DESGAGNÉS INC.

Dara Desgagnés	9040089	TK	1992	D	10,511	405' 10"	58' 01"	34' 09"
Built: MTW Shipyard, Wismar, Germany (Elbestern '92-'93, Diamond Star, '93-'10)								
Esta Desgagnés	9040077	TK	1992	D	10,511	405' 10"	58' 01"	34' 09"
Built: MTW Shipyard, Wismar, Germany (Emsstern '92-'92, Emerald Star '92-'10)								

Manistee at her namesake Michigan port. (Jeff Mast)

CSL Assiniboine loading coal at KCBX in South Chicago, Ill. (Peter Groh)

49

Jana Desgagnés	9046564	TK	1993	D	10,511	405' 10"	58' 01"	34' 09"

Built: MTW Shipyard, Wismar, Germany (Jadestern '93-'94, Jade Star '94-'10)

Maria Desgagnés	9163752	TK	1999	D	13,199	393' 08"	68' 11"	40' 05"

Built: Qiuxin Shipyard, Shanghai, China (Kilchem Asia '99-'99)

Sarah Desgagnés	9352171	TK	2007	D	18,000	483'11"	73' 06"	41' 04"

Built: Gisan Shipyard, Tuzla, Turkey (Besiktas Greenland '07-'08)

Thalassa Desgagnés	7382988	TK	1976	D	9,748	441' 05"	56' 05"	32' 10"

Built: Ankerlokken Verft Glommen, Fredrikstad, Norway (Joasla '76-'79, Orinoco '79-'82, Rio Orinoco '82-'93)

Véga Desgagnés	7927960	TK	1982	D	11,548	461' 11"	69' 07"	35' 01"

Built: Kvaerner Masa-Yards, Helsinki, Finland (Shelltrans '82-'94, Acila '94-'99, Bacalan '99-'01)

THE FOLLOWING VESSELS CHARTERED TO RELAIS NORDIK INC., RIMOUSKI, QC
A SUBSIDIARY OF GROUPE DESGAGNÉS INC.

Bella Desgagnés	9511519	PF/RR	2012	D	1,054	312' 00"	63' 06"	22' 08"

Built: Brodogradil Kraljevica d.d., Kraljevica, Croatia

Nordik Express	7391290	GC/CF	1974	D	1,697	219' 11"	44' 00"	16' 01"

Built: Todd Pacific Shipyards Corp., Seattle, WA (Theriot Offshore IV '74-'77, Scotoil 4 '77-'79, Tartan Sea '79-'87)

TRANSPORT MARITIME ST-LAURENT INC., A SUBSIDIARY OF GROUPE DESGAGNÉS INC.

Espada Desgagnés	9334698	TK	2006	D	42,810*	750' 00"	105' 08"	67' 01"

Built: Brodosplit, Split, Croatia (Stena Poseidon '06-'14)

Laurentia Desgagnés	9334703	TK	2007	D	42,810*	750' 00"	105' 08"	67' 01"

Built: Brodosplit, Split, Croatia (laid down as Neste Polaris, Palva '07-'14)

H-1 HAIMARK LINE, DENVER, CO *(haimarkline.com)*

Saint Laurent	9213129	PA	2001	D	4,954*	298' 05"	49' 02"	13' 00"

Built: Atlantic Marine Inc., Jacksonville, FL (Cape May Light '01-'09, Sea Voyager '09 -'14)

H-2 HAMILTON PORT AUTHORITY, HAMILTON, ON *(hamiltonport.ca)*

Judge McCombs		TB	1948	D	10*	33' 01"	10' 03"	4' 00"

Built: Northern Shipbuilding & Repair Co. Ltd., Bronte, ON (Bronte Sue '48-'50)

H-3 HARBOR LIGHT CRUISE LINES INC., TOLEDO, OH *(sandpiperboat.com)*

Sandpiper		ES	1984	D	37*	65' 00"	16' 00"	3' 00"

H-4 HERITAGE MARINE, KNIFE RIVER, MN *(heritagemarinetug.com)*

Edward H.	8651879	TB	1944	D	142*	86' 00"	23' 00"	10' 03"

Built: Equitable Equipment Co., Madisonville, LA (ST-707 '44-'60, Forney '60-'07)

Helen H.	8624670	TB	1967	D	138*	82' 03"	26' 08"	10' 05"

Built: Bludworth Shipyard, Corpus Christi, TX (W. Douglas Masterson '67-'11)

Nancy J.	6504838	TB	1964	D	186*	92' 17"	29' 05"	14' 00"

Built: Main Iron Works, Houma, La (Horace, Point Comfort-'14)

Nels J.	5126615	TB	1958	D	194*	103' 00"	26 06"	12' 00"

Built: Gulfport Shipbuilding Co., Port Arthur, TX (Gatco Alabama, Ares)

H-5 HORNBLOWER NIAGARA CRUISES, NIAGARA FALLS, ON *(niagaracruises.com)*

Niagara Guardian		PA	2013	D	38*	68' 09"	15' 07"	7' 05"
Niagara Thunder		PA	2014	D	185*	83' 02"	35' 09"	8' 09"
Niagara Wonder		PA	2014	D	185*	83' 02"	35' 09"	8' 09"

H-6 HORNE TRANSPORTATION LTD., WOLFE ISLAND, ON *(wolfeisland.com/ferry.php)*

William Darrell		CF	1952	D	66*	66' 00"	28' 00"	6' 00"

Built: Harry Gamble, Port Dover, ON

H-7 HUFFMAN EQUIPMENT RENTAL INC., EASTLAKE, OH

Benjamin Ridgway		TW	1969	D	51*	53' 00"	18' 05"	7' 00"
Hamp Thomas		TB	1968	D	22*	43' 00"	13' 00"	4' 00"
Paddy Miles		TB	1934	D	16*	45' 04"	12' 04"	4' 07"

H-8 HURON LADY II INC., PORT HURON, MI *(huronlady.com)*

Huron Lady II		ES	1993	D	82*	65' 00"	19' 00"	10' 00"

Built: Navigator Boat Works (Lady Lumina '93-'99)

H-9 HYDRO-QUEBEC, MONTREAL, QC

R.O. Sweezy		TB	1991	D	29*	41' 09"	14' 00"	5' 07"

Built: Jean Fournier, Quebec City, QC (Citadelle I '91-'92)

I-1 INFINITY AND OVATION YACHT CHARTERS LLC, ST. CLAIR SHORES, MI *(infinityandovation.com)*

Infinity		PA	2001	D	82*	117' 00"	22' 00"	6' 00"
Ovation		PA	2005	D	97*	138' 00"	27' 00"	7' 00"

I-2 INLAND LAKES MANAGEMENT INC., ALPENA, MI

Alpena {2}   5206362   CC   1942   T   13,900   519' 06"   67' 00"   35' 00"
Built: Great Lakes Engineering Works, River Rouge, MI; shortened by 120' and converted to a self-unloading cement carrier at Fraser Shipyards, Superior, WI, in '91 (Leon Fraser '42-'91)

J. A. W. Iglehart   5139179   CC   1936   T   12,500   501' 06"   68' 03"   37' 00"
Built: Sun Shipbuilding and Drydock Co., Chester, PA; converted from a saltwater tanker to a self-unloading cement carrier at American Shipbuilding Co., South Chicago, IL, in '65; last operated Oct. 29, 2006; in use as a cement storage/transfer vessel at Superior, WI (Pan Amoco '36-'55, Amoco '55-'60, H. R. Schemm '60-'65)

Paul H. Townsend   5272050   CC   1945   D   7,850   447' 00"   50' 00"   29' 00"
Built: Consolidated Steel Corp., Wilmington, DE; converted from a saltwater cargo vessel to a self-unloading cement carrier at Bethlehem Steel Co., Shipbuilding Div., Hoboken, NJ, and Calumet Shipyard, Chicago, IL, in '52-'53; lengthened at Great Lakes Engineering Works, Ashtabula, OH, in '58; last operated Dec. 5, 2005; in long-term lay-up at Muskegon, MI (USNS Hickory Coll '45-'46, USNS Coastal Delegate '46-'52)

S. T. Crapo   5304011   CC   1927   B   8,900   402' 06"   60' 03"   29' 00"
Built: Great Lakes Engineering Works, River Rouge, MI; last operated Sept. 4, 1996; in use as a cement storage and transfer vessel at Green Bay, WI

I-3 INLAND SEAS EDUCATION ASSOCIATION, SUTTONS BAY, MI *(schoolship.org)*

Inland Seas   RV   1994   W   41*   61' 06"   17' 00"   7' 00"
Built: Treworgy Yachts, Palm Coast, FL

I-4 INLAND TUG & BARGE LTD., BROCKVILLE, ON

Katanni   TB   1991   D   19*   34' 08"   14' 05"   5' 05"

I-5 INTERLAKE STEAMSHIP CO., MIDDLEBURG HEIGHTS, OH *(interlakesteamship.com)*

Dorothy Ann   8955732   AT/TT   1999   D   1,090*   124' 03"   44' 00"   24' 00"
Built: Bay Shipbuilding Co., Sturgeon Bay, WI; paired with self-unloading barge Pathfinder

Herbert C. Jackson   5148417   SU   1959   T   24,800   690' 00"   75' 00"   37' 06"
Built: Great Lakes Engineering Works, River Rouge, MI; converted to a self-unloader at Defoe Shipbuilding Co., Bay City, MI, in '75

Hon. James L. Oberstar   5322518   SU   1959   D   31,000   806' 00"   75' 00"   37' 06"
Built: American Shipbuilding Co., Lorain, OH; lengthened 96' in '72; converted to a self-unloader in '81 at Fraser Shipyards, Superior, WI (Shenango II '59-'67, Charles M. Beeghly '67-'11)

James R. Barker   7390260   SU   1976   D   63,300   1,004' 00"   105' 00"   50' 00"
Built: American Shipbuilding Co., Lorain, OH

Mesabi Miner   7390272   SU   1977   D   63,300   1,004' 00"   105' 00"   50' 00"
Built: American Shipbuilding Co., Lorain, OH

Pathfinder {3}   5166768   SU   1953   B   10,577   606' 00"   70' 03"   36' 03"
Built: Great Lakes Engineering Works, River Rouge, MI; converted from a powered vessel to a self-unloading barge at Bay Shipbuilding Co., Sturgeon Bay, WI, in '98 (J. L. Mauthe '53-'98)

Paul R. Tregurtha   7729057   SU   1981   D   68,000   1,013' 06"   105' 00"   56' 00"
Built: American Shipbuilding Co., Lorain, OH; this is the largest vessel on the lakes (William J. DeLancey '81-'90)

INTERLAKE LEASING III – A SUBSIDIARY OF INTERLAKE STEAMSHIP CO.

Stewart J. Cort   7105495   SU   1972   D   58,000   1,000' 00"   105' 00"   49' 00"
Built: Erie Marine Inc., Erie, PA; built for Bethlehem Steel Corp.; this was the Great Lakes' first 1,000-footer

LAKES SHIPPING CO. INC. – A SUBSIDIARY OF INTERLAKE STEAMSHIP CO.

John Sherwin {2}   5174438   BC   1958   31,500   806' 00"   75' 00"   37' 06"
Built: American Steamship Co., Lorain, OH; lengthened 96' at Fraser Shipyards, Superior, WI, in '73; last operated Nov. 16, 1981; in long-term lay-up at DeTour, MI

Kaye E. Barker   5097450   SU   1952   D   25,900   767' 00"   70' 00"   36' 00"
Built: American Shipbuilding Co., Toledo, OH; lengthened 120' at Fraser Shipyards, Superior, WI, in '76; converted to a self-unloader at American Shipbuilding Co., Toledo, OH, in '81; repowered in '12 (Edward B. Greene '52-'85, Benson Ford {3} '85-'89)

Lee A. Tregurtha   5385625   SU   1942   D   29,360   826' 00"   75' 00"   39' 00"
Built: Bethlehem Shipbuilding and Drydock Co., Sparrows Point, MD; converted from a saltwater tanker to a Great Lakes bulk carrier in '61; lengthened 96' in '76 and converted to a self-unloader in '78, all at American Shipbuilding Co., Lorain, OH; repowered in '06 (laid down as Mobiloil; launched as Samoset; USS Chiwawa [AO-68] '42-'46, Chiwawa '46-'61, Walter A. Sterling '61-'85, William Clay Ford {2} '85-'89)

J-1 J. W. WESTCOTT CO., DETROIT, MI *(jwwestcott.com)*

J. W. Westcott II   MB   1949   D   14*   46' 01"   13' 03"   4' 05"
Built: Paasch Marine Service, Erie, PA; floating post office has its own U.S. ZIP code, 48222

Joseph J. Hogan   MB   1957   D   16*   40' 00"   12' 05"   5' 00"
(USCOE Ottawa '57-'95)

Barge Pere Marquette 41 loading synthetic gypsum at Monroe, Mich. *(Paul C. LaMarre III)*

Edgar B. Speer shows off a fresh paint job in drydock at Bay Ship Building Co., Sturgeon Bay, Wis. *(Chris Mazzella)*

J-2	**JEFF FOSTER, SUPERIOR, WI**							
Sundew		IB	1944	DE	1,025*	180' 00"	37' 05"	17' 04"

Built: Marine Ironworks and Shipbuilding Corp., Duluth, MN; former U.S. Coast Guard cutter WLB-404 was decommissioned in 2004 and turned into a marine museum; vessel was returned to private ownership in 2009

J-3	**JOSEPH B. MARTIN, BEAVER ISLAND, MI**							
Shamrock		TB	1933	D	60*	64' 00"	18' 00"	7' 03"

Built: Pennsylvania Shipyard Inc., Beaumont, TX

Tanker II		TK	1964	B	60*	64' 00"	18' 00"	6' 00"

Built: Christy Corp., Sturgeon Bay, WI

J-4	**JUBILEE QUEEN CRUISES, TORONTO, ON** (jubileequeencruises.ca)							
Jubilee Queen		ES	1986	D	269*	122' 00"	23' 09"	5' 05"

J-5	**JULIO CONTRACTING CO., HANCOCK, MI** (juliocontracting.com)							
Julio		TB	1941	D	84*	65' 05"	18' 00"	9' 01"

K-1	**KEHOE MARINE CONSTRUCTION CO., LANSDOWNE, ON** (tiecomarine.com)							
Houghton		TB	1944	D	15*	45' 00"	13' 00"	6' 00"

Built: Port Houston Iron Works, Houston, TX

Halton		TB	1942	D	15*	42' 08"	14' 00"	5' 08"

Built: Muir Bros. Dry Dock Co. Ltd., Port Dalhousie, ON

K-2	**KELLEYS ISLAND BOAT LINES, MARBLEHEAD, OH** (kelleysislandferry.com)							
Carlee Emily		PA/CF	1987	D	98*	101' 00"	34' 06"	10' 00"

Built: Blount Marine Corp., Warren, RI (Endeavor '87-'02)

Juliet Alicia		PA/CF	1969	D	95*	88' 03"	33' 00"	6' 08"

Built: Blount Marine Corp., Warren, RI (Kelley Islander)

Shirley Irene		PA/CF	1991	D	68*	160' 00"	46' 00"	9' 00"

Built: Ocean Group Shipyard, Bayou La Batre, AL

K-3	**KEWEENAW EXCURSIONS INC., CHARLEVOIX, MI** (keweenawexcursions.com)							
Keweenaw Star	631711	ES	1981	D	97*	110' 00"	23' 04"	6' 03"

Built: Camcraft Inc., Crown Point, LA (Atlantic Star, Privateer, De De Bruce)

K-4	**KINDRA LAKE TOWING LP, CHICAGO, IL** (kindralake.com)							
Buckley		TW	1958	D	94*	95' 00"	26' 00"	11' 00"

Built: Parker Bros. Shipyard, Houston, TX (Linda Brooks '58-'67, Eddie B. {2} '67-'95)

Donald C.	8841967	TB	1962	D	198*	91' 00"	29' 00"	11' 06"

Built: Main Iron Works Inc., Houma, LA (Donald C. Hannah '62-'09)

Ellie		TB	1970	D	29*	39' 07"	16' 00"	4' 06"

Built: Big River Shipbuilding Inc., Vicksburg, MS (Miss Bissy '09)

Morgan		TB	1974	D	134*	90' 00"	30' 00"	10' 06"

Built: Peterson Builders Inc., Sturgeon Bay, WI (Donald O'Toole '74-'86, Bonesey B. '86-'95)

Old Mission		TB	1945	D	94*	85' 00"	23' 00"	10' 04"

Built: Sturgeon Bay Shipbuilding, Sturgeon Bay, WI (U. S. Army ST-880 '45-'47, USCOE Avondale '47-'64, Adrienne B. '64-'95)

Tanner		TW	1977	D	62*	56' 06"	22' 03"	6' 06"

Built: Thrift Shipbuilding, Inc., Sulphur, LA; Owned by Jamattca, Downers Grove, IL (J.H. Tanner 76-'00)

K-5	**KING CO. (THE), HOLLAND, MI**							
Barry J		TB	1943	D	26*	46' 00"	13' 00"	7' 00"

Built: Sturgeon Bay Shipbuilding & Dry Dock Co., Sturgeon Bay, WI

Buxton II		DR	1976	B	147*	130' 02"	28' 01"	7' 00"

Built: Barbour Boat Works Inc., Holland, MI

Carol Ann		TB	1981	D	86*	61' 05"	24' 00"	8' 07"

Built: Rodriguez Boat Builders, Bayou La Batre, AL

John Henry		TB	1954	D	66*	65' 04"	19' 04"	9' 06"

Built: Missouri Valley Steel, Leavenworth, KS (U. S. Army ST-2013 '54-'80)

Julie Dee		TB	1937	D	64*	68' 08"	18' 01"	7' 06"

Built: Herbert Slade, Beaumont, TX (Dernier, Jerry O'Day, Cindy B)

Matt Allen		TB	1961	D	146*	80' 04"	24' 00"	11' 03"

Built: Nolty Theriot Inc., Golden Meadow, LA (Gladys Bea '61-'73, American Viking '73-'83, Maribeth Andrie '83-'05)

Miss Edna		TB	1935	D	13*	36' 08"	11' 02"	4' 08"

Built: Levingston Shipbuilding, Orange, TX

K-6	**KINGSTON 1,000 ISLANDS CRUISES, KINGSTON, ON** (1000islandscruises.on.ca)							
Island Belle I		ES	1988	D	150*	65' 00"	22' 00"	8' 00"

Island Queen III		ES	1975	D	300*	96' 00"	26' 00"	11' 00"

Island Queen III ES 1975 D 300* 96' 00" 26' 00" 11' 00"
  Built: Marlin Yachts Co. Ltd., Summerstown, ON
Papoose III ES 1968 D 110* 64' 08" 23' 03" 7' 03"
  Built: Hike Metal Products Ltd., Wheatley, ON (Peche Island II)

K-7 KK INTEGRATED LOGISTICS, MENOMINEE, MI *(kkil.net)*
William H. Donner CS 1914 B 524' 00" 54' 00" 30' 00"
  Built: Great Lakes Engineering Works, Ashtabula, OH; last operated in 1969; in use as a cargo transfer hull at Marinette, WI

L-1 LAFARGE CANADA INC., POINTE-CLAIRE, QC
  THE FOLLOWING VESSEL MANAGED BY ALGOMA CENTRAL CORP.
English River 5104382 CC 1961 D 7,450 404' 03" 60' 00" 36' 06"
  Built: Canadian Shipbuilding and Engineering Ltd., Collingwood, ON; converted to a self-unloading cement carrier by Port Arthur Shipbuilding, Port Arthur (now Thunder Bay), ON, in '74

L-2 LAFARGE NORTH AMERICA INC., BINGHAM FARMS, MI *(lafargenorthamerica.com)*
J. B. Ford CC 1904 R 8,000 440' 00" 50' 00" 28' 00"
  Built: American Shipbuilding Co., Lorain, OH; converted to a self-unloading cement carrier in '59; last operated Nov. 15, 1985; most recently used as a cement storage and transfer vessel at Superior, WI, and now laid up at that port (Edwin F. Holmes '04-'16, E. C. Collins '16-'59)

Fleet Name / Vessel Name	IMO #	Vessel Type	Year Built	Engine Type	Cargo Cap. or Gross*	Overall Length	Breadth	Depth
THE FOLLOWING VESSELS MANAGED BY ANDRIE INC., MUSKEGON, MI (andrie.com)								
G. L. Ostrander	7501106	AT	1976	D	198*	140' 02"	40' 01"	22' 03"

Built: Halter Marine, New Orleans, LA; paired with barge Integrity (Andrew Martin '76-'90, Robert L. Torres '90-'94, Jacklyn M '94-'04)

Innovation	9082336	CC	2006	B	7,320*	460' 00"	70' 00"	37' 00"

Built: Bay Shipbuilding Co., Sturgeon Bay, WI

Integrity	8637213	CC	1996	B	14,000	460' 00"	70' 00"	37' 00"

Built: Bay Shipbuilding Co., Sturgeon Bay, WI

Samuel de Champlain	7433799	AT	1975	D	299*	140' 02"	39' 02"	20' 00"

Built: Mangone Shipbuilding, Houston, TX; paired with barge Innovation (Musketeer Fury '75- '78, Tender Panther '78- '79, Margarita '79- '83, Vortice '83- '99, Norfolk '99-'06)

L-3 **LAKE ERIE ISLAND CRUISES LLC, SANDUSKY, OH** (goodtimeboat.com)								
Goodtime I		ES	1960	D	81*	111' 00"	29' 08"	9' 05"

Built: Blount Marine Corp., Warren, RI

L-4 **LAKE EXPRESS LLC, MILWAUKEE, WI** (lake-express.com)								
Lake Express	9329253	PA/CF	2004	D	96*	179' 02"	57' 07"	16' 00"

Built: Austal USA, Mobile, AL; high-speed ferry service from Milwaukee, WI, to Muskegon, MI; capacity is 250 passengers, 46 autos

Lower Lakes Towing's Cuyahoga coming off Lake Ontario at Hamilton, Ont. (Ted Wllush)

Fleet Name / Vessel Name	IMO #	Vessel Type	Year Built	Engine Type	Cargo Cap. or Gross*	Overall Length	Breadth	Depth

L-5 **LAKE MICHIGAN CARFERRY SERVICE INC., LUDINGTON, MI** *(ssbadger.com)*

Badger	5033583	PA/CF	1953	S	4,244*	410' 06"	59' 06"	24' 00"

Built: Christy Corp., Sturgeon Bay, WI; traditional ferry service from Ludington, MI, to Manitowoc, WI; capacity is 520 passengers, 180 autos; vessel is the last coal-fired steamship on the Great Lakes

Spartan		PA/CF	1952	S	4,244*	410' 06"	59' 06"	24' 00"

Built: Christy Corp., Sturgeon Bay, WI; last operated Jan. 20, 1979; in long-term lay-up at Ludington, MI

L-6 **LAKE MICHIGAN CONTRACTORS INC., HOLLAND, MI** *(lakemicontractors.com)*

Defiance		TW	1965	D	39*	48' 00	18' 00"	6' 03"
Wisconsin		CS	1965	B	309*	103' 00"	50' 00"	14' 00"

L-7 **LAKE SERVICE SHIPPING, MUSKEGON, MI**

McKee Sons	5216458	SU	1945	B	19,900	579' 02"	71' 06"	38' 06"

Built: Sun Shipbuilding and Drydock Co., Chester, PA; converted from saltwater vessel to a self-unloading Great Lakes bulk carrier by Maryland Drydock, Baltimore, MD, in '52; completed as a self-unloader by Manitowoc Shipbuilding Co., Manitowoc, WI, in '53; converted to a self-unloading barge by Upper Lakes Towing, Escanaba, MI, in '91; laid up at Erie, PA 2012-14 and Muskegon, MI, since Dec. 20, 2014 (USNS Marine Angel '45-'52)

L-8 **LAKES PILOTS ASSOCIATION, PORT HURON, MI** *(lakespilots.com)*

Huron Belle		PB	1979	D	38*	50' 00"	15' 07"	7' 09"

Built: Gladding-Hearn Shipbuilding, Somerset, MA; vessel offers pilot service at Port Huron, MI

Huron Maid		PB	1977	D	26*	46' 00"	12' 05"	3' 05"

Built: Hans Hansen Welding Co., Toledo, OH; vessel offers pilot service at Detroit, MI

L-9 **LAMBTON MARINE LTD., PORT LAMBTON, ON**

Mary Ellen I		TB	2008	D	18*	41' 08"	14' 02"	7' 0

L-10 **LAURENTIAN PILOTAGE AUTHORITY, MONTREAL, QC** *(pilotagestlaurent.gc.ca)*

Charlevoix		PB	1995	D	79*	75' 00"	18' 08"	4' 01
Grandes Eaux		PB	2008	D	63*	62' 06"	17' 02"	9' 05
Taukamaim		PB	2012	D	82*	72' 01"	19' 05"	10' 05

L-11 **LE GROUPE OCÉAN INC., QUÉBEC, QC** *(groupocean.com)*

Andre H.	5404172	TB	1963	D	317*	126' 00"	28' 06"	12' 10"

Built: Davie Shipbuilding Co., Lauzon, QC (Foundation Valiant '63-'73, Point Valiant {1} '73-'95)

Avantage	6828882	TB	1969	D	362*	116' 10"	32' 09"	16' 03"

Built: J. Boel En Zonen, Temse, Belgium (Sea Lion '69-'97)

Basse-Cote	8644620	DB	1932	B	400	201' 00"	40' 00"	12' 00"

Built: Department of Marine and Fisheries Government Shipyard, Sorel, QC (Louis D. '32-'93)

Betsiamites	8644632	SU	1969	B	11,600	402' 00"	75' 00"	24' 00"

Built: Port Weller Dry Docks Ltd., St. Catharines, ON

Duga	7530030	TB	1977	D	382*	114' 02"	32' 10"	16' 05"

Built: Langsten Slip & Båtbyggeri A/S, Lansten, Norway

Escorte	8871027	TT	1964	D	120*	85' 00"	23' 07"	7' 05"

Built: Jakobson Shipyard, Oyster Bay, NY (USS Menasha [YTB / YTM-773, YTM-761] '64-'92, Menasha {1} '92-'95)

Jerry G.	8959788	TB	1960	D	202*	91' 06"	27' 03"	12' 06"

Built: Davie Shipbuilding Co., Lauzon, QC

Josee H.		PB	1961	D	66*	63' 50"	16' 02"	9' 50"

Built: Ferguson Industries Ltd., Pictou, NS (Le Bic '61-'98)

La Prairie	7393585	TB	1975	D	110*	73' 09"	25' 09"	11' 08"

Built: Georgetown Shipyard, Georgetown, PEI

Le Phil D.		TB	1961	D	38*	56' 01"	16' 00"	5' 08"

Océan Abys	8644644	DB	1948	B	1,000	140' 00"	40' 00"	9' 00"

Built: Marine Industries Ltd., Sorel, QC (Omni No. 1 '48-'94)

Océan A. Simard	8000056	TT	1980	D	286*	92' 00"	34' 00"	13' 07"

Built: Georgetown Shipyards Ltd., Georgetown, PEI (Alexis-Simard '80-'11)

Océan Arctique	9261607	TB	2005	TB	512*	102' 08"	39' 05"	17' 00"

Built: Industries Ocean Inc., Ile-Aux-Coudres, QC (Stevns Arctic '05-'13)

Océan Basques	7237212	TB	1972	D	396*	98' 04"	32' 08"	16' 04"

Built: Canadian Shipbuilding & Engineering Co., Collingwood, ON (Pointe Aux-Basques '72-'13)

Océan Bertrand Jeansonne	9521526	TB	2008	D	402*	94' 05"	36' 05"	17' 02"

Built: East Isle Shipyard, Georgetown, PEI

Océan Bravo	7025279	TB	1970	D	320*	110' 00"	28' 06"	17' 00"

Built: Davie Shipbuilding Co., Lauzon, QC (Takis V. '70-'80, Donald P '80-'80, Nimue '80-'83, Donald P. '83-'98)

Océan Charlie	7312024	TB	1973	D	448*	123' 02"	31' 07"	16' 01"

Built: Davie Shipbuilding Co., Lauzon, QC (Leonard W. '73-'98)

Vessel	IMO	Type	Year	Engine	Tonnage	Length	Beam	Depth
Océan Cote-Nord			2001	D	79*	75' 01"	18' 00"	10' 06"
Built: Industries Ocean Inc., Ile-Aux-Coudres, QC (Cote-Nord '01-'14)								
Océan Delta	7235707	TB	1973	D	722*	136' 08"	35' 08"	22' 00"
Built: Ulstein Mek. Verksted A.S., Ulsteinvik, Norway (Sistella '73-'78, Sandy Cape '78-'80, Captain Ioannis S. '80-'99)								
Océan Echo II	6913091	AT	1969	D	438*	104' 08"	34' 05"	18' 00"
Built: Port Weller Dry Docks, Port Weller, ON (Atlantic '69-'75, Laval '75-'96)								
Océan Express		PB	1999	D	29*	47' 02"	14' 00"	7' 05"
Built: Industries Ocean Inc., Charlevoix, QC (H-2000 '99-'00)								
Océan Foxtrot	7101619	TB	1971	D	700*	170' 10"	38' 09"	11' 11"
Built: Cochrane & Sons Ltd., Selby, England (Polar Shore '71-'77, Canmar Supplier VII '77-'95)								
Océan Georgie Bain	9553892	TB	2009	D	204*	75' 02"	29' 09"	12' 09"
Built: Industries Ocean Inc., Ile-Aux-Coudres, QC								
Océan Golf	5146354	TB	1959	D	159*	103' 00"	25' 10"	11' 09"
Built: P.K. Harris & Sons, Appledore, England (launched as Stranton; Helen M. McAllister '59-'97)								
Océan Guide		PB	2001	D	29*	47' 02"	14' 00"	7' 05"
Built: Industries Ocean Inc., Charlevoix, QC								
Océan Henry Bain	9420916	TB	2006	D	402*	94' 08"	30' 01"	14' 09"
Built: East Isle Shipyard, Georgetown, PEI								
Océan Hercule	7525346	TB	1976	D	448*	120' 00"	32' 00"	19' 00"
(Stril Pilot '76-'81, Spirit Sky '81-'86, Ireland '86-'89, Irelandia '89-'95, Charles Antoine '95-'97)								
Océan Intrepide	9203423	TT	1998	D	302*	80' 00"	30' 01"	14' 09"
Built: Industries Ocean Inc., Ile-Aux-Coudres, QC								
Océan Jupiter	9220160	TT	1999	D	178*	74' 07"	30' 00"	13' 03"
Built: Industries Ocean Inc., Ile-Aux-Coudres, QC								
Océan K. Rusby	9345556	TB	2005	D	402*	94' 08"	30' 01"	14' 09"
Built: East Isle Shipyard, Georgetown, PEI								
Océan Lima		TB	1977	D	15*	34' 02"	11' 08"	4' 00"
(VM/S St. Louis III '77-'10)								
Océan Pierre Julien		TB	2013	D	204*	75' 01"	30' 01"	12' 09"
Built: Industries Ocean Inc., Ile-Aux-Coudres, QC								
Océan Raymond Lemay	9420904	TB	2006	D	402*	94' 08"	30' 01"	14' 09"
Built: East Isle Shipyard, Georgetown, PEI								
Océan Sept-Iles	7901162	TB	1980	D	427*	98' 04"	36' 01"	13' 01"
Built: Canadian Shipbuilding & Engineering Co., Collingwood, ON (Pointe Sept-Iles '80-'13)								
Océan Serge Genois	9553907	TB	2010	D	204*	75' 01"	30' 01"	12' 09"
Built: Industries Ocean Inc., Ile-Aux-Coudres, QC								
Océan Stevns	9224960	TB	2002	D	512*	102' 08"	39' 05"	17' 00"
Built: Industries Ocean Inc., Ile-Aux-Coudres, QC (Stevns Ocean '02-'13)								
Océan Traverse Nord	9666534	DR	2012	B	1,165*	210' 00"	42' 06"	14' 07"
Built: Industries Ocean Inc., Ile-Aux-Coudres, QC								
Océan Tundra	9645504	TB	2013	D	710*	118' 01"	42' 03"	22' 09"
Built: Industries Ocean Inc., Ile-Aux-Coudres, QC								
Omni-Atlas	8644668	CS	1913	B	479*	133' 00"	42' 00"	10' 00"
Built: Sir William Arrol & Co. Ltd., Glasgow, Scotland								
Omni-Richelieu	6923084	TB	1969	D	144*	83' 00"	24' 06"	13' 06"
Built: Pictou Industries Ltd., Pictou, NS (Port Alfred II '69-'82)								
R. F. Grant		TB	1934	D	78*	71' 00"	17' 00"	8' 00"
Service Boat No. 1		PB	1965	D	55*	57' 08"	16' 01"	7' 06"
Service Boat No. 2		TB	1934	D	78*	65' 02"	17' 00"	8' 01"
Service Boat No. 4		PB	1959	D	26*	39' 01"	14' 02"	6' 03"

TRAVAUX MARITIMES OCÉAN INC. – AN AFFILIATE OF LE GROUPE OCÉAN INC., QUÉBEC, QC

Vessel	IMO	Type	Year	Engine	Tonnage	Length	Beam	Depth
Mega	7347641	TB	1975	D	768*	125' 03"	42' 03"	22' 09"
Built: Oy Wartsila AB, Helsinki, Finland; mated with articulated barge Motti								
Motti	9072434	DB	1993	B	5,195*	403' 04"	78' 02"	7' 07"
Built: Kvaerner Masa Yards, Turku, Finland								
Océan Ross Gaudreault	9542221	TB	2011	D	402*	94' 04"	36' 05"	17' 00"
Built: East Isle Shipyard, Georgetown, PEI								
Océan Yvan Desgagnés	9542207	TB	2010	D	402*	94' 04"	36' 05"	17' 00"
Built: East Isle Shipyard, Georgetown, PEI								

L-12 LEGEND CRUISES LLC, STURGEON BAY, WI (ridethefireboat.com)

Vessel	IMO	Type	Year	Engine	Tonnage	Length	Beam	Depth
Fred A. Busse		ES	1937	D	99*	92' 00"	22' 04"	9' 06"
Built: Defoe Boat & Motor Works, Bay City, MI; former Chicago fireboat offers cruises at Sturgeon Bay, WI								

Great Lakes Towing tug Superior in lower Lake Huron. *(Wade P. Streeter)*

Jimmy L assisting Larsholmen at Green Bay, Wis. *(Scott Best)*

L-13 LIVERPOOL BAY PACKET CO. LTD., TORONTO, ON

Mist of Avalon		ES	1967	W	91*	74' 02"	20' 01"	9' 08"

L-14 LOWER LAKES TOWING LTD., PORT DOVER, ON (randlogisticsinc.com)
   A SUBSIDIARY OF RAND LOGISTICS INC., NEW YORK, NY

Cuyahoga   5166392   SU   1943   D   15,675   620' 00"   60' 00"   35' 00"
   Built: American Shipbuilding Co., Lorain, OH; converted to a self-unloader by Manitowoc Shipbuilding Co., Manitowoc, WI, in '74; repowered in '01 (J. Burton Ayers '43-'95)

Kaministiqua   8119285   BC   1983   D   34,500   730' 01"   75' 09"   48' 00"
   Built: Govan Shipyards, Glasgow, Scotland (Saskatchewan Pioneer '83-'95, Lady Hamilton '95-'06, Voyageur Pioneer '06-'08)

Manitoba {3}   6702301   BC   1967   D   19,093   607' 09"   62' 00"   36' 00"
   Built: Collingwood Shipyards, Collingwood, ON (Mantadoc '67-'02, Teakglen '02-'05, Maritime Trader '05-'11)

Manitoulin   8810918   SU   1991   D   (New info not available at press time)
   Former saltwater tanker rebuilt for Great Lakes service in 2015 with a new self-unloading bow section.
   ***Bow section** built 2014-15 at Chengxi Shipyards, Jiangyin, China; **Stern section** built in 1991 at Uljanik Shipyard, Pula, Croatia (Trelsi '08-'01, Euro Swan '01-'11, Lalandia Swan '11-'14)*

Michipicoten {2}   5102865   SU   1952   D   22,300   698' 00"   70' 00"   37' 00"
   Built: Bethlehem Shipbuilding & Drydock Co., Sparrows Point, MD; lengthened 72' by American Shipbuilding Co., S. Chicago, IL, in '57; converted to a self-unloader by American Shipbuilding Co., Toledo, OH, in '80; repowered in '11 (Elton Hoyt 2nd '52-'03)

Mississagi   5128467   SU   1943   D   15,800   620' 06"   60' 00"   35' 00"
   Built: Great Lakes Engineering Works, River Rouge, MI; converted to a self-unloader by Fraser Shipyards, Superior, WI, in '67; repowered in '85 (Hill Annex '43-'43, George A. Sloan '43-'01)

Ojibway   5105831   BC   1952   D   20,668   642' 03"   67' 00"   35' 00"
   Built: Defoe Shipbuilding Co., Bay City, MI; repowered in '05 (Charles L. Hutchinson {3} '52-'62, Ernest R. Breech '62-'88, Kinsman Independent '88-'05, Voyageur Independent '05-'08)

Robert S. Pierson   7366403   SU   1974   D   19,650   630' 00"   68' 00"   36' 11"
   Built: American Shipbuilding Co., Lorain, OH (Wolverine {2} '74-'08)

Saginaw {3}   5173876   SU   1953   D   20,200   639' 03"   72' 00"   36' 00"
   Built: Manitowoc Shipbuilding Co., Manitowoc, WI, repowered in '08 (John J. Boland {3} '53-'99)

Tecumseh {2}   7225855   BC   1973   D   29,510   641' 00"   78' 00"   45' 03
   Built: Lockheed Shipbuilding & Construction Co., Seattle, WA (Sugar Islander '73-'96, Islander '96-'96, Judy Litrico '96-'06, Tina Litrico '06-'11)

L-15 LOWER LAKES TRANSPORTATION CO., WILLIAMSVILLE, NY – DIV. OF LOWER LAKES TOWING LTD.
   GRAND RIVER NAVIGATION CO., AVON LAKE, OH – OWNER – AN AFFILIATE OF LOWER LAKES TOWING LTD.

Ashtabula   SU   1982   B   17,982   610' 01"   78' 01"   49' 08"
   Built: Bay Shipbuilding Co., Sturgeon Bay, WI (Mary Turner '82-'12)

Calumet {3}   7329314   SU   1973   D   19,650   630' 00"   68' 00"   36' 11"
   Built: American Shipbuilding Co., Lorain, OH (William R. Roesch '73-'95, David Z. Norton {3} '95-'07, David Z. '07-'08)

CTC No. 1   CC   1943   R   16,300   620' 06"   60' 00"   35' 00"
   Built: Great Lakes Engineering Works, River Rouge, MI; last operated Nov. 12, 1981; former cement storage/transfer vessel is laid up at South Chicago, IL; may be returned to service at a future date (Launched as McIntyre; Frank Purnell {1} '43-'64, Steelton {3} '64-'78, Hull No. 3 '78-'79, Pioneer {4} '79-'82)

Defiance   8109761   ATB   1982   D   196*   145' 01"   44' 00"   21' 00
   Built: Marinette Marine Corp., Marinette, WI; paired with barge Ashtabula (April T. Beker '82-'87, Beverly Anderson '82-'12)

Invincible   7723819   ATB   1979   D   180*   100' 00"   35' 00"   22' 06"
   Built: Atlantic Marine Inc., Fort George Island, FL (R. W. Sesler '79-'91)

James L. Kuber   5293341   SU   1953   B   25,500   703' 08"   70' 00"   36' 00"
   Built: Great Lakes Engineering Works, River Rouge, MI; lengthened 120' by Fraser Shipyards, Superior, WI, in '75; converted to a self-unloader by Bay Shipbuilding, Sturgeon Bay, WI, in '83; converted to a barge by the owners in '07 (Reserve '53-'08)

Lewis J. Kuber   5336351   SU   1952   B   22,300   616' 10"   70' 00"   37' 00"
   Built: Bethlehem Steel Corp., Sparrows Point, MD; lengthened 72' by American Shipbuilding, South Chicago, IL, in '58; converted to a self-unloader by Fraser Shipyards, Superior, WI, in '80; converted to a barge by Erie Shipbuilding, Erie, PA, in '06; (Sparrows Point '52-'90, Buckeye {3} '90-'06)

Manistee   5294307   SU   1943   D   14,900   620' 06"   60' 03"   35' 00"
   Built: Great Lakes Engineering Works, River Rouge, MI; converted to a self-unloader by Manitowoc Shipbuilding Co., Manitowoc, WI, in '64; repowered in '76 (launched as Adirondack; Richard J. Reiss {2} '43-'86, Richard Reiss '86-'05)

Manitowoc   7366398   SU   1973   D   19,650   630' 00"   68' 00"   36' 11"
   Built: American Shipbuilding Co., Lorain, OH (Paul Thayer '73-'95, Earl W. Oglebay '95-'07, Earl W. '07-'08)

Olive L. Moore   8635227   AT   1928   D   524*   125' 00"   39' 02"   13' 09"
Built: Manitowoc Shipbuilding Co., Manitowoc, WI; paired with barge Lewis J. Kuber
(John F. Cushing '28-'66, James E. Skelly '66-'66)

Victory   8003292   TB   1980   D   194*   140' 00"   43' 01"   18' 00"
Built: McDermott Shipyard Inc., Amelia, LA; paired with barge James L. Kuber

L-16   LUEDTKE ENGINEERING CO., FRANKFORT, MI *(luedtke-eng.com)*

Alan K. Luedtke   TB   1944   D   149*   86' 04"   23' 00"   10' 03"
Built: Allen Boat Co., Harvey, LA (U. S. Army ST-527 '44-'55, USCOE Two Rivers '55-'90)

Ann Marie   TB   1954   D   81*   71' 00"   19' 05"   9' 06"
Built: Smith Basin & Drydock, Pensacola, FL (ST-9684 '54- '80, Lewis Castle '80-'97, Apache '97-'01)

Chris E. Luedtke   TB   1936   D   18*   42' 05"   11' 09"   5' 00"

Erich R. Luedtke   TB   1939   D   18*   42' 05"   11' 09"   5' 00"

Gretchen B   TB   1943   D   18*   41' 09"   12' 05"   6' 00"

Karl E. Luedtke   TB   1928   D   32*   55' 02"   14' 09"   6' 00"
Buit: Leathem D. Smith Dock Co., Sturgeon Bay, WI

Krista S   TB   1954   D   93*   67' 09"   20' 01"   7' 07"
Built: Walker Shipyard, Pascagoula, MS (Sea Wolf '54-'01, Jimmy Wray '01-'08)

Kurt R. Luedtke   TB   1956   D   95*   72' 00"   22' 06"   7' 06"
Built: Lockport Shipyard, Lockport, LA (Jere C. '56-'90)

Paul L. Luedtke   TB   1988   D   97*   75' 00"   26' 00"   9' 06"
Built: Terrebonne Shipbuilders Inc., Houma, LA (Edward E. Gillen III '88-'13)

M-1   MCM MARINE INC., SAULT STE. MARIE, MI *(mcmmarine.com)*

Beaver State   TB   1935   D   18*   43' 07"   12' 00"   5' 02"

Drummond Islander II   TB   1961   D   97*   65' 00"   36' 00"   9' 00"
Built: Marinette Marine Corp., Marinette, WI

Madison   TB   1975   D   17*   33' 08"   13' 05"   4' 07"

Mohawk   TB   1945   D   46*   65' 00"   19' 00"   10' 06"

No. 55   DR   1927   DE   721*   165' 00"   42' 08"   12' 00"

No. 56   DS   1928   DE   1,174*   165' 00"   42' 04"   15' 07"

Sioux   DS   1954   B   504*   120' 00"   50' 00"   10' 00"

M-2   MacDONALD MARINE LTD., GODERICH, ON *(mactug.com)*

Debbie Lyn   TB   1950   D   10*   45' 00"   14' 00"   10' 00"
Built: Matheson Boat Works, Goderich, ON (Skipper '50-'60)

Donald Bert   TB   1953   D   11*   45' 00"   14' 00"   10' 00"
Built: Matheson Boat Works, Goderich, ON

Dover   TB   1931   D   70*   84' 00"   17' 00"   6' 00"
Built: Canadian Mead-Morrison Co. Ltd., Welland, ON (Earleejune, Iveyrose)

Ian Mac   TB   1955   D   12*   45' 00"   14' 00"   10' 00"
Built: Matheson Boat Works, Goderich, ON

M-3   MADELINE ISLAND FERRY LINE INC., LaPOINTE, WI *(madferry.com)*

Bayfield {2}   PA/CF   1952   D   83*   120' 00"   43' 00"   10' 00"
Built: Chesapeake Marine Railway, Deltaville, VA (Charlotte '52-'99)

Island Queen {2}   PA/CF   1966   D   90*   75' 00"   34' 09"   10' 00"

Madeline   PA/CF   1984   D   94*   90' 00"   35' 00"   8' 00"

Nichevo II   PA/CF   1962   D   89*   65' 00"   32' 00"   8' 09"

M-4   MAID OF THE MIST STEAMBOAT CO. LTD., NIAGARA FALLS, NY *(maidofthemist.com)*

Maid of the Mist VI   ES   1990   D   155*   78' 09"   29' 06"   7' 00"

Maid of the Mist VII   ES   1997   D   160*   80' 00"   30' 00"   7' 00"

M-5   MALCOLM MARINE, ST. CLAIR, MI *(malcolmmarine.com)*

Capt. Keith   TB   1955   D   39*   53' 03"   15' 06"   6' 04"
Built: Diamond Manufacturing, Savannah GA (Richard Merritt '55-'13)

Debbie Lee   TB   1955   D   13*   32' 00"   11' 00"   4' 04"

Manitou {2}   TB   1942   D   199*   110' 00"   26' 02"   15' 06"
Built: U.S. Coast Guard, Curtis Bay, MD (USCGC Manitou [WYT-60] '43-'84)

M-6   MANITOU ISLAND TRANSIT, LELAND, MI *(leelanau.com/manitou)*

Manitou Isle   PA/PK   1946   D   39*   52' 00"   14' 00"   8' 00"
(Namaycush '46-'59)

Mishe Mokwa   PA/CF   1966   D   49*   65' 00"   17' 06"   8' 00"
Built: J. W. Nolan & Sons, Erie, PA

M-7   MARINE RECYCLING CORP., PORT COLBORNE & PORT MAITLAND, ON *(marinerecycling.ca)*

Algoma Progress	6821999	SU	1968	D	31,637	730' 00"	75' 00"	46' 06"

Built: Port Weller Dry Docks, Port Weller, ON; Scrapping scheduled for 2015 (Canadian Progress '68-'11)

Charlie E.		TB	1943	D	32*	63' 00"	16' 06"	7' 06"

Built: W.F. Kolbe & Co. Ltd., Port Dover, ON (Kolbe '43-'86, Lois T. '86-'02)

M-8   MARINE TECH LLC, DULUTH, MN *(marinetechduluth.com)*

Callie M.		TB	1910	D	51*	64' 03"	16' 09"	8' 06"

Built: Houma Shipbuilding Co., Houma, LA (Chattanooga '10-'79, Howard T. Hagen '79-'94, Nancy Ann '94-'01)

Dean R. Smith		DR	1985	B	338*	120' 00"	48' 00"	7' 00"

(No. 2 '85-'94, B. Yetter '94-'01)

Miss Laura		TB	1943	D	146*	81' 01"	24' 00"	9' 10"

Built: Lawley & Son Corp., Neponset, MA (DPC-3 '43-'46, DS-43 '46-'50, Fresh Kills '50-'69, Richard K. '69-'93, Leopard '93-'03)

M-9   MARIPOSA CRUISE LINE LTD., TORONTO, ON *(mariposacruises.com)*

Capt. Matthew Flinders	8883355	ES	1982	D	746*	144' 00"	40' 00"	8' 06"

Built: North Arm Slipway Pty. Ltd., Port Adelaide, Australia

Klancy II		ES	1989	D	124*	60' 02"	20' 00"	8' 02"
Northern Spirit I	8870073	ES	1983	D	489*	136' 00"	31' 00"	9' 00"

Built: Blount Marine Corp., Warren, RI (New Spirit '83-'89, Pride of Toronto '89-'92)

Oriole	8800054	ES	1987	D	200*	75' 00"	23' 00"	9' 00"

Built: Duratug Shipyard Fabricating Ltd., Port Dover, ON

Rosemary		ES	1960	D	52*	68' 00"	15' 06"	6' 08"

Built: Bender Ship Repairs, Mobile, AL

Showboat		ES	1988	D	135*	74' 00"	21' 00"	4' 00"

Built: Herb Fraser & Associates Ltd., Port Colborne, ON

M-10   MAXIMUS CORP., BLOOMFIELD HILLS, MI *(boblosteamers.com)*

Ste. Claire		PA	1910	R	870*	197' 00"	65' 00"	14' 00"

Built: Toledo Ship Building Co., Toledo, OH; former Detroit to Bob-Lo Island passenger steamer last operated Sept. 2, 1991; undergoing restoration at Detroit, MI

M-11   McASPHALT MARINE TRANSPORTATION LTD., TORONTO, ON *(mcasphalt.com)*

Everlast	7527332	ATB	1976	D	1,361*	143' 04"	44' 04"	21' 04"

Built: Hakodate Dock Co., Hakodate, Japan; paired with barge Norman McLeod (Bilibino '77-'96)

John J. Carrick	9473444	TK	2008	B	11,613	407' 06"	71' 07"	30' 00"

Built: Penglai Bohai Shipyard Co. Ltd., Penglai, China

Norman McLeod	8636219	TK	2001	B	6,809*	379' 02"	71' 06"	30' 02"

Built: Jinling Shipyard, Nanjing, China

Victorious	9473262	ATB	2009	D	1,299	122' 00"	44' 03"	26' 02

Built: Penglai Bohai Shipyard Co. Ltd., Penglai, China; paired with barge John J. Carrick

M-12   McKEIL MARINE LTD., HAMILTON, ON *(mckeil.com)*

Alouette Spirit	8641537	DB	1969	B	10,087*	425' 01"	74' 02"	29' 05"

Built: Gulfport Shipbuilding Co., Port Arthur, TX (KTC 135 '69-'04, Lambert's Spirit '04-'05)

Beverly M 1	9084047	TB	1994	D	450*	114' 06"	34' 04"	17' 04"

Built: Imamura Shipbuilding, Kure, Japan (Shek O, Hunter, Pacific Tycoon)

Blain M	7907099	RV	1981	D	925*	165' 05"	36' 00"	19' 09"

Built: Ferguson Industries, Picton, ON (Wilfred Templeman '81-'11)

Bonnie B III	7017662	TB	1969	D	308*	107' 00"	32' 00"	18' 00"

(Esso Oranjestad '69-'85, Oranjestad '85-'86, San Nicolas '86-'87, San Nicolas I '87-'88)

Carrol C. 1	7017674	TB	1969	D	307*	107' 00"	32' 00"	18' 00"

Built: Gulfport Shipbuilding Corp., Port Arthur, TX (Esso San Nicolas '69-'86, San Nicolas '86-'87, Carrol C '87-'88)

Evans McKeil	8983416	TB	1936	D	284*	110' 06"	25' 06"	14' 08"

Built: Panama Canal Co., Balboa, Panama (Alhajuela '36-'70, Barbara Ann {2} '70-'89)

Florence M.	5118797	TB	1961	D	236*	96' 03"	29' 03"	9' 00"

Built: P.K. Harris & Sons, Appledore, England (Foundation Vibert '61-'73, Point Vibert '73-'06)

Huron Spirit	8646642	SU	1995	B	4,542*	328' 01"	82' 25"	23 06"

Built: Jiangdu Shipyard, Tiangsu Province, China (Mulege, Hasanuddin)

Jarrett M	5030086	TB	1945	D	96*	82' 00"	20' 00"	10' 00"

Built: Russel Brothers Ltd., Owen Sound, ON (Atomic '45-'06)

John Spence	7218735	TB	1972	D	719*	171' 00"	38' 00"	15' 01"

Built: Star Shipyard, New Westminster, BC (Mary B. VI '72-'81, Mary B. '81-'82, Mary B. VI '82-'83, Arctic Tuktu '83-'94)

Lambert Spirit	8641525	DB	1968	B	9,645	400' 01"	70' 02"	27' 06"

Built: Avondale Shipyards Inc., Avondale, LA (KTC 115 '68-'06)

Leonard M.	8519215	TB	1986	D	457*	103' 07"	36' 01"	19' 02"
Built: McTay Marine, Bromborough, England (Point Halifax '86-'12)								
Lois M.	9017616	TT	1991	D	453*	35' 09"	11' 65"	5' 07"
Built: Matsuura Tekko Zosen, Hirashimo, Japan (Lambert '91-'14)								
Niagara Spirit	8736021	DB	1984	D	9,164*	340' 01"	78' 02"	19' 06"
Built: FMC Corp., Portland, OR (Alaska Trader '84-'99, Timberjack '99-'08)								
Nunavut Spirit	8636673	DB	1983	B	6,076*	400' 00"	105' 00"	20' 06"
Built: FMC Corp., Portland, OR (Barge 5001)								
Salvor	5427019	TB	1963	D	407*	120' 00"	31' 00"	18' 06"
Built: Jakobson Shipyard, Oyster Bay, NY (Esther Moran '63-'00)								
Sharon M I	9084059	TB	1993	D	450*	107' 04"	34' 04"	17' 03"
Built: Inamura Shipbuilding, Kure, Japan (Mai Po, Pacific Tempest)								
Stormont	8959893	TB	1953	D	108*	80' 00"	20' 00"	15' 00"
Built: Canadian Dredge & Dock Co., Kingston, ON								
S/VM 86		DB	1958	B	487*	168' 01"	40' 00"	10' 00"
Built: Canadian Shipbuilding & Engineering Ltd., Collingwood, ON (S.L.S. 86)								

Barge Lewis J. Kuber, the former steamer Buckeye, in winter ice, January 2015. (Graham Grattan)

Tim McKeil	9017604	TB	1991	D	453*	107' 07"	34' 04"	17' 03"

Built: Matsuura Tekko Zosen, Hirashimo, Japan (Pannawonica 1 '91-'14)

Tobias	9642253	DB	2012	B	8,870*	393' 09"	105' 07"	26' 07"

Built: Damen Shipyard Gorinchem, Gorinchem, Netherlands

Tony MacKay	7227786	TB	1973	D	366*	117' 00"	30' 02"	14' 05"

Built: Richard Dunston Ltd., Hessle, England (Point Carroll '73-'01)

Viateur's Spirit		DB	2004	D	253*	141' 01"	52' 03"	5' 01"

Built: Port Weller Dry Dock, Port Weller, ON (Traverse René Lavasseur '04-'06)

Wilf Seymour	5215789	TB	1961	D	442*	122' 00"	31' 00"	17' 00"

Built: Gulfport Shipbuilding, Port Arthur, TX (M. Moran '61-'70, Port Arthur '70-'72, M. Moran '72-'00, Salvager '00-'04)

Wyatt M.	8974178	TB	1948	D	123*	85' 00"	20' 00"	10' 00"

Built: Russel Brothers Ltd., Owen Sound, ON (P. J. Murer '48-'81, Michael D. Misner '81-'93, Thomas A. Payette '93-'96, Progress '96-'06)

MAMMOET-MCKEIL LTD., AYR, ON – A SUBSIDIARY OF McKEIL MARINE LTD.

Dowden Spirit		DB	2014	B	2,130*	250' 02"	72' 01"	16' 04"

Built: Glovertown Shipyards Ltd., Glovertown, NL

Glovertown Spirit	9662174	DB	2012	B	2,073*	243' 07"	77' 02"	14' 09"

Built: Damen Shipyards Gorinchem, Netherlands

MM Newfoundland	DB	2011	B	2,165*	260' 00"	72' 00"	16' 01"

Built: Signal International, Pascagoula, MS

MONTREAL BOATMEN LTD., PORT COLBORNE, ON – A SUBSIDIARY OF McKEIL MARINE LTD.

Aldo H.	PB	1979	D	37*	56' 04"	15' 04"	6' 02"
Boatman No. 3	PB	1965	D	13*	33' 08"	11' 00"	6' 00"
Boatman No. 6	PB	1979	D	39*	56' 07"	18' 07"	6' 03"
Primrose	DR	1915	B	916*	136' 06"	42' 00"	10' 02"

M-13 **McMULLEN & PITZ CONSTRUCTION CO., MANITOWOC, WI** (mcmullenandpitz.net)

Dauntless	TB	1937	D	25*	52' 06"	15' 06"	5' 03"

M-14 **McNALLY INTERNATIONAL INC., HAMILTON, ON** (mcnallycorp.com)
A SUBSIDIARY OF WEEKS MARINE INC., CRANFORD, NJ

Bagotville	TB	1964	D	65*	65' 00"	18' 05"	8' 03"

Built: Verreault Navigation, Les Méchins, QC

Beaver Delta II	TB	1959	D	14*	35' 08"	12' 00"	4' 04"

Built: Allied Builders Ltd., Vancouver, BC (Halcyon Bay)

Beaver Gamma	TB	1960	D	17*	37' 01"	12' 09"	6' 00"

Built: Diesel Sales & Service (Burlington) Ltd., Burlington, ON (Burlington Bertie)

Canadian	DR	1954	B	1,087*	173' 08"	49' 08"	13' 04"

Built: Port Arthur Shipbuilding Co. Ltd., Port Arthur (Thunder Bay), ON

Canadian Argosy	DS	1978	B	951*	149' 09"	54' 01"	10' 08"

Built: Canadian Shipbuilding & Engineering Ltd., Collingwood, ON

Cargo Carrier I	DB	1969	B	196*	89' 09"	29' 09"	8' 05"

Built: Halifax Shipyards Ltd., Halifax, NS

Cargo Master	CS	1964	B	562*	136' 00"	50' 00"	9' 00"

Built: Canadian Shipbuilding & Engineering Ltd., Collingwood, ON

Carl M.	TB	1957	D	21*	47' 00"	14' 06"	6' 00"
Dapper Dan	TB	1948	D	21*	41' 03"	12' 07"	5' 09"
D.L. Stanyer	TB	2014	D	14*	40' 03"	11' 08"	6' 02"

Built: Chantier Naval Forillon, Gaspé, QC

F. R. McQueen	DB	1959	B	180*	79' 09"	39' 09"	5' 07"

Built: Manitowoc Engineering Corp., Manitowoc, WI

Handy Andy	DB	1925	B	313*	95' 09"	43' 01"	10' 00"
Idus Atwell	DS	1962	B	366*	100' 00"	40' 00"	8' 05"

Built: Dominion Bridge Co. Ltd., Toronto, ON

Island Sauvage	DB	1969	D	381*	86' 03"	61' 04"	9' 03"

Built: Halifax Shipyards Ltd., Halifax, NS (Cargo Carrier II)

J.F. Whalen	TB	2014	D	14*	0' 03"	11' 08"	6' 02"

Built: Chantier Naval Forillon, Gaspé, QC

Jamie L.	TB	1988	D	25*	36' 04"	14' 07"	5' 09"
John Holden	DR	1954	B	148*	89' 08"	30' 01"	6' 02"

Built: McNamara Construction Co. Ltd., Toronto, ON

Lac Como	TB	1944	D	63*	65' 00"	16' 10"	7' 10"

Built: Canadian Bridge Co., Walkerville, ON (Tanac 74 '44-'64)

Lac Vancouver	TB	1943	D	65*	60' 09"	16' 10"	7' 08"

Built: Central Bridge Co., Trenton, ON (Vancouver '43-'74)

Maggie Girl	TB	1972	D	72*	72' 07	17' 04	8' 05

Built: Alloy Manufacturing Ltd., Lachine, QC (Advent)

Mister Joe	TB	1964	D	70*	61' 00"	19' 00"	7' 02"

Built: Russel Brothers Ltd., Owen Sound, ON (Churchill River -'99)

Oshawa	TB	1969	D	24*	42' 09"	13' 08"	5' 04"
Paula M.	TB	1959	D	12*	48' 02"	10' 05"	3' 01"
Sandra Mary	TB	1962	D	97*	80' 00"	21' 00"	10' 09"

Built: Russel Brothers Ltd., Owen Sound, ON (Flo Cooper '62-'00)

Whitby	TB	1978	D	24*	42' 19"	13' 08"	6' 05"
William B. Dilly	DR	1957	B	473*	116' 00"	39' 10"	9' 01"

Built: Canadian Shipbuilding & Engineering Ltd., Collingwood, ON

Willmac	TB	1959	D	16*	40' 00"	13' 00"	3' 07"

M-15 **MENASHA TUGBOAT CO., SARNIA, ON**

Menasha {2}	TB	1949	D	132*	78' 00"	24' 00"	9' 08"

Built: Bludworth Marine, Houston, TX (W. C. Harms '49-'54, Hamilton '54-'86, Ruby Casho '86-'88, W. C. Harms '88-'97)

M-16	**MERCURY CRUISES, CHICAGO, IL** *(mercuryskylinecruiseline.com)*							
	Skyline Queen		ES	1959	D	45*	61'05"	16'10"	6'00"

M-17 MICHIGAN DEPARTMENT OF NATURAL RESOURCES, LANSING, MI *(michigan.gov/dnr)*

Channel Cat	RV	1968	D	24*	46'00"	13'06"	4'00"
Lake Char	RV	2006	D	26*	56'00"	16'00"	4'05"
Steelhead	RV	1967	D	70*	63'00"	16'04"	6'06"

M-18 MICHIGAN TECHNOLOGICAL UNIVERSITY, HOUGHTON, MI *(mtu.edu/greatlakes/fleet/agassiz)*

Agassiz	RV	2002	D	14*	36'00"	13'00"	4'00"

M-19 MIDLAND TOURS INC., PENETANGUISHENE, ON *(midlandtours.com)*

Miss Midland	7426667	ES	1974	D	106*	68'07"	19'04"	6'04"

M-20 MIDWEST MARITIME CORP., MILWAUKEE, WI

Leona B.	TB	1972	D	99*	59'08"	24'01"	10'03"

(Kings Squire '72-'89, Juanita D. '78-'89, Peggy Ann '89-'93, Mary Page Hannah {2} '93-'04)

M-21 MILLER BOAT LINE, PUT-IN-BAY, OH *(millerferry.com)*

Islander {3}	PA/CF	1983	D	92*	90'03"	38'00"	8'03"
Put-in-Bay {3}	PA/CF	1997	D	97*	136 00"	38'06"	9'06"

Built: Sturgeon Bay Shipbuilding Co., Sturgeon Bay, WI; lengthened by 40' at Cleveland, OH, in '09

South Bass	PA/CF	1989	D	95*	96'00"	38'06"	9'06"
Wm. Market	PA/CF	1993	D	95*	96'00"	38'06"	8'09"

Built: Peterson Builders Inc., Sturgeon Bay, WI

M-22 MILWAUKEE BOAT LINE LLC, MILWAUKEE, WI *(mkeboat.com)*

Iroquois	PA	1922	D	91*	61'09"	21'00"	6'04"
Vista King	ES	1978	D	60*	78'00"	23'00"	5'02"
Voyageur	PA	1988	D	94*	67'02"	21'00"	7'04"

M-23 MILWAUKEE HARBOR COMMISSION, MILWAUKEE, WI *(city.milwaukee.gov/port)*

Harbor Seagull	TB	1961	D	23*	44'05"	16'04"	5'00"
Joey D.	TB	2011	D	65*	60'00"	20'06"	6'06"

Built: Great Lakes Shipyard, Cleveland, OH

M-24 MILWAUKEE RIVER CRUISE LINE, MILWAUKEE, WI *(edelweissboats.com)*

Edelweiss II	ES	1989	D	95*	73'08"	20'00"	2'08"

M-25 MINISTRY OF TRANSPORTATION, DOWNSVIEW, ON *(mto.gov.on.ca)*

Frontenac II	5068875	PA/CF	1962	D	666*	181'00"	45'00"	10'00"

Built: Chantier Maritime de Saint-Laurent, Saint-Laurent, QC (Charlevoix {2} '62-'92)

Frontenac Howe Islander	PF/CF	2004	D	130*	100'00"	32'03"	5'05"

Built: Heddle Marine Service Inc., Hamilton, ON

Glenora	PA/CF	1952	D	189*	127'00"	33'00"	9'00"

Built: Erieau Shipbuilding & Drydock Co. Ltd., Erieau, ON (The St. Joseph Islander '52-'74)

Jiimaan	9034298	PA/CF	1992	D	2,807*	176'09"	42'03"	13'06"

Built: Port Weller Drydock, Port Weller, ON

Pelee Islander	5273274	PA/CF	1960	D	334*	145'00"	32'00"	10'00"

Built: Erieau Shipbuilding & Drydock Co. Ltd., Erieau, ON

Quinte Loyalist	5358062	PA/CF	1954	D	204*	127'00"	32'00"	8'00"

Built: Erieau Shipbuilding & Drydock Co. Ltd., Erieau, ON

Wolfe Islander III	7423079	PA/CF	1975	D	985*	205'00"	68'00"	6'00"

Built: Port Arthur Shipbuilding Co., Port Arthur, ON

M-26 MONTREAL PORT AUTHORITY, MONTREAL, QC *(port-montreal.com)*

Denis M	TB	1942	D	21*	46'07"	12'08"	4'01"

Built: Russel Brothers Ltd., Owen Sound, ON (Marcel D.)

Maisonneuve	7397749	PA	1972	D	84*	63'10"	20'07"	9'03"

Built: Fercraft Marine Inc., Ste. Catherine D'Alexandrie, QC

M-27 MUNISING BAY SHIPWRECK TOURS INC., MUNISING, MI *(shipwrecktours.com)*

Miss Munising	ES	1967	D	50*	60'00"	14'00"	4'04"

M-28 MUSIQUE AQUATIQUE CRUISE LINES INC., TORONTO, ON *(citysightseeingtoronto.com)*

Harbour Star	ES	1978	D	45*	63'06"	15'09"	3'09"

Built: Eastern Equipment Ltd., LaSalle, QC (K. Wayne Simpson '78-'95)

M-29 **MUSKOKA STEAMSHIP & HISTORICAL SOCIETY, GRAVENHURST, ON** *(segwun.com)*

Segwun		PA	1887	R	308*	128' 00"	24' 00"	7' 06"

Built: Melancthon Simpson, Toronto, ON (Nipissing {2} 1887–'25)

Wenonah II	8972003	PA	2001	D	447*	127' 00"	28' 00"	6' 00"

Built: McNally Construction Inc., Belleville, ON

M-30 **M/V ZEUS LC, CHESAPEAKE CITY, MD**

Zeus	9506071	TB	1964	D	98*	104' 02"	29' 03"	13' 05"

Built: Houma Shipbuilding Co., Houma, LA; usually paired with barge Robert F. Deegan, Fleet U-13

M-31 **MYSTIC BLUE CRUISES INC., CHICAGO, IL** *(mysticbluecruises.com)*

Mystic Blue		PA	1998	D	97*	138' 09"	36' 00"	10' 05"

N-1 **NADRO MARINE SERVICES LTD., PORT DOVER, ON** *(nadromarine.com)*

Ecosse	8624682	TB	1979	D	142*	91' 00"	26' 00"	8' 06"

Built: Hike Metal Products Ltd., Wheatley, ON (R & L No. 1 '79–'96)

Intrepid III		TB	1976	D	39*	66' 00"	17' 00"	7' 06"

Built: Halter Marine Ltd., Chalmette, LA

Lac Manitoba		TB	1944	D	51*	64' 00"	16' 07"	7' 10"

Built: Central Bridge Co., Trenton, ON (Tanac 75 '44–'52, Manitoba '52–'57)

Lac St-Jean		DB	1971	B	771*	150' 00"	54' 09"	10' 06"

Built: Canadian Vickers Ltd., Montreal, QC

Molly M. 1	5118838	TB	1962	D	207*	98' 06"	27' 10"	12' 02"

Built: Davie Shipbuilding Co., Lauzon, QC (Foundation Vigour '62–'74, Point Vigour '74–'07)

Seahound		TB	1941	D	57*	65' 00"	18' 00"	8' 00"

Built: Equitable Equipment Co., New Orleans, LA ([Unnamed] '41–'56, Sea Hound '56–'80, Carolyn Jo '80–'00)

Vac		TB	1942	D	36*	65' 00"	20' 04"	4' 03"

Built: George Gamble, Port Dover, ON

Vigilant I		TB	1944	D	111*	79' 06"	20' 11"	10' 02"

Built: Russell Brothers Ltd., Owen Sound, ON (HMCS Glenlivet [W-43] '44–'75, Glenlivet II '75–'77, Canadian Franko '77–'82, Glenlivet II '82–'00)

N-2 **NAUTICA QUEEN CRUISE DINING, CLEVELAND, OH** *(nauticaqueen.com)*

Nautica Queen		ES	1981	D	95*	124' 00"	31' 02"	8' 09"

Built: Blount Marine Corp., Warren, RI (Bay Queen '81–'85, Arawanna Queen '85–'88, Star of Nautica '88–'92)

N-3 **NAUTICAL ADVENTURES, TORONTO, ON** *(nauticaladventure.com)*

Empire Sandy	5071561	ES/3S	1943	D/W	338*	140' 00"	32' 08"	14' 00"

Built: Clellands Ltd., Wellington Quay-on-Tyne, England (Empire Sandy '43–'48, Ashford '48–'52, Chris M. '52–'79)

Wayward Princess		ES	1976	D	325*	92' 00"	26' 00"	10' 00"

Built: Marlin Yacht Co., Summerstown, ON (Cayuga II '76–'82)

Walter J. McCarthy Jr. in the Rock Cut, on the St. Marys River at Barbeau, Mich. *(Neil Johnson)*

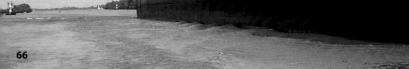

N-4	**NEW YORK POWER AUTHORITY, LEWISTON, NY**							
	Breaker		IB/TB	1962	D	29*	43' 03"	14' 03"	5' 00"
	Daniel Joncaire		IB/TB	1979	D	25*	43' 03"	15' 00"	5' 00"
	William H. Latham		IB/TB	1987	D	77*	61' 00"		

N-5 NEW YORK DEPT. OF ENVIRONMENTAL QUALITY, LAKE ONTARIO UNIT, CAPE VINCENT, NY

Seth Green		RV	1984	D	50*	47' 00"	17' 00"	8' 00"

N-6 NEW YORK STATE MARINE HIGHWAY TRANSPORTATION CO., TROY, NY (nysmarinehighway.com)

Benjamin Elliot		TB	1960	D	27*	47 07'	15' 02"	7' 02

Built: Gladding-Hearn Shipbuilding, Somerset, MA (El-Jean)

Frances	5119246	TB	1957	D	146*	90' 00"	25' 00"	10' 00"

Built: Jakobson Shipyard, Oyster Bay, NY (Frances Turecamo)

Margot	5222043	TB	1958	D	141*	90' 00"	25' 00"	10' 00"

Built: Jakobson Shipyard, Oyster Bay, NY (Jolene Rose, Margot Moran)

N-7 NORTH SHORE SCENIC CRUISES, SILVER BAY, MN (scenicsuperior.com)

Wenonah		ES	1960	D	91*	70' 07"	19' 04"	9' 07"

Built: Dubuque Boat & Boiler, Dubuque, IA (Jamaica '60-'64)

N-8 NORTHERN MARINE TRANSPORTATION INC., SAULT STE. MARIE, MI

Empire State		PB	1951	D	21*	41' 09"	12' 04"	6' 06"
David Allen		PB	1964	D	32*	56' 04"	13' 03"	6' 00"
Linda Jean		PB	1950	D	17*	38' 00"	10' 00"	5' 00"

N-9 NUNAVUT EASTERN ARCTIC SHIPPING INC., MONTREAL, QC (neas.ca)

Vessels offer service between St. Lawrence River ports and the Canadian Arctic between July and November

Avataq	8801618	GC	1989	D	9,653	370' 07"	62' 00"	37' 00"

Built: Miho Shipbuilding Co. Ltd., Shimizu Shizuoka Prefecture, Japan; operated by Spliethoff's, Amsterdam (Poleca, Mekhanik Volkosh, Tiger Speed, Lootsgracht)

Erasmusgracht	9081368	GC	1994	D	12,754	450' 00"	62' 00"	38' 02"

Built: Ulstein Verft, Ulsteinvik, Norway; operated by Spliethoff's, Amsterdam, Netherlands

Mitiq	9081306	GC	1995	D	12,754	447' 04"	62' 00"	38' 03"

Built: Frisian Shipbuilding Welgelegen B.V., Harlingen, Netherlands; operated by Spliethoff's, Amsterdam, Netherlands (Emmagracht '95-'13)

Qamutik	9081289	GC	1995	D	12,760	446' 00"	62' 00"	38' 02"

Built: Frisian Shipbuilding Welgelegen B.V., Harlingen, Netherlands; operated by Spliethoff's, Amsterdam, Netherlands (Edisongracht)

Umiavut	8801591	GC	1988	D	9,653	370' 07"	63' 01"	37' 00"

Built: Miho Shipbuilding Co. Ltd., Shimizu Shizuoka Prefecture, Japan; operated by Spliethoff's, Amsterdam, Netherlands (Completed as Newca; Kapitan Silin '88-'92, Lindengracht '92-'00)

O-1 OAK GROVE MARINE AND TRANSPORTATION INC., CLAYTON, NY

Maple Grove		PK	1954	D	55*	73' 07"	20' 00"	9' 00"

O-2 OFFSHORE DREDGING & CONSTRUCTION INC., MUSKEGON, MI (offshoredredging.com)

Andrew J.		TB	1972	D	31*	43' 08"	14' 03"	7' 05"

O-3 OHIO DEPARTMENT OF NATURAL RESOURCES, COLUMBUS, OH (dnr.state.oh.us)

Explorer II		RV	1999	D		53' 00"	15' 05"	4' 05"
Grandon		RV	1990	D	47*	47' 00"	16' 00"	5' 05"

O-4 OLSON DREDGE & DOCK CO., ALGONAC, MI

John Michael		TB	1913	D	41*	55' 04"	15' 01"	7' 06"

Built: Cowles Shipyard Co., Buffalo, NY (Colonel Ward, Ross Coddington, Joseph J. Olivieri)

O-5 OLYMPIA CRUISE LINE INC., THORNHILL, ON (torontocruises.com)

Enterprise 2000		ES	1998	D	370*	121' 06"	35' 00"	6' 00"

O-6 ONTARIO MINISTRY OF NATURAL RESOURCES, PETERBOROUGH, ON (mnr.gov.on.ca)

Erie Explorer		RV	1981	D	72*	53' 05"	20' 01"	4' 08"

Built: Hopper Fisheries Ltd., Port Stanley, ON (Janice H.X. '81-'97)

Huron Explorer I		RV	2010	D	112*	62' 00"	21' 03"	6' 00"

Built: Hike Metal Products Ltd., Wheatley, ON

Keenosay		RV	1957	D	68*	51' 04"	20' 07"	2' 07"

Built: S.G. Powell Shipyard Ltd., Dunnville, ON

Nipigon Osprey		RV	1990	D	33*	42' 04"	14' 09"	6' 08"

Built: Kanter Yachts Corp., St. Thomas, ON

Ontario Explorer		RV	2009	D	84*	64' 09"	21' 03"	6' 00"

Built: Hike Metal Products Ltd., Wheatley, ON

O-7 ONTARIO POWER GENERATION INC., TORONTO, ON

Niagara Queen II		IB	1992	D	58*	56' 01"	18' 00"	6' 08"

Built: Hike Metal Products Ltd., Wheatley, ON

O-8 OSBORNE MATERIALS CO., GRAND RIVER, OH (osbornecompaniesinc.com)

Emmett J. Carey		SC	1948	D	900	114' 00"	23' 00"	11' 00"

Built: Hugh E. Lee Iron Works, Saginaw, MI; laid up at Fairport, OH (Beatrice Ottinger '48-'63, James B. Lyons '63-'88)

F. M. Osborne {2}		SC	1910	D	500	150' 00"	29' 00"	11' 03"

Built: J. Baterman & T. Horn, Buffalo, NY; laid up at Fairport, OH (Grand Island {1} '10-'58, Lesco '58-'75)

O-9 OWEN SOUND TRANSPORTATION CO. LTD., OWEN SOUND, ON (ontarioferries.com)

Chi-Cheemaun	7343607	PA/CF	1974	D	6,991*	365' 05"	61' 00"	21' 00"

Built: Canadian Shipbuilding and Engineering Ltd., Collingwood, ON

P-1 PERE MARQUETTE SHIPPING CO., LUDINGTON, MI (pmship.com)

Pere Marquette 41	5073894	SU	1941	B	3,413*	403' 00"	58' 00"	23' 05"

Built: Manitowoc Shipbuilding Co., Manitowoc, WI; converted from powered train/car ferry to a self-unloading barge in '97 (City of Midland 41 '41-'97)

Undaunted	8963210	AT	1943	DE	569*	143' 00"	38' 00"	18' 00"

Built: Gulfport Boiler/Welding, Port Arthur, TX; paired with barge Pere Marquette 41 (USS Undaunted [ATR-126, ATA-199] '44-'63, USMA Kings Pointer '63-'93, Krystal K. '93-'97)

P-2 PICTURED ROCKS CRUISES INC., MUNISING, MI (picturedrocks.com)

Grand Island {2}		ES	1989	D	52*	68' 00"	16' 01"	7' 01"
Grand Portal		ES	2004	D	76*	64' 08"	20' 00"	8' 08"
Miners Castle		ES	1974	D	82*	68' 00"	16' 06"	6' 04"
Miss Superior		ES	1984	D	83*	68' 00"	16' 09"	10' 04"
Pictured Rocks		ES	1972	D	53*	55' 07"	13' 07"	4' 04"

P-3 PLAUNT TRANSPORTATION CO. INC., CHEBOYGAN, MI (bbiferry.com)

Kristen D		CF	1987	D	83*	94' 11"	36' 00"	4' 06"

P-4 PEARL SEAS CRUISES LLC., GUILFORD, CT (pearlseascruises.com)

Pearl Mist	9412701	PA	2009	D	5,109*	335' 00"	56' 00"	12' 00"

P-5 PORT CITY CRUISE LINE INC., NORTH MUSKEGON, MI (portcityprincesscruises.com)

Port City Princess		ES	1966	D	79*	64' 09"	30' 00"	5' 06"

Built: Blount Marine Corp., Warren, RI (Island Queen {1} '66-'87)

P-6 PORTOFINO ON THE RIVER, WYANDOTTE, MI (portofinoontheriver.com)

Friendship		ES	1968	D	76*	85' 00"	23' 04"	7' 03"

Built: Hike Metal Products Ltd., Wheatley, ON (Peche Island V '68-'71, Papoose V '71-'82)

Tall and the Paul:
The 1,014-foot Paul
R. Tregurtha and the
tall ship Niagara pass
at Monroe, Mich.
(Paul C. LaMarre III)

Fleet Name / Vessel Name	IMO #	Vessel Type	Year Built	Engine Type	Cargo Cap. or Gross*	Overall Length	Breadth	Depth

P-7 PRESQUE ISLE BOAT TOURS, ERIE, PA *(piboattours.com)*

Vessel	IMO	Type	Year	Eng	Cap	Length	Breadth	Depth
Lady Kate {2}		ES	1952	D	11*	59' 03"	15' 00"	3' 09"

Built: J. W. Nolan & Sons, Erie, PA (G. A. Boeckling II, Cedar Point III, Island Trader '89-'97)

P-8 PURVIS MARINE LTD., SAULT STE. MARIE, ON *(purvismarine.com)*

Vessel	IMO	Type	Year	Eng	Cap	Length	Breadth	Depth
Adanac III		TB	1913	D	108*	80' 03"	19' 03"	9' 10"

Built: Western Drydock & Shipbuilding Co., Port Arthur, ON (Edward C. Whalen '13-'66, John McLean '66-'95)

Anglian Lady	5141483	TB	1953	D	398*	132' 00"	31' 00"	14' 00"

Built: John I. Thornecroft & Co., Southampton, England (Hamtun '53-'72, Nathalie Letzer '72-'88)

Avenger IV	5401297	TB	1962	D	291*	120' 00"	30' 00"	19' 00"

Built: Cochrane & Sons Ltd., Selby, Yorkshire, England (Avenger '62-'85)

G.L.B. No. 2		DB	1953	B	3,215	240' 00"	50' 00"	12' 00"

Built: Ingalls Shipbuilding Corp., Birmingham, AL (Jane Newfield '53-'66, ORG 6502 '66-'75)

Malden		DB	1946	B	1,075	150' 00"	41' 09"	10' 03"

Built: Russel Brothers Ltd., Owen Sound, ON

Martin E. Johnson		TB	1959	D	26*	47' 00"	16' 00"	7' 00"

Built: Russel Brothers Ltd., Owen Sound, ON

PML 357		DB	1932	B	363*	138' 00"	38' 00"	11' 00"
PML 2501		TK	1980	B	1,954*	302' 00"	52' 00"	17' 00"

Built: Cenac Shipyard, Houma, LA (CTCO 2505 '80-'96)

PML 9000		DB	1968	B	4,285*	400' 00"	76' 00"	20' 00"

Built: Bethlehem Steel – Shipbuilding Division, San Francisco, CA (Palmer '68-'00)

PML Alton		DB	1933	B	150	93' 00"	30' 00"	8' 00"

Built: McClintic-Marshall, Sturgeon Bay, WI

PML Ironmaster		DB	1962	B	7,437*	360' 00"	75' 00"	25' 00"

Built: Yarrows Ltd., Esquimalt, BC (G.T. Steelmaster, Ceres, American Gulf VII, Seaspan 241, G.T. Ironmaster)

PML Tucci		CS	1958	B	601*	150' 00"	52' 00"	10' 00"

Built: Calumet Shipyard & Drydock Co., Chicago, IL (MCD '58-'73, Minnesota '73-'88, Candace Andrie '88-'08)

PML Tucker		DS	1971	B	477*	140' 00"	50' 00"	9' 00"

Built: Twin City Shipyard, St. Paul, MN (Illinois '71-'02, Meredith Andrie '02-'08)

Reliance	7393808	TB	1974	D	708*	148' 03"	35' 07"	21' 07"

Built: Ulstein Hatlo A/S, Ulsteinvik, Norway (Sinni '74-'81, Irving Cedar '81-'96, Atlantic Cedar '96-'02)

Rocket		TB	1901	D	40*	73' 00"	16' 00"	7' 00"

Built: Buffalo Shipbuilding Co., Buffalo, NY

Tecumseh II		DB	1976	B	2,500	180' 00"	54' 00"	12' 00"
Wilfred M. Cohen	7629271	TB	1947	D	284*	102' 06"	28' 00"	15' 00"

Built: Newport News Shipbuilding and Drydock Co., Newport News, VA (A. T. Lowmaster '48-'75)

W. I. Scott Purvis	5264819	TB	1938	D	203*	96' 00"	26' 00"	10' 00"

Built: Marine Industries, Sorel, QC (Orient Bay '38-'75, Guy M. No. 1 '75-'90)

W.J. Isaac Purvis	318726	TB	1962	D	71*	72' 00"	19' 00"	12' 00"

Built: McNamara Marine Ltd., Toronto, ON (Angus M. '62-'92, Omni Sorel '92-'02, Joyce B. Gardiner '02-'09)

W. J. Ivan Purvis	5217218	TB	1938	D	190*	100' 00"	26' 00"	10' 00"

Built: Marine Industries, Sorel, QC (Magpie '38-'66, Dana T. Bowen '66-'75)

Yankcanuck {2}	5409811	CS	1963	D	4,760	324' 03"	49' 00"	26' 00"

Built: Collingwood Shipyards, Collingwood, ON; in lay-up at Sault Ste. Marie, ON, since 2008

P-9 PUT-IN-BAY BOAT LINE CO., PORT CLINTON, OH *(jet-express.com)*

Vessel	IMO	Type	Year	Eng	Cap	Length	Breadth	Depth
Jet Express		PF/CA	1989	D	93*	92' 08"	28' 06"	8' 04"
Jet Express II		PF/CA	1992	D	85*	92' 06"	28' 06"	8' 04"
Jet Express III		PF/CA	2001	D	70*	78' 02"	27' 06"	8' 02"
Jet Express IV		PF/CA	1995	D	71*	77' 02"	28' 05"	7' 07"

Q-1 QUEBEC PORT AUTHORITY, QUÉBEC, QC *(portquebec.ca)*

Vessel	IMO	Type	Year	Eng	Cap	Length	Breadth	Depth
Le Cageux		TB	2011	D	24*	42' 06"	16' 01"	7' 07"

Q-2 QUEEN CITY FERRY CO., BUFFALO, NY *(queencityferry.com)*

Vessel	IMO	Type	Year	Eng	Cap	Length	Breadth	Depth
River Queen		ES	1972	D	88*	81' 09"	24' 00"	6' 0

(Miss Buffalo II '72-'14)

R-1 RDK LLC, HOLLAND, MI

Vessel	IMO	Type	Year	Eng	Cap	Length	Breadth	Depth
Bonnie G. Selvick		TB	1981	D	45*	57' 08"	17' 00"	6' 01"

(Captain Robbie '81-'90, Philip M. Pearse '90-'97, Chris Ann '97-'09)

Mary E. Hannah		TB	1945	D	612*	149' 00"	33' 00"	16' 00"

Built: Marietta Manufacturing, Marietta, GA (U. S. Army LT-821 '45-'47, Brooklyn '47-'66, Lee Reuben '66-'75)

R-2	**RIO TINTO-ALCAN INC., LA BAIE, QC** (riotintoalcan.com)							
	Fjord Éternité	9364348	TT	2006	D	381*	94' 00"	36' 05"	16' 04"
	Built: East Isle Shipyard, Georgetown, PEI (Svitzer Njord, Stevns Iceflower)							
	Fjord Saguenay	9351012	TT	2006	D	381*	94' 00"	36' 05"	16' 04"
	Built: East Isle Shipyard, Georgetown, PEI (Svitzer Nanna, Stevns Icecap)							

R-3	**ROCKPORT BOAT LINE LTD., ROCKPORT, ON** (rockportcruises.com)							
	Chief Shingwauk		ES	1965	D	109*	70' 00"	24' 00"	4' 06"
	Ida M.		ES	1970	D	29*	55' 00"	14' 00"	3' 00"
	Ida M. II		ES	1973	D	121*	63' 02"	22' 02"	5' 00"
	Sea Prince II		ES	1978	D	172*	83' 00"	24' 02"	6' 08"

R-4	**ROEN SALVAGE CO., STURGEON BAY, WI** (roensalvage.com)							
	Chas. Asher		TB	1967	D	39*	49' 02"	17' 06"	6' 10"
	John R. Asher		TB	1943	D	93*	68' 09"	20' 00"	8' 00"
	Built: Platzer Boat Works, Houston, TX (U. S. Army ST-71 '43-'46, Russell 8 '46-'64, Reid McAllister '64-'67, Donegal '67-'85)							
	Louie S.		TB	1956	D	10*	37' 00"	12' 00"	4' 05"
	Spuds		TB	1944	D	19*	42' 00"	12' 05"	5' 04"
	Stephan M. Asher		TB	1954	D	60*	65' 00"	19' 01"	5' 04"
	Built: Burton Shipyard Inc., Port Arthur, TX (Captain Bennie '54-'82, Dumar Scout '82-'87)							
	Timmy A.		TB	1953	D	12*	33' 06"	10' 08"	5' 02"

R-5	**RUSSELL ISLAND TRANSIT CO., ALGONAC, MI**							
	Islander {2}		PA/CF	1967	D	38*	41' 00"	15' 00"	3' 06"

R-6	**RYBA MARINE CONSTRUCTION CO., CHEBOYGAN, MI** (rybamarine.com)							
	Amber Mae		TB	1922	D	67*	65' 00"	14' 01"	10' 00"
	Built: Glove Shipyard Inc., Buffalo, NY (E. W. Sutton '22-'52, Venture '52- '00)							
	Kathy Lynn	8034887	TB	1944	D	140*	85' 00"	24' 00"	9' 06"
	Built: Decatur Iron & Steel Co., Decatur, AL (U. S. Army ST-693 '44-'79, Sea Islander '79-'91)							
	Rochelle Kaye		TB	1963	D	52*	51' 06"	19' 04"	7' 00"
	Built: St. Charles Steel Works Inc., Thibodeaux, LA (Jaye Anne '63-?, Katanni ?-'97)							
	Tenacious	5238004	TB	1960	D	149*	79' 01"	25' 06"	12' 06"
	Built: Ingalls Shipbuilding Corp., Pascagoula, MS (Mobil 8 '60-'91, Tatarrax '91-'93, Nan McKay '93-'95)							
	Thomas R. Morrish		TB	1980	D	88*	64' 00"	14' 05"	8' 06"
	Built: Houma Shipbuilding Co., Houma, LA. (Lady Ora '80- '99, Island Eagle '99- '04, Captain Zeke '01- '14)							

S-1	**SAIL DOOR COUNTY, SISTER BAY, WI** (saildoorcounty.com)							
	Edith M. Becker		PA	1984	D/W	22*	62' 00"	24' 00"	8' 06"

S-2	**SAND PRODUCTS CORP., MUSKEGON, MI**							

MICHIGAN-OHIO BARGE LLC, MUSKEGON, MI

	Cleveland Rocks		SU	1957	B	6,280*	390' 00"	71' 00"	27' 00"
	Built: Todd Shipyards Corp., Houston, TX (M-211 '57-'81, Virginia '81-'88, C-11 '88-'93, Kellstone 1 '93-'04)							

PORT CITY MARINE SERVICES, MUSKEGON, MI

	St. Marys Challenger	5009984	CC	1906	B	N/A	N/A	56' 00"	31' 00"
	Built: Great Lakes Engineering Works, Ecorse, MI; repowered in '50; converted to a self-unloading cement carrier by Manitowoc Shipbuilding Co., Manitowoc, WI, in '67; converted to a barge by Bay Shipbuilding Co., Sturgeon Bay, WI, over the winter of 2013-'14 (William P. Snyder '06-'26, Elton Hoyt II {1} '26-'52, Alex D. Chisholm '52-'66, Medusa Challenger '66-'99, Southdown Challenger '99-'04)							
	St. Marys Conquest	5015012	CC	1937	B	8,500	437' 06"	55' 00"	28' 00"
	Built: Manitowoc Shipbuilding Co., Manitowoc, WI; converted from a powered tanker to a self-unloading cement barge by Bay Shipbuilding, Sturgeon Bay, WI, in '87 (Red Crown '37-'62, Amoco Indiana '62-'87, Medusa Conquest '87-'99, Southdown Conquest '99-'04)							

PORT CITY TUG INC., MUSKEGON, MI

	Bradshaw McKee	7644312	ATB	1977	D	174*	121' 06"	34' 06"	18' 02"
	Built: Toche Enterprises Inc., Ocean Springs, MS; paired with barge St. Marys Challenger (Lady Elda '77-'78, Kings Challenger '78-'78, ITM No. 1 '78-'81, Kings Challenger '81-'86, Susan W. Hannah '86-'11)							
	Prentiss Brown	7035547	TB	1967	D	197*	123' 05"	31' 06"	19' 00"
	Built: Gulfport Shipbuilding, Port Arthur, TX; paired with barge St. Marys Conquest (Betty Culbreath, Micheala McAllister)							

S-3	**SEA SERVICE LLC, SUPERIOR, WI**							
	Sea Bear		PB	1959	D	28*	45' 08"	13' 08"	7' 00"
	Built: Gladding-Hearn Shipbuilding, Somerset, MA (Narrows)							

Move over! Joseph H. Thompson getting chased up the St. Marys River by Thunder Bay. (Roger LeLievre)

S-4 SEAWAY MARINE GROUP LLC, CLAYTON, NY *(seawaymarinegroup.com)*

Seaway Supplier		GC	1952	D	97*	73' 06"	21' 00"	9' 04"

(Jeremy Kellogg, Elizabeth)

S-5 SELVICK MARINE TOWING CORP., STURGEON BAY, WI

Cameron O		TB	1955	D	26*	50' 00"	15' 00"	7' 03"

Built: Peterson Builders Inc., Sturgeon Bay, WI (Escort II '55-'06)

Donny S	7436234	TB	1950	DE	461*	143' 00"	33' 01"	14' 06"

Built: Levingston Shipbuilding, Orange, TX (U. S. Army ATA-230 '49-'72, G. W. Codrington '72-'73,
William P. Feeley {2} '73-'73, William W. Stender '73-'78, Mary Page Hannah '78-'14)

Jacquelyn Nicole		TB	1913	D	96*	71' 00"	20' 01"	11' 02"

Built: Great Lakes Towing Co., Cleveland, OH (Michigan {4} '13-'78, Ste. Marie II '78-'81, Dakota '81-'92, Ethel E. '92-'02)

Jimmy L		TB	1939	D	148*	110' 00"	25' 00"	13' 00"

Built: Defoe Shipbuilding Co., Bay City, MI (USCGC Naugatuck [WYT / WYTM-92] '39-'80, Timmy B. '80-'84)

Sharon M. Selvick		TB	1945	D	28*	45' 05"	12' 10"	7' 01"

Built: Kewaunee Shipbuilding & Engineering, Kewaunee, WI (USACE Judson)

Susan L		TB	1944	D	133*	86' 00"	23' 00"	10' 04"

Built: Equitable Equipment Co., New Orleans, LA (U. S. Army ST-709 '44-'47, USCOE Stanley '47-'99)

William C. Selvick		TB	1944	D	142*	85' 00"	23' 00"	9' 07"

Built: Platzer Boat Works, Houston, TX (U. S. Army ST-500 '44-'49, Sherman H. Serre '49-'77)

S-6 SHELL CANADA LIMITED, CALGARY, AB

Arca	5411761	RT	1963	D	1,296	175' 00"	36' 00"	14' 00"

Built: Port Weller Dry Docks, Port Weller, ON; serves vessels near Montreal, QC (Imperial Lachine '63-'03, Josee M. '03-'03)

S-7 SHEPARD MARINE CONSTRUCTION, CLINTON TOWNSHIP, MI

Robin Lynn	7619769	TB	1952	D	148*	85' 00"	25' 00"	11' 00"

Built: Alexander Shipyard Inc., New Orleans, LA; company reported out of business as of 2013
(Bonita '52-'85, Susan Hoey {2} '85-'95, Blackie B '95-'97, Susan Hoey {3 } '97-'98)

S-8 SHEPLER'S MACKINAC ISLAND FERRY, MACKINAW CITY, MI *(sheplersferry.com)*

Capt. Shepler		PF	1986	D	71*	84' 00"	21' 00"	7' 10"
Felicity		PF	1972	D	65*	65' 00"	18' 01"	8' 03"
Sacré Bleu		PK	1959	D	98*	94' 10"	31' 00"	9' 09"
The Hope		PF	1975	D	87*	77' 00"	20' 00"	8' 03"
The Welcome		PF	1969	D	66*	60' 06"	16' 08"	8' 02"
Wyandot		PF	1979	D	83*	77' 00"	20' 00"	8' 00"

S-9 SHORELINE CHARTERS, GILLS ROCK, WI *(shorelinecharters.net)*

The Shoreline		ES	1973	D	12*	33' 00"	11' 4"	3' 00"

S-10 SHORELINE CONTRACTORS INC., WELLINGTON, OH *(shorelinecontractors.com)*

Eagle		TB	1943	D	31*	57' 07"	35' 09"	6' 08"

Built: Defoe Shipbuilding Co., Bay City, MI (Jack Boyce, Jan B., Sea Search II)

General		TB	1964	D	125*	63' 08"	15' 04"	6' 05"

S-11 SHORELINE SIGHTSEEING CO., CHICAGO, IL *(shorelinesightseeing.com)*

Blue Dog		ES	1981	D	31*	47' 07"	18' 00"	5' 05"
Bright Star		ES	2003	D	93*	79' 03"	23' 00"	7' 01"
Cap Streeter		ES	1987	D	28*	63' 06"	24' 04"	7' 07"
Evening Star		ES	2001	D	93*	83' 00"	23' 00"	7' 00"
Marlyn		ES	1961	D	70*	65' 00"	25' 00"	7' 00"
Shoreline II		ES	1987	D	89*	75' 00"	26' 00"	7' 01"
Star of Chicago {2}		ES	1999	D	73*	64' 10"	22' 08"	7' 05"
Voyageur		ES	1983	D	98*	65' 00"	35' 00"	7' 00"

S-12 SOCIÉTÉ DES TRAVERSIERS DU QUÉBEC, QUÉBEC, QC *(traversiers.gouv.qc.ca)*

Alphonse-Desjardins	7109233	CF	1971	D	1,741*	214' 00"	71' 06"	20' 00"

Built: Davie Shipbuilding Co., Lauzon, QC

Armand-Imbeau	7902269	CF	1980	D	1,285*	203' 07"	72' 00"	18' 04"

Built: Marine Industries Ltd., Sorel, QC

Camille-Marcoux	7343578	CF	1974	D	6,122*	310' 09"	62' 09"	39' 00"

Built: Marine Industries Ltd., Sorel, QC

Catherine-Legardeur	8409355	CF	1985	D	1,348*	205' 09"	71' 10"	18' 10"

Built: Davie Shipbuilding Co., Lauzon, QC

F.-A.-Gauthier		CF	2014	DE		436' 03"	72' 01"	

Built: Fincantieri Castellammare di Stabia, Naples, Italy

Felix-Antoine-Savard	9144706	CF	1997	D	2,489*	272' 00"	70' 00"	21' 09"
Built: Davie Shipbuilding Co., Lauzon, QC								
Grue-des-Iles	8011732	CF	1981	D	447*	155' 10"	41' 01"	12' 06"
Built: Bateaux Tur-Bec Ltd., Ste-Catherine, QC								
Ivan-Quinn	9554028	CF	2008	D	241*	83' 07"	26' 09"	11' 03"
Built: Meridien Maritime Reparation Inc., Matane, QC								
Jos-Deschenes	391571	CF	1980	D	1,287*	203' 07"	72' 00"	18' 04"
Built: Marine Industries Ltd., Sorel, QC								
Joseph-Savard	8409343	CF	1985	D	1,445*	206' 00"	71' 10"	18' 10"
Built: Davie Shipbuilding Co., Lauzon, QC								
Lomer-Gouin	7109221	CF	1971	D	1,741*	214' 00"	71' 06"	20' 00"
Built: Davie Shipbuilding Co., Lauzon, QC								
Lucien-L.	6721981	CF	1967	D	867*	220' 10"	61' 06"	15' 05"
Built: Marine Industries Ltd., Sorel, QC								
Peter-Fraser		CF	2012	DE	292*	110' 02"	39' 03"	7' 03"
Built: Chantier Naval Forillon, Gaspé, QC								
Radisson {1}		CF	1954	D	1,037*	164' 03"	72' 00"	10' 06"
Built: Davie Shipbuilding Co., Lauzon, QC								

S-13 SOO LOCKS BOAT TOURS, SAULT STE. MARIE, MI *(soolocks.com)*

Bide-A-Wee {3}		ES	1955	D	99*	64' 07"	23' 00"	7' 11"
Built: Blount Marine Corp., Warren, RI								
Hiawatha {2}		ES	1959	D	99*	64' 07"	23' 00"	7' 11"
Built: Blount Marine Corp., Warren, RI								
Holiday		ES	1957	D	99*	64' 07"	23' 00"	7' 11"
Built: Blount Marine Corp., Warren, RI								
Le Voyageur		ES	1959	D	70*	65' 00"	25' 00"	7' 00"
Built: Sturgeon Bay Shipbuilding and Drydock Co., Sturgeon Bay, WI								
Nokomis		ES	1959	D	70*	65' 00"	25' 00"	7' 00"
Built: Sturgeon Bay Shipbuilding and Drydock Co., Sturgeon Bay, WI								

S-14 SOO MARINE SUPPLY INC., SAULT STE. MARIE, MI *(soomarine.com)*

Ojibway		SB	1945	D	53*	53' 00"	28' 00"	7' 00"
Built: Great Lakes Engineering Works, Ashtabula, OH								

S-15 SPIRIT CRUISES LLC, CHICAGO, IL *(spiritcruises.com/chicago)*

Chicago Elite		ES	1988	D	96*	115' 00"	27' 00"	7' 06"

A friendly wave from Capt. Joe Walters, International Shipmasters' Association Grand Lodge president, aboard the research vessel Kiyi. (Roger LeLievre)

	Mystic Blue	ES	1998	D	97*	138' 09"	36' 00"	10' 05"
	Odyssey II	ES	1993	D	88*	162' 05"	40' 00"	13' 05"
	Spirit of Chicago	ES	1988	D	92*	156' 00"	35' 00"	7' 01"

S-16 SPIRIT OF THE SOUND SCHOONER CO., PARRY SOUND, ON (spiritofthesound.ca)

Chippewa III	PA	1954	D	47*	65' 00"	16' 00"	6' 06"

    Built: Russel-Hipwell Engines Ltd., Owen Sound, ON (Maid of the Mist III '54-'56, Maid of the Mist '56-'92)

S-17 ST. JAMES MARINE CO. / FOGG TOWING & MARINE, BEAVER ISLAND, MI (stjamesmarine.com)

American Girl	TB	1922	D	63*	62' 00"	14' 00"	6' 05"
Wendy Anne	TB	1955	D	89*	71' 00"	20' 00"	8' 05"

    Built: Smith Basin Drydock, Port Everglades, FL (ST-2199, Four Point)

S-18 ST. LAWRENCE CRUISE LINES INC., KINGSTON, ON (stlawrencecruiselines.com)

Canadian Empress	PA	1981	D	463*	108' 00"	30' 00"	8' 00"

    Built: Algan Shipyards Ltd., Gananoque, ON

S-19 ST. LAWRENCE SEAWAY DEVELOPMENT CORP., MASSENA, NY (seaway.dot.gov)

Grasse River	GL	1958	GL		150 00"	65' 08"	5' 06"
Performance	TB	1997	D		50' 00"	16' 06"	7' 05"

    Built: Marine Builders Inc., Utica, IN

Robinson Bay	TB	1958	DE	213*	103' 00"	26' 10"	14' 06"

    Built: Christy Corp., Sturgeon Bay, WI

S-20 ST. LAWRENCE SEAWAY MANAGEMENT CORP., CORNWALL, ON (greatlakes-seaway.com)

VM/S Hercules	GL	1962	D	2,107*	200' 00"	75' 00"	18' 08"
VM/S Maisonneuve	SV	1974	D	56*	58' 03"	20' 03"	6' 05"
VM/S St. Lambert	TB	1974	D	20*	30' 08"	13' 01"	6' 05"

S-21 ST. MARYS CEMENT INC. (CANADA), TORONTO, ON (stmaryscement.com)

Sea Eagle II	7631860	ATB	1979	D	560*	132' 00"	35' 00"	19' 00"

    Built: Modern Marine Power Co., Houma, LA; paired with barge St. Marys Cement II
    (Sea Eagle '79-'81, Canmar Sea Eagle '81-'91)

St. Marys Cement		CC	1986	B	9,400	360' 00"	60' 00"	23' 03"

    Built: Merce Industries East, Cleveland, OH

St. Marys Cement II	8879914	CC	1978	B	19,513	496' 06"	76' 00"	35' 00"

    Built: Galveston Shipbuilding Co., Galveston, TX (Velasco '78-'81, Canmar Shuttle '81-'90)

Tug Océan Bertrand Jeansonne helping a tanker through Seaway ice. (Paul Beesley)

THE FOLLOWING VESSEL CHARTERED BY ST. MARYS CEMENT GROUP FROM GREAT LAKES AND INTERNATIONAL TOWING & SALVAGE CO., BURLINGTON, ON

Petite Forte	6826119	TB	1969	D	368*	127' 00"	32' 00"	14' 06"

Built: Cochrane and Sons Ltd., Selby, Yorkshire, England; paired with barge St. Marys Cement
(E. Bronson Ingram '69-'72, Jarmac 42 '72-'73, Scotsman '73-'81, Al Battal '81-'86)

S-22 STAR LINE MACKINAC ISLAND FERRY, ST. IGNACE, MI *(mackinacferry.com)*

Anna May		ES	1947	D	94*	64' 10"	30' 00"	7' 03"

Built: Sturgeon Bay Shipbuilding Co., Sturgeon Bay, WI *(West Shore '47-'12)*

Cadillac {5}		PF	1990	D	73*	64' 07"	20' 00"	7' 07"
Joliet {3}		PF	1993	D	83*	64' 08"	22' 00"	8' 03"
La Salle {4}		PF	1983	D	55*	65' 00"	20' 00"	7' 05"
Marquette II {2}		PF	2005	D	65*	74' 00"	23' 06"	8' 00"
Radisson {2}		PF	1988	D	97*	80' 00"	23' 06"	7' 00"

S-23 STERLING FUELS (HAMILTON) LTD., HAMILTON, ON *(mcasphalt.com)*
A DIVISION OF McASPHALT INDUSTRIES LTD.

Hamilton Energy	6517328	RT	1965	D	1,282	201' 05"	34' 01"	14' 09"

Built: Grangemouth Dockyard Co., Grangemouth, Scotland; serves vessels in the vicinity of Hamilton and
Toronto, ON, and the Welland Canal (Partington '65-'79, Shell Scientist '79-'81, Metro Sun '81-'85)

Provmar Terminal	5376521	TK	1959	B	7,300	403' 05"	55' 06"	28' 05"

Built: Sarpsborg Mekaniske, Verksted, Norway; last operated in 1984; in use as a fuel storage barge at Hamilton, ON,
(Varangnes '59-'70, Tommy Wiborg '70-'74, Ungava Transport '74-'85)

Sterling Energy	9277058	RT	2002	D	749*	226' 03"	32' 10"	14' 09"

Built: Selahattin Alsan Shipyard, Istanbul Turkey (Melisa D '02-'13)

T-1 TALL SHIP ADVENTURES OF CHICAGO, CHICAGO, IL *(tallshipwindy.com)*

Windy		ES/4S	1996	W	75*	148' 00"	25' 00"	8' 00"

T-2 TALL SHIP RED WITCH LLC, CHICAGO, IL *(redwitch.com)*

Red Witch		ES/2S	1986	W	41*	77' 00"	17' 06"	6' 05"

T-3 TGL MARINE HOLDINGS ULC, TORONTO, ON

Jane Ann IV	7802809	ATB	1978	D	954*	150' 11"	42' 08"	21' 04"

Built: Mitsui Engineering & Shipbuilding Co., Tokyo, Japan; paired with barge Sarah Spencer; in long-term lay-up at
Toledo, OH (Ouro Fino '78-'81, Bomare '81-'93, Tignish Sea '93-'98)

Sarah Spencer	5002223	SU	1959	B	21,844	693' 10"	72' 00"	40' 00"

Built: Manitowoc Shipbuilding Co., Manitowoc, WI; engine removed, converted to a self-unloading barge by
Halifax Dartmouth Industries, Halifax, NS, in '89; in long-term lay-up at Toledo, OH (Adam E. Cornelius {3} '59-'89,
Capt. Edward V. Smith '89-'91, Sea Barge One '91-'96)

T-4 THOUSAND ISLANDS & SEAWAY CRUISES, BROCKVILLE, ON *(1000islandscruises.com)*

General Brock III		ES	1977	D	56*	56' 05"	15' 04"	5' 02"

Built: Gananoque Boat Line Ltd., Gananoque, ON (Miss Peterborough)

Sea Fox II		ES	1988	D	55*	39' 08"	20' 00"	2' 00"

T-5 THUNDER BAY TUG SERVICES LTD., THUNDER BAY, ON

Glenada		TB	1943	D	107*	80' 06"	25' 00"	10' 01"

Built: Russel Brothers Ltd., Owen Sound, ON (HMCS Glenada [W-30] '43-'45)

Miseford		TB	1915	D	116*	85' 00"	20' 00"	9' 06"

Built: M. Beatty & Sons Ltd., Welland, ON

Point Valour		TB	1958	D	246*	97' 08"	28' 02"	13' 10"

Built: Davie Shipbuilding Co., Lauzon, QC (Foundation Valour '58-'83)

Robert W.		TB	1949	D	48*	60' 00"	16' 00"	8' 06"

Built: Russel Brothers Ltd., Owen Sound, ON

Rosalee D.		TB	1943	D	22*	55' 00"	12' 07"	4' 11"

T-6 TNT DREDGING INC., CALEDONIA, MI

Joyce Marie		TB	1960	D	36*	46' 02"	15' 02"	6' 03"

Built: Kremer Motor Co. (Kendee '60-'71, Morelli, Michelle B, Debra Ann '98-'03)

T-7 TORONTO BOAT CRUISES, TORONTO, ON *(torontoboatcruises.com)*

Aurora Borealis		ES	1983	D	277*	108' 00"	24' 00"	6' 00"

Built: Ralph Hurley, Port Burwell, ON

T-8 TORONTO BRIGANTINE INC., TORONTO, ON *(torontobrigantine.org)*

Pathfinder		W/TV	1963	D/W	32*	59' 08"	15' 00"	8' 00"
Playfair		W/TV	1973	D/W	33*	59' 08"	15' 00"	8' 00"

T-9 **TORONTO DRYDOCK LTD., TORONTO, ON** *(torontodrydock.com)*

M. R. Kane		TB	1945	D	51*	60' 06"	16' 05"	6' 07"

Built: Central Bridge Co. Ltd., Trenton, ON (Tanac V-276 '45–'47)

Menier Consol		FD	1962	B	2,575*	304' 05"	49' 06"	25' 06"

Built: Davie Shipbuilding Co., Lauzon, QC; former pulpwood carrier is now a floating dry dock at Toronto, ON

Radium Yellowknife	5288956	TB	1948	D	235*	120' 00"	28' 00"	6' 06"

Built: Yarrows Ltd., Esquimalt, BC

Salvage Monarch	5308275	TB	1959	D	219*	97' 09"	29' 00"	13' 06"

Built: P.K. Harris Ltd., Appledore, England

T-10 **TORONTO FIRE DEPARTMENT, TORONTO, ON** *(toronto.ca/fire)*

2014-0 *(New name expected)*		FB	1982	D	55*	70' 10"	18' 00"	8' 09"

Built: Breton Industrial & Marine Ltd., Port Hawkesbury, NS (Cape Hurd '82–'14)

Wm. Lyon Mackenzie	6400575	FB	1964	D	102*	81' 01"	20' 00"	10' 00"

Built: Russel Brothers Ltd., Owen Sound, ON

T-11 **TORONTO PADDLEWHEEL CRUISES LTD., NORTH YORK, ON** *(pioneercruises.com)*

Pioneer Princess		ES	1984	D	96*	56' 00"	17' 01"	3' 09"
Pioneer Queen		ES	1968	D	110*	85' 00"	30' 06"	7' 03"

T-12 **TORONTO PORT AUTHORITY, TORONTO, ON** *(torontoport.com)*

Brutus I		TB	1992	D	10*	36' 01"	11' 09"	4' 04"
David Hornell VC		PA/CF	2006	D	219*	95' 10"	37' 07"	7' 05"

Built: Hike Metal Products, Wheatley, ON (TCCA 2 '09–'10)

Maple City		PA/CF	1951	D	135*	70' 06"	36' 04"	5' 11"

Built: Muir Brothers Dry Dock Co. Ltd., Port Dalhousie, ON

Marilyn Bell I		PA/CF	2009	D	270*	95' 10"	37' 07"	7' 05"

Built: Hike Metal Products, Wheatley, ON (TCCA 2 '09–'10)

William Rest		TB	1961	D	62*	65' 00"	18' 06"	10' 06"
Windmill Point		PA/CF	1954	D	118*	65' 00"	36' 00"	10' 00"

T-13 **TORONTO HARBOUR TOURS INC., TORONTO, ON** *(harbourtourstoronto.ca)*

Miss Kim Simpson		ES	1960	D	33*	90' 02"	13' 04"	3' 09"
New Beginnings		ES	1961	D	28*	41' 09"	13' 01"	4' 09"
Shipsands		ES	1972	D	23*	58' 03"	12' 01"	4' 07"

T-14 **TRAVERSE TALL SHIP CO., TRAVERSE CITY, MI** *(tallshipsailing.com)*

Manitou {1}		ES/2S	1983	W	78*	114' 00"	21' 00"	9' 00"

T-15 **30,000 ISLANDS CRUISE LINES INC., PARRY SOUND, ON** *(island-queen.com)*

Island Queen V		ES	1990	D	526*	130' 00"	35' 00"	6' 06"

T-16 **TRIDENT MARINE CORP., CLEVELAND, OH** *(holidaycleveland.com)*

Holiday		PA	1964	D	25*	60' 00"	16' 01"	5' 06"

U-1 **UNCLE SAM BOAT TOURS, ALEXANDRIA, NY** *(usboattours.com)*

Alexandria Belle		ES	1988	D	92*	82' 00"	32' 00"	8' 00"
Island Duchess		ES	1988	D	73*	90' 03"	27' 08"	9' 00"
Island Wanderer		ES	1971	D	57*	62' 05"	22' 00"	7' 02"
Uncle Sam 7		ES	1976	D	55*	60' 04"	22' 00"	7' 01"

U-2 **U.S. ARMY CORPS OF ENGINEERS – GREAT LAKES AND OHIO RIVER DIV., CINCINNATI, OH** *(usace.army.mil)* **U.S. ARMY CORPS OF ENGINEERS – BUFFALO DISTRICT**

Cheraw		TB	1970	D	356*	109' 00"	30' 06"	16' 03"

Built: Southern Shipbuilding Corp., Slidell, LA (USS Cheraw [YTB-802] '70–'96)

McCauley		CS	1948	B		112' 00"	52' 00"	4' 25"
Mike Donlon		TB	1999	TB	64*	53' 00"	19' 02"	7' 07"
Simonsen		CS	1954	B		142' 00"	58' 00"	5' 00"

U.S. ARMY CORPS OF ENGINEERS – DETROIT DISTRICT, LAKE MICHIGAN AREA OFFICE, KEWAUNEE SUB-OFFICE

Kenosha		TB	1954	D	82*	70' 00"	20' 00"	9' 08"

Built: Missouri Valley Bridge & Iron Works, Leavenworth, KS (U. S. Army ST-2011 '54–'65)

Manitowoc		CS	1976	B		132' 00"	44' 00"	8' 00"
Racine		TB	1931	D	61*	66' 03"	18' 05"	7' 08"

U.S. ARMY CORPS OF ENGINEERS – DETROIT DISTRICT, DETROIT AREA OFFICE

Demolen		TB	1974	D	356*	109' 00"	30' 06"	16' 03"

Built: Marinette Marine Corp., Marinette, WI (USS Metacom [YTB-829] '74–'01, Metacom '01–'02)

Tug Massachusetts helps Algoma Progress negotiate the Calumet River at South Chicago. Federal Mackinac is the saltie at right. (Lou Gerard)

		Type	Year		Tonnage	Length	Beam	Depth
Veler		CS	1991	B	613*	150'00"	46'00"	10'06"

U.S. ARMY CORPS OF ENGINEERS – DETROIT DISTRICT, DULUTH AREA OFFICE

		Type	Year		Tonnage	Length	Beam	Depth
D. L. Billmaier		TB	1968	D	356*	109'00"	30'06"	16'03"

Built: Southern Shipbuilding Corp., Slidell, LA (USS Natchitoches [YTB-799] '68-'95)

		Type	Year		Tonnage	Length	Beam	Depth
H. J. Schwartz		DB	1995	B		150'00"	48'00"	11'00"
Hammond Bay		TB	1953	D	23*	45'00"	13'00"	7'00"

U.S. ARMY CORPS OF ENGINEERS – DETROIT DISTRICT, SOO AREA OFFICE

		Type	Year		Tonnage	Length	Beam	Depth
Harvey		DB	1961	B		120'00"	40'00"	8'00"
Nicolet		DB	1971	B		120'00"	40'00"	8'00"
Owen M. Frederick		TB	1942	D	56*	65'00"	17'00"	7'06"

Built: Sturgeon Bay Shipbuilding Co., Sturgeon Bay, WI

		Type	Year		Tonnage	Length	Beam	Depth
Paul Bunyan		GL	1945	B		150'00"	65'00"	12'06"

Built: Wiley Equipment Co., Port Deposit, MD

		Type	Year		Tonnage	Length	Beam	Depth
Whitefish Bay		TB	1953	D	23*	45'00"	13'00"	7'00"

U-3   U.S. COAST GUARD 9TH COAST GUARD DISTRICT, CLEVELAND, OH *(uscg.mil/d9)*

		Type	Year		Tonnage	Length	Beam	Depth
Alder [WLB-216]		BT	2004	D	2,000*	225'09"	46'00"	19'08"

Built: Marinette Marine Corp., Marinette, WI; stationed at Duluth, MN

		Type	Year		Tonnage	Length	Beam	Depth
Biscayne Bay [WTGB-104]		IB	1979	D	662*	140'00"	37'06"	12'00"

Built: Tacoma Boatbuilding Co., Tacoma, WA; stationed at St. Ignace, MI

		Type	Year		Tonnage	Length	Beam	Depth
Bristol Bay [WTGB-102]		IB	1979	D	662*	140'00"	37'06"	12'00"

Built: Tacoma Boatbuilding Co., Tacoma, WA; stationed at Detroit, MI

		Type	Year		Tonnage	Length	Beam	Depth
Buckthorn [WLI-642]		BT	1963	D	200*	100'00"	24'00"	4'08"

Built: Mobile Ship Repair Inc., Mobile, AL; stationed at Sault Ste. Marie, MI

		Type	Year		Tonnage	Length	Beam	Depth
CGB-12001		BT	1991	B	700*	120'00"	50'00"	6'00"
CGB-12002		BT	1992	B	700*	120'00"	50'00"	6'00"
Hollyhock [WLB-214]		BT	2003	D	2,000*	225'09"	46'00"	19'08"

Built: Marinette Marine Corp., Marinette, WI; stationed at Port Huron, MI

		Type	Year		Tonnage	Length	Beam	Depth
Katmai Bay [WTGB-101]		IB	1978	D	662*	140'00"	37'06"	12'00"

Built: Tacoma Boatbuilding Co., Tacoma, WA; stationed at Sault Ste. Marie, MI

		Type	Year		Tonnage	Length	Beam	Depth
Mackinaw [WLBB-30]		IB	2005	D	3,407*	240'00"	58'00"	15'05"

Built: Marinette Marine Corp., Marinette, WI; stationed at Cheboygan, MI

		Type	Year		Tonnage	Length	Beam	Depth
Mobile Bay [WTGB-103]		IB	1979	D	662*	140'00"	37'06"	12'00"

Built: Tacoma Boatbuilding Co., Tacoma, WA; stationed at Sturgeon Bay, WI

		Type	Year		Tonnage	Length	Beam	Depth
Morro Bay [WTGB-106]		IB	1979	D	662*	140'00"	37'06"	12'00"

Built: Tacoma Boatbuilding Co., Tacoma, WA; stationed at Cleveland, OH

		Type	Year		Tonnage	Length	Beam	Depth
Neah Bay [WTGB-105]		IB	1980	D	662*	140'00"	37'06"	12'00"

Built: Tacoma Boatbuilding Co., Tacoma, WA; stationed at Cleveland, OH

U-4   U.S. ENVIRONMENTAL PROTECTION AGENCY, DULUTH, MN & CHICAGO, IL *(epa.gov)*

		Type	Year		Tonnage	Length	Beam	Depth
Lake Explorer II		RV	1966	D	150*	86'09"	22'00"	7'02"

Built: Jackobson Shipyard, Oyster Bay, New York (NOAA Rude '66-'08)

		Type	Year		Tonnage	Length	Beam	Depth
Lake Guardian	8030609	RV	1981	D	959*	180'00"	40'00"	14'00"

Built: Halter Marine Inc., Moss Point MS (Marsea Fourteen '81-'90)

U-5   U.S. FISH & WILDLIFE SERVICE, JORDAN RIVER NATIONAL FISH HATCHERY, ELMIRA, MI

		Type	Year		Tonnage	Length	Beam	Depth
Spencer F. Baird		RV	2006	D	256*	95'00"	30'00"	9'05"

Built: Conrad Industries, Inc., Morgan City, LA

U-6   U.S. NATIONAL PARK SERVICE - ISLE ROYALE NATIONAL PARK, HOUGHTON, MI *(nps.gov)*

		Type	Year		Tonnage	Length	Beam	Depth
Greenstone II		TK	2003	B	114*	70'01"	24'01"	8'00"

Built: Fraser Shipyards Inc., Superior, WI

		Type	Year		Tonnage	Length	Beam	Depth
Ranger III	7618234	PK	1958	D	648*	152'08"	34'00"	13'00"

Built: Christy Corp., Sturgeon Bay, WI

U-7   U.S. NAVAL SEA CADET CORPS *(seacadets.org)*

		Type	Year		Tonnage	Length	Beam	Depth
Grayfox [TWR-825]		TV	1985	D	213*	120'00"	25'00"	12'00"

Built: Marinette Marine, Marinette, WI; based at Port Huron, MI (USS TWR-825 '85-'97)

		Type	Year		Tonnage	Length	Beam	Depth
Manatra [YP-671]		TV	1974	D	67*	80'05"	17'09"	5'04"

Based at Chicago, IL; name stands for MArine NAvigation and TRaining Association (USS YP-671 '74-'89)

		Type	Year		Tonnage	Length	Beam	Depth
Pride of Michigan [YP-673]		TV	1977	D	70*	80'06"	17'08"	5'03"

Built: Peterson Builders Inc., Sturgeon Bay, WI; based at Mount Clemens, MI (USS YP-673 '77-'89)

U-8   U.S. OIL, A DIVISION OF U.S. VENTURE INC., APPLETON, WI *(usoil.com)*

		Type	Year		Tonnage	Length	Beam	Depth
Great Lakes {2}		TK	1982	B	5,024*	414'00"	60'00"	30'00"

Built: Bay Shipbuilding Co., Sturgeon Bay, WI (Amoco Great Lakes '82-'85)

Michigan {10}   8121795   AT   1982   D   292*   107'08"   34'00"   16'00"
Built: Bay Shipbuilding Co., Sturgeon Bay, WI (Amoco Michigan '82–'85)

U-9   UNIVERSITY OF MINNESOTA-DULUTH, DULUTH, MN *(d.umn.edu)*
Blue Heron   RV   1985   D   175*   87'00"   23'00"   11'00"*
Built: Goudy and Stevens, East Boothbay, ME (Fairtry '85–'97)

U-10   UNIVERSITY OF WISCONSIN, GREAT LAKES WATER INSTITUTE, MILWAUKEE, WI *(glwi.uwm.edu)*
Neeskay   RV   1952   D   75*   71'00"   17'06"   7'06"

U-11   UNIVERSITY OF WISCONSIN, SUPERIOR, WI *(uwsuper.edu)*
L. L. Smith Jr.   RV   1950   D   38*   57'06"   16'06"   6'06"

U-12   UPPER LAKES TOWING CO., ESCANABA, MI
Joseph H. Thompson   SU   1944   B   21,200   706'06"   71'06"   38'06"
Built: Sun Shipbuilding & Drydock Co., Chester, PA; converted from a saltwater vessel to a Great Lakes bulk carrier by Maryland Dry Dock, Baltimore, MD, and American Shipbuilding Co., South Chicago, IL, in '52; converted to a self-unloading barge by the owners in '91 (USNS Marine Robin '44–'52)
Joseph H. Thompson Jr.   5175745   ATB   1990   D   841*   146'06"   38'00"   30'00"
Built at Marinette, WI, from steel left over from the conversion of Joseph H. Thompson (above)

U-13   USS GREAT LAKES LLC, NEW YORK, NY
Robert F. Deegan   TK   1968   B   2,424*   225'08"   60'00"   18'00"
Built: Wyatt Industries, Houston, TX; usually paired with tug Zeus, Fleet M-30

V-1   VANENKEVORT TUG & BARGE INC., ESCANABA MI *(vtbarge.com)*
     GREAT LAKES MARINE LEASING LLC, PORTLAND, OR – OWNER
Great Lakes Trader   8635966   SU   2000   B   39,600   740'00"   78'00"   45'00"
Built: Halter Marine, Pearlington, MS
Joyce L. VanEnkevort   8973033   AT   1998   D   1,179*   135'04"   50'00"   26'00"
Built: Bay Shipbuilding Co., Sturgeon Bay, WI; paired with barge Great Lakes Trader

V-2   VICTORIAN PRINCESS CRUISE LINES INC., ERIE, PA *(victorianprincess.com)*
Victorian Princess   ES   1985   D   46*   67'00"   24'00"   4'05"

V-3   VIKING I LLC, MENOMINEE, MI
Viking I   5018246   DB   1925   B   2,713*   360'00"   56'03"   21'06"
Built: Manitowoc Shipbuilding Co., Manitowoc, WI; laid up at Menominee, MI; converted to a flat deck barge at Menominee, MI, by the owners in 2013 (Ann Arbor No. 7 '25–'64, Viking {2} '64–'96)

V-4   VISTA FLEET, DULUTH, MN *(vistafleet.com)*
Vista Queen   ES   1987   D   97*   64'00"   16'00"   6'02"
Built: Mid-City Steel Fabricating Inc., La Crosse, WI (Queen of Excelsior)
Vista Star   ES   1987   D   95*   91'00"   24'09"   5'02"
Built: Freeport Shipbuilding Inc., Freeport, FL (Island Empress '87–'88)

V-5   VOIGHT'S MARINE SERVICES LTD., ELLISON BAY AND GILLS ROCK, WI *(islandclipper.com)*
Island Clipper {2}   ES   1987   D   71*   65'00"   20'00"   8'00"
Yankee Clipper   ES   1971   D   41*   46'06"   17'00"   6'00"

W-1   WALPOLE-ALGONAC FERRY LINE, PORT LAMBTON, ON *(walpolealgonacferry.com)*
City of Algonac   CF   1990   D   82*   62'06"   27'09"   5'09"
Walpole Islander   CF   1986   D   72*   54'05"   27'09"   6'03"

W-2   WALSTROM MARINE, HARBOR SPRINGS, MI *(walstrom.com)*
Elizabeth   TB   1945   D   21*   42'02"   12'01"   5'05"
Built: Burger Boat Co., Manitowoc, WI (Charles F. Liscomb, Jason, Lydie Rae)

W-3   WHITE LAKE DOCK & DREDGE INC., MONTAGUE, MI *(wlddi.com)*
Captain George   TB   1929   D   61*   60'09"   16'07"   7'07"
Built: Charles Ward Engine Works, Charleston, WV (Captain George '29–'73, Kurt R. Luedtke '73–'91)

W-4   WARNER PETROLEUM CORP., CLARE, MI *(warnerpetroleum.com)*
Coloma L. Warner   7337892   TB   1955   D   134*   86'00"   24'00"   10'00"
Built: Sturgeon Bay Shipbuilding, Sturgeon Bay, WI; paired with the barge Warner Provider (Harbor Ace '55–'61, Gopher State '61–'71, Betty Gale '71–'93, Hannah D. Hannah '93–'10)
Warner Provider   RT   1962   B   1,698*   264'00"   52'05"   12'00"
Built: Port Houston Iron Works, Houston, TX (Hannah 2903); in use as a fueling barge at south Lake Michigan ports
William L. Warner   7322055   RT   1973   D   492*   120'00"   40'00"   14'00"
Built: Halter Marine, New Orleans, LA; (Jos. F. Bigane '73–'04); in use as a vessel fueling barge at Detroit, MI

Cedarglen and southbound geese. (Roger LeLievre)

Tug Nebraska and barge Alouette Spirit. (Marc Dease)

W-5	**WASHINGTON ISLAND FERRY LINE INC., WASHINGTON ISLAND, WI** *(wisferry.com)*							
	Arni J. Richter	PA/CF	2003	D	92*	104' 00"	38' 06"	10' 11"
	Built: Bay Shipbuilding Co., Sturgeon Bay, WI							
	Eyrarbakki	PA/CF	1970	D	95*	87' 00"	36' 00"	7' 06"
	Built: Bay Shipbuilding Co., Sturgeon Bay, WI							
	Karfi	PA/CF	1967	D	23*	36' 00"	16' 00"	4' 08"
	Built: T.D. Vinette Co., Escanaba, MI							
	Robert Noble	PA/CF	1979	D	97*	90' 04"	36' 00"	8' 03"
	Built: Peterson Builders Inc., Sturgeon Bay, WI							
	Washington {2}	PA/CF	1989	D	97*	100' 00"	37' 00"	9' 00"
	Built: Peterson Builders Inc., Sturgeon Bay, WI							
W-6	**WENDELLA BOAT TOURS, CHICAGO, IL** *(wendellaboats.com)*							
	Linnea	ES	2010	D	77*	85' 05"	30' 00"	7' 01"
	Ouilmette	ES	2001	D	43*	65' 00"	22' 04"	4' 05"
	Wendella	ES	2007	D	77*	85' 05"	30' 00"	7' 01"
	Wendella LTD	ES	1992	D	66*	68' 00"	20' 00"	4' 09"
W-7	**WILLY'S CONTRACTING CO., SOUTHAMPTON, ON** *(willyscontracting.com)*							
	Howard W. Fitzpatrick	FB	1971	D	97*	78' 00"	20' 05"	4' 09"
	Built: Grafton Boat Co. Inc., Grafton, IL (Fireboat No. 1)							
	Pride	TB	1957	D	47*	52' 06"	29' 08"	5' 01"
	Built: Strege Fisheries Inc., Racine, WI							
W-8	**WINDSOR RIVER CRUISES LTD., WINDSOR, ON** *(windsorrivercruises.com)*							
	Macassa Bay	8624709	ES	1986	D	210*	93' 07"	29' 07"	10' 04"
	Built: Boiler Pump & Marine Works Ltd., Hamilton, ON							
W-9	**WOHLLEB-SOCIE CO., TOLEDO, OH**							
	Bessie B	TB	1947	D	30*	52' 03"	13' 09"	5' 05"
W-10	**WISCONSIN DEPARTMENT OF NATURAL RESOURCES, BAYFIELD AND STURGEON BAY, WI**							
	Coregonus	RV	2011	D	37*	60' 00"	16' 00"	5' 09"
	Gaylord Nelson	RV	1992	D	12*	45' 09"	16' 00"	5' 05"
	Hack Noyes	RV	1947	D	50*	56' 00"	14' 05"	4' 00"

Lee A. Tregurtha and John G. Munson in ice at the lower end of Lake Huron, January 2015. (Marc Dease)

Wilfred Sykes inbound at Grand Haven, Mich. (Sam Hankinson)

Vessel Name	Engine Manufacturer & Model #	Engine Type	Total Engines	Total Cylinders	Rated HP	Total Props	Speed MPH
Adam E. Cornelius	GM EMD - 20-645-E7B	Diesel	2	20	7,200 bhp	1 cpp	16.1
Alder (USCG)	Caterpillar - 3608TA	Diesel	2	6	3,100 bhp	1 cpp	
Algocanada	MaK - 9M32C	Diesel	1	9	6,118 bhp	1 cpp	16.1
Algolake	Pielstick - 10PC2-2V-400	Diesel	2	10	9,000 bhp	1 cpp	17.3
Algoma Conveyor	Wartsila 5RT-flex50-D	Diesel	1	5	11,863 bhp	1 cpp	16.1
Algoma Dartmouth	MAN-B&W - 6L23/30A	Diesel	2	6	2,310 bhp	2 cpp	13.3
Algoma Discovery	Sulzer - 6RTA62	Diesel	1	6	15,499 bhp	1 cpp	16.4
Algoma Enterprise	MAN - 7L40/45	Diesel	2	7	8,804 bhp	1 cpp	13.8
Algoma Equinox	Wartsila 5RT-flex50-D	Diesel	1	5	11,863 bhp	1 cpp	16.1
Algoma Guardian	Sulzer - 6RTA62	Diesel	1	6	15,499 bhp	1 cpp	16.4
Algoma Hansa	Wartsila - 6L46A	Diesel	1	6	6,525 bhp	1 cpp	15.8
Algoma Harvester	Wartsila 5RT-flex50-D	Diesel	1	5	11,863 bhp	1 cpp	16.1
Algoma Mariner	MAN-B&W - 6L48/60CR	Diesel	1	6	9,792 bhp	1 cpp	
Algoma Niagara	Wartsila 5RT-flex50-D	Diesel	1	5	11,863 bhp	1 cpp	16.1
Algoma Navigator	Doxford Engines Ltd.- 76J4	Diesel	1	4	9,680 bhp	1	16.7
Algoma Olympic	MAN - 8L40/54A	Diesel	2	8	10,000 bhp	1 cpp	15.0
Algoma Sault	Wartsila 5RT-flex50-D	Diesel	1	5	11,863 bhp	1 cpp	16.1
Algoma Spirit	Sulzer - 6RTA62	Diesel	1	6	11,284 bhp	1 cpp	16.4
Algoma Transport	MAN - 8L40/45	Diesel	2	8	10,000 bhp	1 cpp	13.8
Algomarine	Sulzer - 6RND76	Diesel	1	6	9,600 bhp	1 cpp	17.0
Algonova	MaK - 9M32C	Diesel	1	9	6,118 bhp	1 cpp	16.1
Algorail	Fairbanks Morse - 10-38D8-1/8	Diesel	4	10	6,662 bhp	1 cpp	13.8
Algosar	Alco - 16V251E	Diesel	2	16	5,150 bhp	2	14.4
Algoscotia	Wartsila - 6L46C	Diesel	1	6	8,445 bhp	1 cpp	16.0
Algosoo	Pielstick - 10PC2-V-400	Diesel	2	10	9,000 bhp	1 cpp	15.0
Algosea	Wartsila - 6L46A	Diesel	1	6	6,434 bhp	1 cpp	15.0
Algosteel	Sulzer - 6RND76	Diesel	1	6	9,599 bhp	1	17.0
Algoway	Fairbanks Morse - 10-38D8-1/8	Diesel	4	10	6,662 bhp	1 cpp	13.8
Algowood	MaK - 6M552AK	Diesel	2	6	10,200 bhp	1 cpp	13.8
Alpena	De Laval Steam Turbine Co.	Turbine	1	**	4,400 shp	1	14.1
Amelia Desgagnés	Allen - 12PVBCS12-F	Diesel	2	12	4,000 bhp	1 cpp	16.1
American Century	GM - EMD - 20-645-E7B	Diesel	4	20	14,400 bhp	2 cpp	17.3
American Courage	GM - EMD - 20-645-E7	Diesel	2	20	7,200 bhp	1 cpp	16.1
American Integrity	GM EMD - 20-645-E7	Diesel	4	20	14,400 bhp	2 cpp	18.4
American Mariner	GM EMD - 20-645-E7	Diesel	2	20	7,200 bhp	1 cpp	15.0
American Spirit	Pielstick - 16PC2-2V-400	Diesel	2	16	16,000 bhp	2 cpp	17.3
American Valor	Westinghouse Elec. Corp.	Turbine	1	**	7,700 shp	1	16.1
American Victory	Bethlehem Steel Corp.	Turbine	1	**	7,700 shp	1	19.0
Amundsen (CCG)	Alco - 16V251F	Diesel	6	16	17,700 bhp	2	18.6
Anglian Lady *	Deutz - SBA12M528	Diesel	2	12	3,480 bhp	2 cpp	15.5
Anna Desgagnés	MAN - K5SZ70/125B	Diesel	1	5	10,332 bhp	1	17.8
Arctic	MAN - 14V52/55A	Diesel	1	14	14,769 bhp	1	17.8
Arthur M. Anderson	Westinghouse Elec. Corp.	Turbine	1	**	7,700 shp	1	16.1
Atlantic Erie	Sulzer - 6RLB66	Diesel	1	6	11,100 bhp	1 cpp	16.1
Atlantic Huron	Sulzer - 6RLB66	Diesel	1	6	11,094 bhp	1 cpp	17.3
Avenger IV *	British Polar	Diesel	1	9	2,700 bhp	1 cpp	12.0
Badger **	Skinner Engine Co. - Steeple Compound Uniflow	Steam	2	4	8,000 ihp	2	18.4
Baie Comeau	MAN B&W - 6S50ME-B9	Diesel	1	6	11,897 bhp	1	15.5
Baie St. Paul	MAN B&W - 6S50ME-B9	Diesel	1	6	11,897 bhp	1	15.5
Barbara Andrie *	GM EMD 16-645-EF	Diesel	1	16	2,000 bhp	1	
Bella Desgagnés	Wartsila - 9L20CR	Diesel	4	9	8,320 bhp	2 azimuth	17.3
Beverly M 1 *	Niigata - 6L28HX	Diesel	2	6	1,971 bhp	2	16.0

* = tug ** = ferry

bhp: brake horsepower, a measure of diesel engine output measured at the crankshaft before entering gearbox or any other power take-out device

ihp: indicated horsepower, based on an internal measurement of mean cylinder pressure, piston area, piston stroke and engine speed; used for reciprocating engines

shp: shaft horsepower, a measure of engine output at the propeller shaft at the output of the reduction gearbox; used for steam and diesel-electric engines

cpp: controllable pitch propeller

Birchglen	Sulzer 4RLB76	Diesel	1	4	10,880 bhp	1 cpp	13.8
Biscayne Bay (USCG)	Fairbanks Morse - 10-38D8-1/8	Diesel	2	10	2,500 bhp	1	13.8
Bradshaw McKee *	GM EMD - 12-645-E5	Diesel	2	12	4,320 bhp	2	11.5
Bristol Bay (USCG)	Fairbanks Morse - 10-38D8-1/8	Diesel	2	10	2,500 bhp	1	13.8
Buffalo	GM EMD - 20-645-E7	Diesel	2	20	7,200 bhp	1 cpp	16.1
Burns Harbor	GM EMD - 20-645-E7	Diesel	4	20	14,400 bhp	2 cpp	18.4
Calumet	Alco - 16V251E	Diesel	2	16	5,600 bhp	1	16.1
Camilla Desgagnés	Werkspoor - 12TM410	Diesel	1	12	7,797 bhp	1 cpp	
Capt. Henry Jackman	MaK - 6M552AK	Diesel	2	6	9,465 bhp	1 cpp	17.3
Cason J. Callaway	Westinghouse Elec. Corp.	Turbine	1	**	7,700 shp	1	16.1
Catherine Desgagnés	Sulzer - 6SAD60	Diesel	1	6	3,841 bhp	1	15.5
Cedarglen	B&W - 7-74VTBF-160	Diesel	1	7	8,750 bhp	1 cpp	15.5
Chi-Cheemaun **	Caterpillar - C280-6	Diesel	4	6	9,280 bhp	2	
Claude A. Desgagnés	MaK/Caterpillar - 6M43C	Diesel	1	6	7,342 bhp	1 cpp	17.8
CSL Assiniboine	MaK/Caterpillar - 6M32C	Diesel	2	6	8,060 bhp	1 cpp	
CSL Laurentien	MaK/Caterpillar - 6M32C	Diesel	2	6	8,060 bhp	1 cpp	
CSL Niagara	MaK/Caterpillar - 6M32C	Diesel	2	6	8,060 bhp	1 cpp	
CSL St-Laurent	MAN B&W 6S50ME-B	Diesel	1	6	11,897 bhp	1 cpp	15.5
CSL Tadoussac	Sulzer - 6RND76	Diesel	1	6	9,600 bhp	1	17.0
CSL Welland	MAN B&W 6S50ME-B	Diesel	1	6	11,897 bhp	1 cpp	15.5
Cuyahoga	Caterpillar - 3608	Diesel	1	8	3,000 bhp	1 cpp	12.6
CWB Marquis	Wartsila 5RT-flex50-D	Diesel	1	5	11,863 bhp	1 cpp	16.1
CWB Strongfield	Wartsila 5RT-flex50-D	Diesel	1	5	11,863 bhp	1 cpp	16.1
Dara Desgagnés	B&W - 6L35MC	Diesel	1	6	5,030 bhp	1 cpp	14.4
Defiance *	GM EMD - 20-645-E7	Diesel	2	20	7,200 bhp	2	15.0
Des Groseilliers (CCG)	Alco - 16V251F	Diesel	6	16	17,700 bhp	2	18.6
Donny S *	GM -12-278A	Diesel	2	12	1,850 bhp	2	
Dorothy Ann *	GM EMD - 20-645-E7B	Diesel	2	20	7,200 bhp	2 Z-drive cpp	16.1
Ecosse *	GM Detroit - 16V92 N	Diesel	2	16	1,800 bhp	2	13.8
Edgar B. Speer	Pielstick - 18PC2-3V-400	Diesel	2	18	19,260 bhp	2 cpp	17.0
Edward L. Ryerson	General Electric Co.	Turbine	1	**	9,900 shp	1	19.0
Edwin H. Gott	MaK - 8M43C	Diesel	2	8	19,578 bhp	2 ccp	16.7
English River	Werkspoor - TMAB-390	Diesel	1	8	1,850 bhp	1 cpp	13.8
Espada Desgagnés	B&W - 6S60MC-C	Diesel	1	5	18,605 bhp	1 cpp	18.4
Esta Desgagnés	B&W - 6L35MC	Diesel	1	6	5,030 bhp	1 cpp	14.4
Evans McKeil *	GM EMD - 16-645C	Diesel	1	16	2,150 bhp	1	11.5
Everlast *	Daihatsu - 8DSM-32	Diesel	2	8	6,000 bhp	2	16.5
Federal Asahi	B&W - 6S46MC-C	Diesel	1	6	10,710 bhp	1	16.1
Federal Danube	B&W - 6S46MC-C	Diesel	1	6	10,686 bhp	1	16.1
Federal Elbe	B&W - 6S46MC-C	Diesel	1	6	10,686 bhp	1	16.1
Federal Ems	B&W - 6S46MC-C	Diesel	1	6	10,686 bhp	1	16.1
Federal Hudson	B&W - 6S46MC-C	Diesel	1	6	10,710 bhp	1	15.5
Federal Hunter	B&W - 6S46MC-C	Diesel	1	6	10,710 bhp	1	15.5
Federal Kivalina	B&W - 6S46MC-C	Diesel	1	6	10,710 bhp	1	16.1
Federal Kumano	B&W - 6S46MC-C	Diesel	1	6	10,710 bhp	1	16.1
Federal Kushiro	Mitsubishi - 6UEC52LA	Diesel	1	6	9,626 bhp	1	16.6
Federal Leda	B&W - 6S46MC-C	Diesel	1	6	10,686 bhp	1	16.1
Federal Maas	B&W - 6S50MC	Diesel	1	6	11,640 bhp	1	16.1
Federal Mackinac	B&W - 6S46MC-C	Diesel	1	6	10,540 bhp	1	16.1
Federal Margaree	B&W - 6S46MC-C	Diesel	1	6	10,686 bhp	1	16.1
Federal Mayumi	MAN B&W - 6S46MC-C	Diesel	1	6	10,686 bhp	1	16.1
Federal Miramichi	B&W - 6S46MC-C	Diesel	1	6	10,686 bhp	1	16.1
Federal Nakagawa	B&W - 6S46MC-C	Diesel	1	6	10,710 bhp	1	16.1
Federal Oshima	B&W - 6S46MC-C	Diesel	1	6	10,710 bhp	1	16.1
Federal Rhine	B&W - 6S50MC	Diesel	1	6	11,640 bhp	1	16.1
Federal Rideau	B&W - 6S46MC-C	Diesel	1	6	10,710 bhp	1	16.1
Federal Saguenay	B&W - 6S50MC	Diesel	1	6	11,665 bhp	1	16.1
Federal Satsuki	MAN B&W - 6S46MC-C	Diesel	1	6	8,960 bhp	1	16.1
Federal Schelde	B&W - 6S50MC	Diesel	1	6	11,640 bhp	1	16.1
Federal Seto	MAN B&W - 6S46MC-C	Diesel	1	6	10,711 bhp	1	16.7
Federal Shimanto	Mitsubishi - 6UEC52LA	Diesel	1	6	9,600 bhp	1	16.6
Federal St. Laurent	B&W - 6S50MC	Diesel	1	6	11,640 bhp	1	16.1

Federal Welland	B&W - 6S46MC-C	Diesel	1	6	10,710 bhp	1	16.1
Federal Weser	B&W - 6S46MC-C	Diesel	1	6	10,686 bhp	1	18.0
Federal Yoshino	Mitsubishi - 6UEC52LA	Diesel	1	6	9,600 bhp	1	16.6
Federal Yukon	B&W - 6S46MC-C	Diesel	1	6	10,710 bhp	1	15.5
Florence M. *	Fairbanks Morse - 8-28D8-1/4	Diesel	2	8	1,450 bhp	2	
Frontenac	Sulzer - 6RND76	Diesel	1	6	9,600 bhp	1 cpp	17.0
G.L. Ostrander *	Caterpillar - 3608-DITA	Diesel	2	8	6,008 bhp	2	17.3
Great Republic	GM EMD - 20-645-E7	Diesel	2	20	7,200 bhp	2 cpp	15.0
Grayfox (USNCS)	Caterpillar - 3512 TAC	Diesel	2	12	2,350 bhp.	2	20.7
Griffon (CCG)	Fairbanks Morse - 8-38D8-1/8	Diesel	4	8	5,332 bhp	2	13.0
H. Lee White	GM EMD - 20-645-E7B	Diesel	2	20	7,200 bhp	1 cpp	15.0
Hamilton Energy	GM EMD - 12-534-E6	Diesel	1	12	1,500 bhp	1 cpp	13.8
Hamburg	Wartsila MaK - 6L32	Diesel	4	6	3,540 bhp	2 cpp	20.7
Herbert C. Jackson	General Electric Co.	Turbine	1	**	6,600 shp	1	16.0
Hollyhock (USCG)	Caterpillar - 3608TA	Diesel	2	6	3,100 bhp	1 cpp	
Hon. James L. Oberstar	Rolls-Royce Bergen - B32:40L6P	Diesel	2	6	8,160 shp	1 ccp	17.0
Indiana Harbor	GM EMD - 20-645-E7	Diesel	4	20	14,400 bhp	2 cpp	16.1
Invincible *	GM EMD - 16-645-E7B	Diesel	2	16	5,750 bhp	2	13.8
J. A. W. Iglehart	De Laval Steam Turbine Co.	Turbine	1	**	4,400 shp	1	15.0
J. S. St. John	GM EMD - 8-567	Diesel	1	8	850 bhp	1	
James R. Barker	Pielstick - 16PC2-2V-400	Diesel	2	16	16,000 bhp	2 cpp	15.5
Jana Desgagnés	B&W - 6L35MC	Diesel	1	6	5,030 bhp	1 cpp	14.4
Jane Ann IV *	Pielstick - 8PC2-2L-400	Diesel	2	8	8,000 bhp	2	15.8
Jiimaan **	Ruston Paxman Diesels Ltd. - 6RK215	Diesel	2	6	2,839 bhp	2 cpp	15.0
John B. Aird	MaK - 6M552AK	Diesel	2	6	9,460 bhp	1 cpp	13.8
John D. Leitch	B&W - 5-74VT2BF-160	Diesel	1	5	7,500 bhp	1 cpp	16.1
John G. Munson	General Electric Co.	Turbine	1	**	7,700 shp	1	17.3
John J. Boland	GM EMD - 20-645-E7B	Diesel	2	20	7,200 bhp	1 cpp	15.0
John Spence *	GM EMD 16-567-C	Diesel	2	16	3,280 bhp	2	13.8
Joseph H. Thompson Jr. *	Caterpillar	Diesel	2			1	
Joseph L. Block	GM EMD - 20-645-E7	Diesel	2	20	7,200 bhp	1 cpp	17.3
Joyce L. VanEnkevort *	Caterpillar - 3612	Diesel	2	12	10,200 bhp	2 cpp	
Kaministiqua	Sulzer - 4RLB76	Diesel	4	4	10,880 bhp	1cpp	15.5
Karen Andrie *	GM EMD - 8-710G7C	Diesel	2	8	4,000 bhp	2	19
Katmai Bay (USCG)	Fairbanks Morse - 10-38D8-1/8	Diesel	2	10	2,500 bhp	1	13.8
Kaye E. Barker	Rolls-Royce Bergen - B32:40L6P	Diesel	2	6	8,160 shp	1 ccp	17.0
Ken Boothe Sr. *	Cat-MaK - 8M32C	Diesel	2	8	10,876 bhp	2 cpp	18.4
Lake Express **	MTU 16V4000M70	Diesel	4	16	12,616 bhp	4 water jet	40.0
Laurentia Desgagnés	B&W - 6S60MC-C	Diesel	1	5	18,605 bhp	1 cpp	18.4
Lee A. Tregurtha	Rolls-Royce Bergen B32:40L6P	Diesel	2	6	8,160 shp	1 ccp	17.0
Leonard M	Ruston P - 6RK270M	Diesel	2	6	2,097 bhp	2	13.8
Mackinaw (USCG)	Caterpillar - 3612	Diesel	3	12	9,119 bhp	2 Azipod	17.3
Manistee	GM EMD - 20-645-E6	Diesel	1	20	2,950 bhp	1	
Manitoba	Fairbanks Morse - 8-38D8-1/8	Diesel	4	8	5,332 bhp	1 cpp	16.1
Manitoulin	B&W - 5L50MC	Diesel	1	5	8,113 bhp	1 cpp	14.4
Manitowoc	Alco - 16V251E	Diesel	2	16	5,600 bhp	1	16.1
Mapleglen	B&W - 6K67GF	Diesel	1	6	11,600 bhp	1	16.1
Maria Desgagnés	B&W - 6S42MC	Diesel	1	6	8,361 bhp	1 cpp	16.1
Martha L. Black (CCG)	Alco - 16V251F	Diesel	3	16	8,973 bhp	2	13.8
Mary E. Hannah *	GM EMD - 16-567C	Diesel	2	16	3,200 bhp	2	15.0
Melissa Desgagnés	Allen - 12PVBCS12-F	Diesel	2	12	4,000 bhp	1 cpp	13.8
Mesabi Miner	Pielstick - 16PC2-2V-400	Diesel	2	16	16,000 bhp	2 cpp	15.5
Michigan *	GM EMD - 20-645-E6	Diesel	2	16	3,900 bhp	2	13.2
Michipicoten	MaK - 6M32C	Diesel	2	6	8,160 bhp	1 cpp	14.0
Mississagi	Caterpillar - 3612-TA	Diesel	1	12	4,500 bhp	1 cpp	13.8
Mobile Bay (USCG)	Fairbanks Morse - 10-38D8-1/8	Diesel	2	10	2,500 bhp	1	13.8
Morro Bay (USCG)	Fairbanks Morse - 10-38D8-1/8	Diesel	2	10	2,500 bhp	1	13.8
Neah Bay (USCG)	Fairbanks Morse - 10-38D8-1/8	Diesel	2	10	2,500 bhp	1	13.8
Nordik Express	GM EMD - 20-645-E7	Diesel	2	20	7,200 bhp	2 ccp	16.0
Oakglen	B&W - 6K67GF	Diesel	1	6	11,600 bhp	1	15.5
Ojibway	GE - 7FDM EFI	Diesel	1	16	4,100 bhp	1 cpp	
Olive L. Moore *	Alco - 16V251	Diesel	2	16	5,830 bhp	1	

Name	Engine	Type			Power		
Paul H. Townsend	Nordberg - TSM-216	Diesel	1	6	2,150 bhp	1	12.1
Paul R. Tregurtha	MaK - 6M43C	Diesel	2	6	17,120 bhp	2 cpp	15.5
Pearl Mist	Caterpillar - 3516C-DITA	Diesel	2	16	3,386 bhp	2	
Pelee Islander **	Caterpillar - 3408	Diesel	2	8	910 bhp	2	
Peter R. Cresswell	MaK - 6M552AK	Diesel	2	6	9,460 bhp	1 cpp	13.8
Petite Forte *	Ruston - 8ATC	Diesel	2	8	4,200 bhp	2	15.5
Philip R. Clarke	Westinghouse Elec. Corp.	Turbine	1	**	7,700 shp	1	16.1
Pierre Radisson (CCG)	Alco - 16V251F	Diesel	6	16	17,700 bhp	2	18.4
Pineglen	MaK - 6M601AK	Diesel	1	6	8,158 bhp	1 cpp	15.5
Prentiss Brown *	GM EMD - 12-645-E2	Diesel	2	12	3,900 bhp	1	
Presque Isle *	Mirrlees Blackstone Ltd. - KVMR-16	Diesel	2	16	14,840 bhp	2 cpp	
Quinte Loyalist **	Caterpillar - 3196	Diesel	2	6	770 bhp		
Radcliffe R. Latimer	MaK - 8M32C	Diesel	2	8	10,442 bhp	1 cpp	
Rebecca Lynn *	GM EMD - 16-567-BC	Diesel	2	16	3,600 bhp	2	
Reliance *	A.B. Nohab - SVI 16VS-F	Diesel	2	16	5,600 bhp	1 cpp	17.6
Robert S. Pierson	Alco - 16V251E	Diesel	2	16	5,600 bhp	1	17.8
Roger Blough	Pielstick - 16PC2V-400	Diesel	2	16	14,200 bhp	1 cpp	16.7
Rosaire A. Desgagnés	MaK/Caterpillar - 6M43	Diesel	1	6	7,344 bhp	1 cpp	17.8
Rt. Hon. Paul J. Martin	MaK/Caterpillar - 6M32C	Diesel	2	6	8,060 bhp (est)	1 cpp	
Saginaw	MaK - 6M43C	Diesel	1	6	8,160 bhp	1 cpp	16.1
Saint Laurent	Caterpillar 3516TA-B	Diesel	2	16	4,000 bhp	2	11,5
Salarium	Pielstick - 10PC2-2V-400	Diesel	2	10	10,700 bhp	1 cpp	13.8
Salvor *	GM EMD - 16-645-E7	Diesel	2	16	5,750 bhp	2	13.8
Sam Laud	GM EMD - 20-645-E7	Diesel	2	20	7,200 bhp	1	16.1
Samuel de Champlain *	GM EMD - 20-645-E5	Diesel	2	20	7,200 bhp	2 cpp	17.3
Samuel Risley (CCG)	Wartsila - VASA 12V22HF	Diesel	4	12	8,836 bhp	2 cpp	17.3
Sarah Desgagnés	MaK - 7M43	Diesel	1	7	9,517 bhp	1 cpp	15.0
Sea Eagle II *	GM EMD - 20-645-E7	Diesel	2	20	7,200 bhp	2	13.8
Sedna Desgagnés	MaK/Caterpillar - 6M43	Diesel	1	6	7,344 bhp	1 cpp	17.8
Sharon M 1 *	Niigata - 6L38HX	Diesel	2	6	1,934 bhp	2	16.0
Spruceglen	Sulzer - 4RLB76	Diesel	1	4	10,880 bhp	1 cpp	13.8
St. Clair	GM EMD - 20-645-E7	Diesel	3	20	10,800 bhp	1 cpp	16.7
Stephen B. Roman	Total	Diesel			5,996 bhp	1 cpp	18.4
(Center)	Fairbanks Morse - 10-38D8-1/8	Diesel	2	10	3,331 bhp		
(Wing)	Fairbanks Morse - 8-38D8-1/8	Diesel	2	8	2,665 bhp		
Sterling Energy	GUASCOR - F360TA-SP	Diesel	1	12	900 bhp	1	
Stewart J. Cort	GM EMD - 20-645-E7	Diesel	4	20	14,400 bhp	2 cpp	18.4
Sugar Islander II **	Caterpillar - 3412	Diesel	2	12	1,280 bhp		
Tecumseh	Pielstick - 12PC-2V-400	Diesel	2	12	12,000 bhp	1 cpp	16.1
Thalassa Desgagnés	B&W - 8K42EF	Diesel	1	8	5,000 bhp	1 cpp	16.4
Tim McKeil*	Niigata 6L38HX	Diesel	2	6	2,400 bhp	2	15.3
Tim S. Dool	MaK - 8M43C	Diesel	1	8	10,750 bhp	1 cpp	17.3
Tony MacKay *	Ruston - 12C-5VM	Diesel	2	12	2,800 bhp	1 cpp	15.0
Thunder Bay	MAN-B&W - 6S50ME-B9	Diesel	1	6	11,897 bhp	1	15.5
Umiak I	M.A.N.-B&W - 7S70ME-C	Diesel	1	7	29,598 bhp	1 cpp	16.5
Umiavut	Hanshin - 6LF58	Diesel	1	6	6,000 bhp	1 cpp	16.2
Undaunted *	Cummins K38-M	Diesel	2				
Véga Desgagnés	Wartsila 9R32	Diesel	2	9	7,560bhp	1 cpp	16.1
Victorious *	MaK - 6M25	Diesel	2	6	5,384 bhp	2 cpp	12.1
Victory *	MaK - 6MU551AK	Diesel	2	6	7,880 bhp	2	16.1
Walter J. McCarthy Jr.	GM EMD - 20-645-E7B	Diesel	4	20	14,400 bhp	2 cpp	16.1
Whitefish Bay	MAN-B&W - 6S50ME-B9	Diesel	1	6	11,897 bhp	1	15.5
Wilfred Sykes	Westinghouse Elec. Corp.	Turbine	1	**	7,700 shp	1	16.1
Wilf Seymour *	GM EMD - 16-645-E7	Diesel	2	16	5,750 bhp	2	13.8
Wolfe Islander III **	Caterpillar - 3412E	Diesel	4	12	2,284 bhp	2 x 2	13.8
Yankcanuck	Cooper-Bessemer Corp.	Diesel	1	8	1,860 bhp	1	11.5
Zélada Desgagnés	MaK/Caterpillar - 6M43	Diesel	1	6	7,344 bhp	1 cpp	17.8
Zeus *	Caterpillar - D399	Diesel	2	8	2,250 bhp	2	

1906-'37

1906: St. Marys Challenger (re:'67,'14) **1936**: J.A.W. Iglehart (re:'65)***1937**: St. Marys Conquest (re:'87)

1941-'49

1941: Pere Marquette 41 (re:'97) **1942**: Alpena (re:'91), American Victory (re:'61,'82)** Lee A. Tregurtha (re:'61) **1943**: Cuyahoga (re:'74), Manistee (re:'64), Mississagi (re:'67) **1944**: Joseph H. Thompson (re '52,'91), McKee Sons (re:'53,'91) **1945**: Paul H. Townsend (re:'52)* **1949**: Wilfred Sykes

1952-'59

1952: Arthur M. Anderson (re: '75,'82), Kaye E. Barker (re:'76, '81), Cason J. Callaway (re: '74,'82), Philip R. Clarke (re: '74,'82), Lewis J. Kuber (re:'06), Michipicoten (re: '57,'80), Ojibway, John G. Munson **1953**: American Valor (re: '74,'82)**, Badger, James L. Kuber (re:'07), Pathfinder (re:'98), Saginaw **1958**: John Sherwin** **1959**: Cedarglen (re:'77), Hon. James L. Oberstar (re:'72, '81), Herbert C. Jackson (re:'75), Sarah Spencer (re:'89)**

1960-'69

1960: Edward L. Ryerson** **1961**: English River (re:'74) **1962**: Catherine Desgagnés, **1963**: Yankcanuck** **1965**: Stephen B. Roman (re:'83) **1966**: Algosteel (re:'89) **1967**: Tim S. Dool (re:'96), Canadian Navigator (re:'80,'97), John D. Leitch (re:'02), Manitoba **1968**: Algomarine (re:'89), Algorail, Frontenac (re:'73) **1969**: CSL Tadoussac (re:'01)

1972-'79

1972: Algoway, Roger Blough, CSL Niagara (re:'99), Stewart J. Cort **1973**: Adam E. Cornelius, Calumet, Manitowoc, John J. Boland, Rt. Hon. Paul J. Martin (re: '00), Presque Isle, Tecumseh **1974**: Algosoo, H. Lee

White, Robert S. Pierson **1975**: Melissa Desgagnés, Sam Laud **1976**: James R. Barker, Joseph L. Block, Algoma Olympic, Amelia Desgagnés, Thalassa Desgagnés, St. Clair **1977**: Algoeast, Algolake, CSL Assiniboine (re:'05), CSL Laurentien (re:'01), Walter J. McCarthy Jr., Mesabi Miner **1978**: Radcliffe R. Latimer (re:'09), Algosar, American Integrity, American Spirit, Buffalo **1979**: American Courage, Algoma Enterprise, Algoma Transport, Edwin H. Gott, Indiana Harbor

1980-'87

1980: American Mariner, Burns Harbor, Salarium, Edgar B. Speer, Oakglen **1981**: Algowood (re:'00), American Century, Great Republic, Capt. Henry Jackman (re:'96), Mapleglen, Saguenay, Paul R. Tregurtha **1982**: Camilla Desgagnés, Peter R. Cresswell (re:'98), Michigan, Véga Desgagnés, Ashtabula **1983**: John B. Aird, Birchglen, Spruceglen, Kaministiqua **1984**: Atlantic Huron (re: '89,'03) **1985**: Atlantic Erie, Pineglen **1986**: Anna Desgagnés, Algoma Spirit **1987**: Algoma Discovery, Algoma Guardian

1992-'99

1991: Manitoulin re: '15 **1992**: Dara Desgagnés, Esta Desgagnés **1993**: Jana Desgagnés **1996**: Integrity **1998**: Algosea **1999**: Maria Desgagnés

2000-'15

2000: Great Lakes Trader **2001**: Norman McLeod **2004**: Algoscotia, Lake Express **2006**: Innovation **2007**: Rosaire A. Desgagnés **2008**: Algocanada, Algonova, John J. Carrick, Zélada Desgagnés **2009**: Sedna Desgagnés **2011**: Algoma Mariner, Claude A. Desgagnés **2012**: Lakes Contender, Bella Desgagnés, Baie St. Paul **2013**: Algoma Equinox, Thunder Bay, Whitefish Bay, Baie Comeau **2014**: Algoma Harvester, CWB Marquis, CSL Welland, CSL St-Laurent **2015**: CWB Strongfield

(re = major rebuild; * storage barge; ** long-term lay-up)

John G. Munson of 1952 vintage unloading stone. *(Chris Mazzella)*

Saltwater Fleets

Jumbo Spirit in the St. Marys River. (Roger LeLievre)

Fleet Name / Vessel Name	IMO #	Vessel Type	Year Built	Engine Type	Cargo Cap. or Gross*	Overall Length	Breadth	Depth
IA-1 ABC MARITIME, NYON, SWITZERLAND (abcmaritime.ch)								
Adfines Sea	9580962	TK	2011	D	19,118	530' 05"	75' 06"	40' 08"
(Osttank Norway '11-'12)								
Adfines Star	9580974	TK	2011	D	19,118	530' 05"	75' 06"	40' 08"
(Osttank Denmark '11-'11, Osttank Sweden '11-'11)								
IA-2 ACE TANKERS CV, AMSTERDAM, NETHERLANDS (ace-tankers.com)								
Chem Hydra	9486180	TK	2009	D	17,055	475' 01"	75' 06"	40' 08"
Chem Norma	9486192	TK	2009	D	17,055	475' 01"	75' 06"	40' 08"
IA-3 ALLIANCE TANKERS, HAMILTON, BERMUDA (alliance-tankers.com)								
Askholmen	9436381	TK	2009	D	16,850	472' 05"	74' 02"	42' 00"
(Hellespont Charger '09-'14)								
Brentholmen	9436393	TK	2010	D	16,850	472' 05"	74' 02"	42' 00"
(Hellespont Chieftan '10-'14)								
Kirkeholmen	9553402	TK	2010	D	16,730	473' 02"	75' 06"	40' 08"
(CF Sophia '10-'12)								
Larsholmen	9436410	TK	2009	D	16,850	472' 05"	74' 02"	42' 00"
(Hellespont Centurion '10-'14)								
Lokholmen	9433303	TK	2010	D	16,850	472' 05"	74' 02"	42' 00"
(Hellespont Crusader '10-'14)								
Morholmen	9553414	TK	2011	D	16,500	472' 05"	75' 06"	40' 08"
IA-4 ALVTANK REDERI AB, DONSO, SWEDEN (alvtank.se)								
Ramira	9362152	TK	2008	D	12,164	472' 07"	75' 07"	40' 08"
IA-5 ARA GROUP, WERKENDAM, NETHERLANDS (aragroup.nl)								
ARA Rotterdam	9240471	BC	2002	D	10,500	468' 02"	59' 10"	33' 04"
(Sabrina '02-'02, MSC Rades '02-'04, Sabrina '04-'04, SCM Olympic '04-'05 , **Sabrina** '05-'14)								
IA-6 ARDMORE SHIPPING LTD., CORK, IRELAND (ardmoreshipping.com)								
Ardmore Calypso	9512123	TK	1983	D	12,334	423' 03"	65' 08"	36' 09"
(Samho Leader '83-'11)								
IA-7 ARMADOR GEMI ISLETMECILIGI TICARET LTD., ISTANBUL, TURKEY (armadorshipping.com)								
Pochard S	9262534	BC	2003	D	37,384	655' 10"	77' 09"	50' 02"
(**Pochard** '03-'14)								
IA-8 ATLANTSKA PLOVIDBA D.D., DUBROVNIK, REPUBLIC OF CROATIA (atlant.hr)								
Orsula	9110901	BC	1996	D	34,372	656' 02"	77' 01"	48' 10"
(*Federal Calumet* {2} '96-'97)								
IB-1 BD-SHIPSNAVO GMBH & CO., HAREN-EMS, GERMANY (bergesen.no)								
Active	9343821	BC	2008	D	12,523	378' 03"	64' 04"	37' 05"
(Antilles VII '08-'14)								
IB-2 BERGESEN WORLDWIDE LTD., OLSO, NORWAY								
Bold World	9141417	TK	1998	D	19,125	486' 10"	75' 06"	42' 04"
(Cambridgeshire '98-'98, **Stolt Kent** '98-'07, Stolt Bold World '07-'08)								
IB-3 BERNHARD SCHULTE GROUP OF COMPANIES, HAMBURG, GERMANY (schultegroup.com)								
Edzard Schulte	9439852	TK	2011	D	16,658	476' 02"	75' 06"	41' 00"
Elisabeth Schulte	9439840	TK	2010	D	16,658	476' 02"	75' 06"	41' 00"
Elisalex Schulte	9439876	TK	2011	D	16,418	476' 02"	76' 05"	41' 00"
Everhard Schulte	9439838	TK	2010	D	16,658	476' 02"	75' 06"	41' 00"
IB-4 BESIKTAS LIKID TASIMACILIK DENIZCILIK TICARET, ISTANBUL, TURKEY (besiktasgroup.com)								
Mainland	9431056	TK	2008	D	7,724	402' 05"	56' 05"	28' 10"
Purple Gem	9403827	TK	2009	D	6,824	390' 09"	55' 05"	27' 07"
IB-5 BIGLIFT SHIPPING BV, AMSTERDAM, NETHERLANDS (bigliftshipping.com)								
Happy River	9139294	HL	1997	D	15,593	452' 09"	74' 10"	42' 06"
Happy Rover	9139309	HL	1997	D	15,593	452' 09"	74' 10"	42' 06"
Tracer	9204702	HL	2000	D	8,874	329' 09"	73' 06"	26' 11"
Tramper	9204697	HL	2000	D	8,874	329' 09"	73' 06"	26' 11"
Transporter	9204714	HL	1999	D	8,469	329' 09"	80' 01"	36' 05"

Fleet Name Vessel Name	IMO #	Vessel Type	Year Built	Engine Type	Cargo Cap. or Gross*	Overall Length	Breadth	Depth
IB-6	**BLUE SHIPMANAGEMENT CORP., ATHENS, GREECE**							
Blue Phoenix I	9134816	BC	1998	D	20,142	472' 05"	75' 09"	44' 03"
(Elise Oldendorff '98-'07, Pacific Grace '07-'10, Birch 2 '10-'13, Blue Phoenix '13-'14)								
IB-7	**BLYSTAD TANKERS INC., OSLO, NORWAY** *(blystad.no)*							
FOLLOWING VESSELS UNDER CHARTER TO SONGA SHIPMANAGEMENT								
Songa Challenge	9409510	TK	2009	D	17,596	472' 05"	74' 02"	41' 00"
Songa Diamond	9460459	TK	2009	D	17,596	472' 05"	74' 02"	41' 00"
Songa Eagle	9461714	TK	2008	D	13,250	423' 03"	67' 00"	37' 09"
Songa Emerald	9473937	TK	2009	D	17,596	472' 05"	74' 02"	41' 00"
Songa Jade	9473925	TK	2009	D	17,596	472' 05"	74' 02"	41' 00"
Songa Opal	9473913	TK	2009	D	17,596	472' 05"	74' 02"	41' 00"
Songa Peace	9409522	TK	2009	D	17,596	472' 05"	74' 02"	41' 00"
(Global Peace '09-'13)								
Songa Ruby	9444479	TK	2008	D	17,596	472' 05"	74' 02"	41' 00"
Songa Sapphire	9444467	TK	2008	D	17,596	472' 05"	74' 02"	41' 00"
Songa Topaz	9460461	TK	2009	D	17,596	472' 05"	74' 02"	41' 00"
IB-8	**BRIESE SCHIFFAHRTS GMBH & CO. KG, LEER, GERMANY** *(briese.de)*							
BBC Austria	9433327	GC	2009	D	7,530	393' 00"	66' 03"	32' 02"
BBC Balboa	9501667	GC	2012	D	8,129	423' 01"	54' 02"	32' 10"
BBC Elbe	9347059	GC	2006	D	17,348	469' 07"	75' 11"	42' 08"
(Horumersiel '06-'06)								
BBC Ems	9347035	GC	2006	D	17,348	469' 07"	75' 11"	42' 08"
BBC Europe	9266308	GC	2003	D	7,409	391' 09"	66' 03"	32' 02"
BBC Fuji	9508419	GC	2011	D	9,310	412' 09"	72' 02"	35' 05"
BBC Greenland	9427079	GC	2007	D	7,530	393' 00"	66' 03"	32' 02"
BBC Houston	9331593	GC	2005	D	7,530	393' 00"	66' 03"	32' 02"
*(**BBC Australia** '05-'05, Wesier Hiede '05-'05, **BBC Australia** '05-'10)*								
BBC Jade	9421116	GC	2007	D	12,000	469' 00"	62' 00"	35' 11"
BBC Kibo	9508421	GC	2011	D	9,310	412' 09"	72' 02"	35' 05"
BBC Kwiatkowski	9436953	GC	2008	D	7,733	401' 09"	59' 09"	31' 02"
(Eugeniusz Kwiatkowski '08-'08)								
BBC Mississippi	9347061	GC	2006	D	17,348	469' 07"	75' 11"	42' 08"
(Greetsiel '06-'07)								
BBC Rushmore	9508469	GC	2012	D	9,310	412' 09"	72' 02"	35' 05"
BBC Scandinavia	9362633	GC	2007	D	7,530	393' 00"	66' 03"	32' 02"
(Rysum '07-'07)								
BBC Sweden	9278600	GC	2003	D	4,325	324' 06"	45' 03"	24' 03"
BBC Switzerland	9433315	GC	2008	D	7,530	393' 00"	66' 03"	32' 02"
BBC Volga	9436329	GC	2009	D	17,300	469' 07"	74' 10"	43' 08"
(Ocean Breeze '09-'09)								
BBC Xingang	9508483	GC	2013	D	9,310	412' 09"	72' 02"	35' 05"
Kurt Paul	9435856	GC	2009	D	17,300	469' 07"	74' 10"	43' 08"
Peter Ronna	9198628	GC	2002	D	4,303	324' 03"	49' 10"	24' 03"
(Peter Ronna '02-'03, Svend '03-'05)								
Sjard	9303314	GC	2007	D	17,348	469' 07"	75' 11"	42' 08"

EDITOR'S NOTE: Observers will likely spot saltwater vessels not included in this book. These may be newcomers to the Great Lakes/Seaway system, recent renames or new construction. This is not meant to be an exhaustive listing of every saltwater vessel that could potentially visit the Great Lakes and St. Lawrence Seaway. To attempt to do so, given the sheer number of world merchant ships, would be space and cost prohibitive.

This list reflects vessels whose primary trade routes are on saltwater but which also regularly visit Great Lakes and St. Lawrence Seaway ports above Montreal. Fleets listed may operate other vessels worldwide than those included herein; additional vessels may be found on fleet websites, which have been included where available. **Former names listed in boldface type indicate the vessel visited the Seaway system under that name.**

C

Fleet Name Vessel Name	IMO #	Vessel Type	Year Built	Engine Type	Cargo Cap. or Gross*	Overall Length	Breadth	Depth

IC-1 **CANADIAN FOREST NAVIGATION CO. LTD., MONTREAL, QUEBEC, CANADA** (canfornav.com)

At press time, Canadian Forest Navigation Co. Ltd. had the following vessels under long or short-term charter. Please consult their respective fleets for details: **Andean, Barnacle, Blacky, Bluebill, Bluewing, Brant, Chestnut, Cinnamon, Eider, Emilie, Gadwall, Garganey, Greenwing, Heloise, Labrador, Maccoa, Mandarin, Mottler, Orna, Puffin, Redhead, Ruddy, Shoveler, Torrent, Tufty, Tundra, Whistler, Wigeon.**

IC-2 **CARISBROOKE SHIPPING LTD., COWES, UNITED KINGDOM** (carisbrookeshipping.net)

Charlotte C	9528706	GC	2009	D	13,517	447' 06"	69' 07"	37' 01"

IC-3 **CHEMFLEET SHIPPING LTD., ISTANBUL, TURKEY** (chemfleet.org)

Mehmet A	9418822	TK	2011	D	20,000	530' 04"	73' 06"	34' 01"
(Aldemar '11-'11)								

IC-4 **CHEMIKALIEN SEETRANSPORT GMBH, HAMBURG, GERMANY** (chemikalien-seetransport.de)

Chemtrans Elbe	9439345	TK	2008	D	13,073	421' 11"	66' 11"	37' 09"
Chemtrans Havel	9439333	TK	2009	D	13,073	421' 11"	66' 11"	37' 09"
Chemtrans Mabuhay	9232369	TK	2000	D	17,427	455' 01"	66' 11"	39' 04"
Oste	9435557	TK	2008	D	13,073	421' 11"	66' 11"	37' 09"
(Chemtrans Oste '08-'13)								
Weser	9439307	TK	2009	D	13,073	421' 11"	66' 11"	37' 09"
(Chemtrans Weser '09-'13)								

IC-5 **CHEMNAV INC., ATHENS, GREECE** (chemnav.gr)

Commencement	9388211	TK	2008	D	13,091	421' 11"	66' 11"	37' 09"

IC-6 **CLIPPER GROUP AS, COPENHAGEN, DENMARK** (clipper-group.com)

Clipper Legacy	9307437	TK	2005	D	10,098	388' 04"	62' 04"	33' 02"

Fionia Swan at anchor off the Lake Ontario end of the Welland Canal. (Jeff Cameron)

Fleet Name / Vessel Name	IMO #	Vessel Type	Year Built	Engine Type	Cargo Cap. or Gross*	Overall Length	Breadth	Depth
IC-7	**COASTAL SHIPPING LTD., GOOSE BAY, NEWFOUNDLAND, CANADA** *(woodwards.nf.ca)*							
Alsterstern	9053220	TK	1994	D	17,078	528' 03"	75' 06"	38' 05"
Havelstern	9053218	TK	1994	D	17,078	528' 03"	75' 06"	38' 05"
IC-8	**COLUMBIA SHIPMANAGEMENT, HAMBURG, GERMANY** *(csm-d.com)*							
Cape Egmont	9262819	TK	2003	D	12,950	417' 04"	67' 00"	37' 09"
Rio Dauphin	9449417	TK	2009	D	12,835	399' 07"	67' 00"	39' 00"
(Ida Theresa '09-'13)								
IC-9	**CONTI REEDEREI MANAGEMENT, MUNICH, GERMANY** *(conti-shipping.com)*							
	OPERATED BY PLANTOURS KREUZFAHRTEN, BREMEN, GERMANY *(plantours-partner.de)*							
Hamburg	9138329	PA	1997	D	15,067	472' 07"	75' 06"	40' 08"
(c. Columbus '97-'12)								
IC-10	**CORSO LOGISTIC SOLUTIONS, SLIEMA, MALTA**							
Corso Dream	9008122	BC	1992	D	6,273	365' 02"	57' 01"	24' 11"
(Putyatin '92-'92, Socofl Pearl '92-'04, CIC Brasil '04-'11)								
IC-11	**COSCO SOUTHERN ASPHALT SHIPPING CO., LTD, GUANGZHOU, CHINA** *(www.coscogz.com.cn/en)*							
Zhuang Yuan Ao	9650339	TK	2012	D	12,000	479' 00"	72' 02"	35' 05"
ID-1	**DAIICHI CHUO KISEN KAISHA, TOKYO, JAPAN** *(www.firstship.co.jp)*							
	FOLLOWING VESSEL UNDER CHARTER TO FEDNAV LTD.							
Federal Yukina	9476977	BC	2010	D	35,868	656' 01"	78' 01"	48' 09"
ID-2	**DANSER VAN GENT, DELFZIJL, NETHERLANDS** *(danservangent.nl)*							
	FOLLOWING VESSELS UNDER CHARTER TO WAGENBORG SHIPPING							
Marietje Deborah	9481594	BC	2011	D	8,200	413' 10"	50' 06"	30' 02"
Marietje Marsilla	9458248	BC	2010	D	8,200	413' 10"	50' 06"	30' 02"

Fleet Name / Vessel Name	IMO #	Vessel Type	Year Built	Engine Type	Cargo Cap. or Gross*	Overall Length	Breadth	Depth
ID-3 DUZGIT GEMI INSA SANAYI, ISTANBUL, TURKEY *(duzgit.com)*								
Duzgit Dignity	9581019	TK	2014	D	8,488	390' 09"	56' 05"	30' 02"
Duzgit Endeavour	9581007	TK	2013	D	16,004	509' 09"	71' 02"	36' 05"
IE-1 EASTERN PACIFIC SHIPPING, SINGAPORE *(epshipping.com.sg)*								
Ebony Ray	9363857	TK	2008	D	19,998	477' 05"	77' 09"	43' 10"
(Millennium Park '08-'14)								
IE-2 EITZEN CHEMICAL ASA, OSLO, NORWAY *(eitzen-chemical.com)*								
North Contender	9352585	TK	2005	D	19,998	481' 00"	77' 09"	42' 08"
North Fighter	9352597	TK	2006	D	19,998	481' 00"	77' 09"	42' 08"
Sichem Beijing	9397042	TK	2007	D	13,073	421' 11"	66' 11"	37' 09"
Sichem Challenge	9196448	TK	1998	D	17,485	382' 06"	62' 04"	33' 02"
*(Queen of Montreaux '98-'99, **North Challenge** '99-'06, Songa Challenge '06-'07)*								
Sichem Contester	9416020	TK	2007	D	19,998	481' 00"	77' 09"	42' 08"
Sichem Defiance	9244374	TK	2001	D	17,369	442' 11"	74' 10"	41' 00"
*(**North Defiance** '01-'06, **Songa Defiance** '06-'07)*								
Sichem Dubai	9376933	TK	2007	D	12,956	417' 04"	67' 00"	37' 09"
Sichem Edinburgh	9352066	TK	2007	D	13,073	421' 11"	66' 11"	37' 09"
Sichem Hiroshima	9361483	TK	2008	D	13,073	421' 11"	66' 11"	37' 09"
Sichem Hong Kong	9397054	TK	2007	D	13,073	421' 11"	66' 11"	37' 09"
Sichem Melbourne	9376921	TK	2007	D	12,936	417' 04"	67' 00"	37' 09"
Sichem Montreal	9404900	TK	2008	D	13,073	421' 11"	66' 11"	37' 09"
Sichem Mumbai	9322085	TK	2006	D	13,141	421' 11"	66' 11"	37' 09"
Sichem New York	9337834	TK	2007	D	12,956	417' 04"	67' 00"	37' 09"
Sichem Onomichi	9361471	TK	2005	D	13,091	421' 11"	66' 11"	37' 09"
Sichem Paris	9404895	TK	2008	D	13,073	421' 11"	66' 11"	37' 09"
IE-3 ELBE SHIPPING GMBH, DROCHTERSEN, GERMANY *(reederei-elbe-shipping.de)*								
BBC Celina	9468102	GC	2010	D	12,744	452' 11"	68' 11"	36' 01"
(Beluga Maturity '10-'10, Beluga Firmament '10-'11)								
BBC Rhine	9368338	GC	2008	D	12,782	468' 06"	70' 06"	43' 08"
(Beluga Gratification '08-'08)								
BBC Steinhoeft	9358046	GC	2006	D	12,744	452' 11"	68' 11"	36' 01"
*(**Beluga Fusion** '06-'11)*								

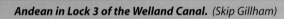

Andean in Lock 3 of the Welland Canal. *(Skip Gillham)*

Fleet Name / Vessel Name	IMO #	Vessel Type	Year Built	Engine Type	Cargo Cap. or Gross*	Overall Length	Breadth	Depth
IE-4 ENERGY SHIPPING SPA, GENOA, ITALY								
Sundaisy E	9609902	BC	2011	D	15,300	477' 08"	68' 11"	37' 01"
IE-5 ENZIAN SHIP MANAGEMENT, ZÜRICH, SWITZERLAND (www.enzian-shipping.com)								
Celine	9214185	BC	2001	D	8,600	423' 03"	52' 00"	32' 00"
Sabina	9205718	BC	2000	D	9,231	416' 08"	52' 00"	32' 00"
SCL Bern	9304461	BC	2005	D	12,680	459' 03"	70' 06"	38' 03"
IF-1 FAIRFIELD CHEMICAL CARRIERS, WILTON, CONNECTICUT, USA (fairfieldchemical.com)								
Fairchem Charger	9367401	TK	2009	D	19,998	477' 04"	77' 10"	43' 10"
Fairchem Steed	9311256	TK	2005	D	19,998	477' 04"	77' 10"	43' 10"
Fairchem Yuka	9477505	TK	2010	D	19,998	477' 04"	77' 10"	43' 10"
IF-2 FEDNAV LTD., MONTREAL, QUEBEC, CANADA (fednav.com)								
CANARCTIC SHIPPING CO. LTD. – DIVISION OF FEDNAV LTD.								
Arctic	7517507	GC	1978	D	26,440	692' 04"	75' 05"	49' 05"
Built: Port Weller Dry Docks, Port Weller, ON								
Umiak I	9334715	BC	2006	D	31,992	619' 04"	87' 02"	51' 50"
Built: Universal Shipbuilding Corp., Kawasaki, Japan								
FEDNAV INTERNATIONAL LTD. - DIVISION OF FEDNAV LTD.								
Federal Asahi {2}	9200419	BC	2000	D	36,563	656' 02"	77' 11"	48' 09"
Federal Hudson {3}	9205902	BC	2000	D	36,563	656' 02"	77' 11"	48' 09"
Federal Hunter {2}	9205938	BC	2001	D	36,563	656' 02"	77' 11"	48' 09"
Federal Kivalina	9205885	BC	2000	D	36,563	656' 02"	77' 11"	48' 09"
Federal Kumano	9244257	BC	2001	D	32,787	624' 08"	77' 05"	49' 10"
Federal Kushiro	9284702	BC	2003	D	32,787	624' 08"	77' 05"	49' 10"
Federal Maas {2}	9118135	BC	1997	D	34,372	656' 02"	77' 01"	48' 10"
Federal Mackinac	9299460	BC	2004	D	27,000	606' 11"	77' 09"	46' 25"
Federal Margaree	9299472	BC	2005	D	27,000	606' 11"	77' 09"	46' 25"
Federal Mayumi	9529578	BC	2012	D	35,300	655' 06"	78' 09"	48' 09"
Federal Nakagawa	9278791	BC	2005	D	36,563	656' 02"	77' 11"	48' 09"
Federal Oshima	9200330	BC	1999	D	36,563	656' 02"	77' 11"	48' 09"
Federal Rhine {2}	9110925	BC	1997	D	34,372	656' 02"	77' 01"	48' 10"
Federal Rideau	9200445	BC	2000	D	36,563	656' 02"	77' 11"	48' 09"

Federal St. Laurent passes Detroit / Windsor. (Wade P. Streeter)

Fleet Name Vessel Name	IMO #	Vessel Type	Year Built	Engine Type	Cargo Cap. or Gross*	Overall Length	Breadth	Depth
Federal Saguenay {2}	9110913	BC	1996	D	34,372	656' 02"	77' 01"	48' 10"
Federal Satsuki	9529578	BC	2012	D	35,300	655' 06"	78' 09"	48' 09"
Federal Schelde {3}	9118147	BC	1997	D	34,372	656' 02"	77' 01"	48' 10"
Federal Seto	9267209	BC	2004	D	36,563	656' 02"	77' 11"	48' 09"
Federal Shimanto	9218404	BC	2001	D	32,787	624' 08"	77' 05"	49' 10"
Federal St. Laurent {3}	9110896	BC	1996	D	34,372	656' 02"	77' 01"	48' 10"
Federal Welland	9205926	BC	2000	D	36,563	656' 02"	77' 11"	48' 09"
Federal Weser	9229972	BC	2002	D	37,372	652' 11"	78' 05"	50' 02"
Federal Yoshino	9218416	BC	2001	D	32,787	624' 08"	77' 05"	49' 10"
Federal Yukon	9205897	BC	2000	D	36,563	656' 02"	77' 11"	48' 09"

At press time, FedNav Ltd. also had the following vessels under charter. Please consult their respective fleets for details: **Federal Danube, Federal Elbe, Federal Ems, Federal Katsura, Federal Leda, Federal Mattawa, Federal Miramichi, Federal Sakura, Federal Yukina.**

IF-3	**FINBETA, SAVONA, ITALY** *(finbeta.com)*							
Sapphire	9114969	TK	1997	D	14,015	467' 06"	72' 02"	36' 01"
IF-4	**FLINTER SHIPPING BV, BARENDRECHT, THE NETHERLANDS** *(flinter.nl)*							
Flinter America	9504114	GC	2010	D	11,000	434' 08"	52' 01"	35' 04"
Flinter Arctic	9504126	GC	2010	D	11,000	434' 08"	52' 01"	35' 04"
Flintermar	9327322	GC	2006	D	7,750	393' 00"	50' 07"	27' 11"
(Flintermar '06-'06, UAL Malabo '06-'09)								
Flintersky	9250385	GC	2002	D	9,122	424' 06"	55' 09"	32' 10"
Flinterstar	9243758	GC	2002	D	9,122	424' 06"	55' 09"	32' 10"
(Flinterstar '02-'03, UAL Africa '03-'11)								
Flinterstream	9415040	GC	2009	D	9,122	424' 06"	55' 09"	32' 10"
Flintersun	9243746	GC	2002	D	9,122	424' 06"	55' 09"	32' 10"
Zeus	9190212	GC	2000	D	9,150	427' 01"	52' 01"	33' 06"
IF-5	**FREESE SHIPPING, STADE, GERMANY** *(freeseship.com)*							
Pacific Huron	9546796	GC	2010	D	30,000	623' 04"	77' 11"	47' 11"
(Seven Islands '10-'10)								
Three Rivers	9546784	GC	2010	D	30,000	623' 04"	77' 11"	47' 11"

HHL Elbe unloads wind turbine parts at Muskegon, Mich. (Tyler Fairfield)

Fleet Name / Vessel Name	IMO #	Vessel Type	Year Built	Engine Type	Cargo Cap. or Gross*	Overall Length	Breadth	Depth

IH-1 HAMMONIA REEDEREI GMBH & CO., HAMBURG, GERMANY *(www.hammonia-reederei.de)*

Vessel	IMO #	Type	Built	Engine	Cargo/Gross	Length	Breadth	Depth
HR Constitution	9273791	BC	2006	D	12,477	514' 04"	70' 06"	30' 06"
(Beluga Constitution '06-'11)								
HR Maria	9164017	BC	1998	D	17,539	465' 10"	70' 06"	43' 08"
(Maria Green '98-'04, BBC India '04-'08, Maria Green '08-'10, SE Viridian '08-'12)								
HR Resolution	9267754	BC	2005	D	10,536	441' 04"	70' 06"	30' 06"
(Beluga Resolution '05-'11)								

IH-2 HANSA HEAVY LIFT GMBH, BREMEN, GERMANY *(hansaheavylift.com)*

Vessel	IMO #	Type	Built	Engine	Cargo/Gross	Length	Breadth	Depth
BBC Elbe	9433262	GC	2008	D	12,840	454' 05"	68' 11"	36' 01"
(BBC Alaska '08-'13, Elbe '13-'14)								
HHL Amazon	9466996	GC	2009	D	12,700	453' 00"	68' 11"	36' 01"
(Beluga Fairy '09-'11)								
HHL Amur	9435753	HL	2007	D	12,744	452' 11"	68' 11"	36' 01"
(Beluga Fidelity '07-'11)								
HHL Congo	9467005	GC	2011	D	12,700	453' 00"	68' 11"	36' 01"
(Beluga Fealty '11-'11)								
HHL Mississippi	9435765	HL	2009	D	12,744	452' 11"	68' 11"	36' 01"
(Beluga Fantasy '09-'11, OXL Fantasy '11-'11)								
HHL Nile	9443669	GC	2009	D	12,700	453' 00"	68' 11"	36' 01"
(Beluga Faculty '09-'11)								

IH-3 HARREN & PARTNER SCHIFFAHRTS GMBH, BREMEN, GERMANY *(harren-partner.de)*

FOLLOWING VESSELS UNDER CHARTER TO COMBI LIFT

Vessel	IMO #	Type	Built	Engine	Cargo/Gross	Length	Breadth	Depth
Palabora	9501875	HL	2010	D	10,052	436' 04"	75' 06"	37' 05"
Palau	9501899	HL	2010	D	10,052	436' 04"	75' 06"	37' 05"
Palembang	9501887	HL	2010	D	10,052	436' 04"	75' 06"	37' 05"
Palmerton	9501863	HL	2009	D	10,052	436' 04"	75' 06"	37' 05"
Panagia	9305295	HL	2004	D	7,846	393' 00"	66' 03"	32' 02"
Pangani	9318943	HL	2004	D	7,846	393' 00"	66' 03"	32' 02"
Panthera	9226700	TK	2001	D	7,072	386' 11"	63' 08"	31' 00"

FOLLOWING VESSELS UNDER CHARTER TO CANADIAN FOREST NAVIGATION LTD.

Vessel	IMO #	Type	Built	Engine	Cargo/Gross	Length	Breadth	Depth
Puffin	9262522	BC	2003	D	37,384	655' 10"	77' 09"	50' 02"

IH-4 HARTMAN SEATRADE, URK, NETHERLANDS *(hartmanseatrade.com)*

Vessel	IMO #	Type	Built	Engine	Cargo/Gross	Length	Breadth	Depth
Deo Volente	9391658	BC	2006	D	3,750	343' 10"	52' 06"	24' 03"
Pacific Dawn	9558464	BC	2010	D	3,750	343' 10"	52' 06"	24' 03"

IH-5 HELLAS MARINE SERVICES LTD., PIRAEUS, GREECE *(hellasmarine.gr)*

Vessel	IMO #	Type	Built	Engine	Cargo/Gross	Length	Breadth	Depth
Sir Henry	9151383	BC	1996	D	18,315	486' 03"	74' 10"	40' 00"
(Rubin Lark '96-'05)								

IH-6 HERMANN BUSS GMBH, LEER, GERMANY *(gbshipping.de)*

Vessel	IMO #	Type	Built	Engine	Cargo/Gross	Length	Breadth	Depth
BBC Carolina	9402043	GC	2007	D	12,744	452' 11"	68' 11"	36' 01"
(Beluga Fantastic '07-'11)								

IH-7 HERNING SHIPPING AS, HERNING, DENMARK *(herning-shipping.dk)*

Vessel	IMO #	Type	Built	Engine	Cargo/Gross	Length	Breadth	Depth
Charlotte Theresa	9400708	TK	2008	D	11,000	424' 10"	63' 00"	27' 11"
Ina Theresa	9449455	TK	2010	D	12,592	399' 07"	67' 00"	39' 00"
(Rio Delaware '10-'10)								
Jette Theresa	9406582	TK	2009	D	11,000	424' 10"	63' 00"	27' 11"
Tina Theresa	9478298	TK	2009	D	7,902	332' 08"	62' 06"	34' 05"

II-1 INTERMARINE, HOUSTON, TEXAS, USA *(intermarineusa.com)*

Vessel	IMO #	Type	Built	Engine	Cargo/Gross	Length	Breadth	Depth
Industrial Eagle	9407574	GC	2008	D	10,340	456' 00"	65' 07"	27' 03"
(Aspus J. '08-'08)								
Ocean Crescent	9258193	GC	2002	D	8,097	393' 01"	65' 07"	37' 01"
(Pollux J. '02-'02, Industrial Crescent '02-'10)								

II-2 INTERNAUT SHIPPING GMBH, BREMEN, GERMANY *(internaut-shipping.de)*

Vessel	IMO #	Type	Built	Engine	Cargo/Gross	Length	Breadth	Depth
Alert	9177789	GC	1999	D	12,947	420' 01"	69' 07"	37' 01"

II-3 INTERSEE SCHIFFAHRTS-GESELLSCHAFT MBH & CO., HAREN EMS, GERMANY *(intersee.de)*

Vessel	IMO #	Type	Built	Engine	Cargo/Gross	Length	Breadth	Depth
Alexia	9369083	GC	2008	D	11,211	477' 09"	60' 03"	33' 10"
Fritz	9415155	BC	2010	D	29,635	622' 04"	77' 05"	47' 11"

Fleet Name / Vessel Name	IMO #	Vessel Type	Year Built	Engine Type	Cargo Cap. or Gross*	Overall Length	Breadth	Depth
Hermann Schoening	9413901	BC	2010	D	29,635	622' 04"	77' 05"	47' 11"
Jan S	9415143	BC	2010	D	29,635	622' 04"	77' 05"	47' 11"
Jana	9255725	GC	2001	D	8,994	433' 09"	52' 01"	31' 08"
Luebbert	9415167	BC	2010	D	29,635	622' 04"	77' 05"	47' 11"
Serena	9294977	GC	2004	D	10,500	468' 02"	59' 10"	33' 04"
Sofia	9312690	GC	2005	D	5,726	348' 02"	47' 03"	26' 07"
Victoria	9290074	GC	2004	D	10,500	468' 02"	59' 10"	33' 04"

II-4   INTERSHIP NAVIGATION CO. LTD., LIMASSOL, CYPRUS (intership-cyprus.com)
 FOLLOWING VESSELS UNDER CHARTER TO FEDNAV LTD.

Federal Danube	9271511	BC	2003	D	37,372	652' 11"	78' 05"	50' 02"
Federal Elbe	9230000	BC	2003	D	37,372	652' 11"	78' 05"	50' 02"
Federal Ems	9229984	BC	2002	D	37,372	652' 11"	78' 05"	50' 02"
Federal Leda	9229996	BC	2003	D	37,372	652' 11"	78' 05"	50' 02"

II-5   INTREPID SHIPPING LLC., STAMFORD, CONNECTICUT, USA

Intrepid Canada	9466740	TK	2011	D	16,427	476' 02"	75' 06"	41' 00"
Intrepid Republic	9466752	TK	2011	D	16,427	476' 02"	75' 06"	41' 00"

IJ-1   JO TANKERS BV, SPIJKENISSE, NETHERLANDS (jotankers.com)

Jo Spirit	9140841	TK	1998	D	6,248	352' 02"	52' 02"	30' 02"

IJ-2   JOHANN M. K. BLUMENTHAL GMBH & CO., HAMBURG, GERMANY (blueships.com)

Ida	9109536	GC	1995	D	18,796	486' 03"	74' 10"	40' 00"
Lita	9117416	GC	1995	D	18,796	486' 03"	74' 10"	40' 00"

IJ-3   JSM SHIPPING GMBH & CO.,JORK, GERMANY

BBC Chile	9290048	GC	2004	D	10,385	468' 02"	59' 10"	33' 10"

*(Ile de Molene '04-'04, **S Pacific** '04-'10, Batz '10-'12)*

IJ-4   JUMBO SHIPPING CO. SA, ROTTERDAM, NETHERLANDS (jumboshipping.nl)

Fairlift	8806905	HL	1990	D	7,780	330' 08"	68' 10"	43' 08"
Fairload	9083134	HL	1995	D	5,198	314' 00"	60' 03"	37' 02"
Jumbo Spirit	9083122	HL	1995	D	5,198	314' 00"	60' 03"	37' 02"

Colorful Edenborg in the Welland Canal. (John C. Knecht)

Fleet Name Vessel Name	IMO #	Vessel Type	Year Built	Engine Type	Cargo Cap. or Gross*	Overall Length	Breadth	Depth
Jumbo Vision	9153642	HL	2000	D	7,123	361' 03"	68' 05"	44' 03"
Stellaprima	8912326	HL	1991	D	7,780	330' 08"	68' 10"	43' 08"

IK-1 KALLIANIS BROS SHIPPING, ATHENS, GREECE (www.kallianisbros.gr)

| **Dimitrios K** | 9216602 | BC | 2001 | D | 24,765 | 574' 02" | 75' 09" | 44' 09" |

    (Cedar '01-'03, Atlantic Castle '03-'07, Ladytramp '07-'13)

IK-2 KNUTSEN O.A.S. SHIPPING AS, HAUGESUND, NORWAY (knutsenoas.com)

| **Kristin Knutsen** | 9141405 | TK | 1998 | D | 19,152 | 477' 05" | 75' 06" | 42' 06" |

IK-3 KOYO KAIUN CO. LTD., TOKYO, JAPAN (koyoline.com)
    FOLLOWING VESSELS UNDER CHARTER TO FEDNAV LTD.

| **Federal Katsura** | 9293923 | BC | 2005 | D | 32,787 | 624' 08" | 77' 05" | 49' 10" |
| **Federal Sakura** | 9288291 | BC | 2005 | D | 32,787 | 624' 08" | 77' 05" | 49' 10" |

IK-4 KOYO LINE LTD., TOKYO, JAPAN (koyotky.co.jp)

| **Maemi** | 9416044 | TK | 2008 | D | 19,998 | 481' 00" | 77' 09" | 42' 08" |

IL-1 LAURANNE SHIPPING BV, GHENT, NETHERLANDS (lauranne-shipping.com)

| **LS Christine** | 9302009 | TK | 2007 | D | 8,400 | 411' 05" | 59' 01" | 27' 07" |
| **LS Jacoba** | 9334428 | TK | 2006 | D | 15,602 | 485' 07" | 70' 10" | 37' 01" |

IL-2 LIAMARE SHIPPING BV, MAARTENSDIJK, NETHERLANDS (liamareshipping.nl)

| **Liamare** | 9166481 | GC | 1999 | D | 5,842 | 351' 03" | 50' 02" | 27' 03" |

IL-3 LITHUANIAN SHIPPING COMPANY, KLAIPEDA, LITHUANIA (ljl.lt)

| **Deltuva** | 8908832 | BC | 1994 | D | 17,064 | 490' 02" | 75' 04" | 39' 08" |

    (Clipper Eagle '94-'07)

IL-4 LLOYD FONDS SINGAPORE PTE LTD., SINGAPORE, SINGAPORE (lloydfonds.de)

| **Ben** | 9311646 | TK | 2006 | D | 12,950 | 417' 04" | 67' 00" | 37' 09" |

    (Songa Diamond '06-'03, Brovig Bay '03-'07, Liquid Velvet '07-'07)

| **Dale** | 9340398 | TK | 2007 | D | 13,032 | 421' 11" | 66' 11" | 37' 09" |
| **Fen** | 9359600 | TK | 2006 | D | 12,950 | 417' 04" | 67' 00" | 37' 09" |

    (Launched as Songa Onyx, Brovig Ocean '06-'07, Liquid Blue '07-'07)

Federal Ems and Federal Miramichi at Cleveland. *(Alain Gindroz)*

Fleet Name / Vessel Name	IMO #	Vessel Type	Year Built	Engine Type	Cargo Cap. or Gross*	Overall Length	Breadth	Depth
Glen	9311634	TK	2005	D	12,950	417' 04"	67' 00"	37' 09"
*(Launched as Songa Pearl, **Brovig Fjord** '06-'07)*								
Vale	9340350	TK	2007	D	13,032	421' 11"	66' 11"	37' 09"

IL-5   LORENTZENS REDERI CO., OSLO, NORWAY

Songa Falcon	9482653	TK	2009	D	13,226	419' 07"	67' 00"	37' 09"

IM-1   MARIDA TANKERS INC., NORWALK, CONNECTICUT, USA *(womarpools.com)*

Marida Melissa	9438169	TK	2009	D	13,132	421' 11"	67' 00"	37' 09"
Marida Mulberry	9474151	TK	2008	D	13,226	419' 07"	67' 00"	37' 09"

IM-2   MARSHIP BEREEDERUNGS GMBH & CO., HAREN EMS, GERMANY *(marship.de)*

Thorco Arctic	9484209	BC	2009	D	8,500	433' 09"	52' 01"	31' 08"
(Beluga Notion '09-'09, BBC Newcastle '09-'11)								

IM-3   MASSOEL LTD., GENEVA, SWITZERLAND *(massoel.com)*

Lugano	9244087	BC	2002	D	20,000	509' 00"	77' 09"	42' 08"
(DS Regent '02-'06)								

IM-4   MASTERMIND SHIPMANAGEMENT LTD., LIMASSOL, CYPRUS *(mastermind-cyprus.com)*

MSM Douro	9519028	GC	2012	D	6,500	357' 08"	49' 10"	25' 11"
(Dourodiep '12-'12)								
Onego Bora	9613604	GC	2011	D	7,658	383' 10"	64' 08"	27' 11"
(MSM Omodos '11-'11)								

IM-5   MEGA CHEMICAL TANKERS LTD., SINGAPORE, SINGAPORE *(www.mega-chemicals.ch)*

MCT Breithorn	9298375	TK	2007	D	19,950	539' 02"	76' 01"	42' 00"
MCT Monte Rosa	9298363	TK	2007	D	19,950	539' 02"	76' 01"	42' 00"
MCT Stockhorn	9298387	TK	2008	D	19,950	539' 02"	76' 01"	42' 00"

IM-6   MST MINERALIEN SCHIFFAHRT, SCHNAITTENBACH, GERMANY *(minship.com)*

Cornelia	9216597	BC	2001	D	16,807	574' 02"	75' 09"	44' 09"
(Pine '01-'04)								
Lady Doris	9459955	BC	2011	D	30,930	606' 11"	77' 09"	47' 11"
(Merganser '11-'11)								
Yulia	9459967	BC	2011	D	30,930	606' 11"	77' 09"	47' 11"

IN-1   NAVARONE SA MARINE ENTERPRISES, LIMASSOL, CYPRUS
FOLLOWING VESSELS UNDER CHARTER TO CANADIAN FOREST NAVIGATION LTD.

Andean	9413925	BC	2009	D	30,930	606' 11"	77' 09"	47' 11"
Barnacle	9409742	BC	2009	D	30,807	606' 11"	77' 09"	47' 11"
Blacky	9393149	BC	2008	D	30,801	607' 04"	77' 09"	47' 11"
Bluebill	9263306	BC	2004	D	37,200	632' 10"	77' 09"	50' 10"
Brant	9393151	BC	2008	D	30,807	606' 11"	77' 09"	47' 11"
Chestnut	9477866	BC	2009	D	30,807	606' 11"	77' 09"	47' 11"
Greenwing	9230921	BC	2002	D	26,737	611' 08"	77' 09"	46' 07"
Labrador	9415222	BC	2010	D	30,899	606' 11"	77' 09"	47' 11"
Maccoa	9413913	BC	2009	D	30,930	606' 11"	77' 09"	47' 11"
Mandarin	9239812	BC	2003	D	26,747	611' 00"	77' 09"	46' 07"
Mottler	9477828	BC	2009	D	30,807	606' 11"	77' 09"	47' 11"
Ruddy	9459981	BC	2009	D	30,930	606' 11"	77' 09"	47' 11"
Shoveler	9459979	BC	2009	D	30,930	606' 11"	77' 09"	47' 11"
Torrent	9415210	BC	2010	D	30,930	606' 11"	77' 09"	47' 11"
Tufty	9393163	BC	2009	D	30,807	606' 11"	77' 09"	47' 11"
Tundra	9415208	BC	2009	D	30,930	606' 11"	77' 09"	47' 11"

IN-2   NAVIGATION MARITIME BULGARE LTD., VARNA, BULGARIA *(navbul.com)*

Bogdan	9132492	BC	1997	D	13,960	466' 04"	72' 10"	36' 07"
Kom	9132480	BC	1997	D	13,960	466' 04"	72' 10"	36' 07"
Lyulin	9498248	BC	2011	D	30,688	610' 03"	77' 09"	48' 01"
Osogovo	9498250	BC	2010	D	30,688	610' 03"	77' 11"	47' 11"
Perelik	9132507	BC	1998	D	13,960	466' 04"	72' 10"	36' 07"
Strandja	9564140	BC	2010	D	30,688	610' 03"	77' 11"	47' 11"
(Eastwind York '10-'10, Federal Yangtze '10-'10)								
Vitosha	9564138	BC	2010	D	30,688	610' 03"	77' 11"	47' 11"

Fleet Name Vessel Name	IMO #	Vessel Type	Year Built	Engine Type	Cargo Cap. or Gross*	Overall Length	Breadth	Depth

O

IN-3 NESTE SHIPPING OY, ESPOO, FINLAND *(nesteoil.com)*

Futura	9255282	TK	2004	D	25,084	556'01"	77'11"	48'11"

IN-4 NGM ENERGY S.A., PIRAEUS, GREECE

El Zorro	9344801	TK	2007	D	13,073	451'11"	66'11"	37'09"

IN-5 NICHOLAS G. MOUNDREAS SHIPPING S.A., PIRAEUS, GREECE

Spring	9416812	TK	2009	D	13,073	421'11"	66'11"	37'09"
Winter	9416800	TK	2009	D	13,073	421'11"	66'11"	37'09"

IN-6 NORBULK SHIPPING CO. LTD., HAMILTON, BERMUDA *(norbulkshipping.com)*

Anuket Ruby	9393668	TK	2008	D	7,315	332'08"	62'06"	34'05"

IN-7 NORDANA SHIPPING CO., COPENHAGEN, DENMARK *(nordana.com)*

Aggersborg	9646455	HL	2012	D	12,645	454'04"	68'11"	36'01"

IN-8 NORDIC TANKERS A/S, COPENHAGEN, DENMARK *(nordictankers.dk)*

Harbour Clear	9230012	TK	2001	D	16,875	453'01"	75'06"	40'02"
(Jo Chiara D '01-'04, Chiara '04-'06, Nora '06-'09)								
Harbour Cloud	9291066	TK	2004	D	16,875	453'01"	75'06"	40'02"
(Fase D '04-'04, Fase '04-'09)								
Harbour Fashion	9473080	TK	2011	D	16,909	473'02"	75'06"	40'08"
Harbour Feature	9473092	TK	2011	D	16,909	473'02"	75'06"	40'08"
(Nordtank Lerner '11-'11)								
Harbour First	9473119	TK	2011	D	16,909	473'02"	75'06"	40'08"
Harbour Fountain	9473107	TK	2011	D	16,909	473'02"	75'06"	40'08"
Harbour Kira	9337286	TK	2007	D	11,259	382'03"	66'07"	38'05"
(Clipper Kira '07-'12)								
Harbour Krystal	9330020	TK	2006	D	11,259	382'03"	66'07"	38'05"
(Clipper Krystal '06-'11)								
Harbour Leader	9286451	TK	2004	D	10,098	388'04"	62'04"	33'02"
(Panam Trinity '04-'06, Clipper Leader '06-'11)								
Harbour Legend	9305403	TK	2004	D	10,098	388'04"	62'04"	33'02"
(Clipper Legend '04-'11)								
Harbour Loyalty	9373929	TK	2007	D	10,098	388'04"	62'04"	33'02"
(Clipper Loyalty '07-'11)								
Harbour Pioneer	9572757	TK	2010	D	19,122	530'05"	75'06"	40'08"
(Harbour Pioneer '10-'10, Nordtank Franklin '10-'10)								
Harbour Progress	9572745	TK	2010	D	19,122	530'05"	75'06"	40'08"
Nordic Copenhagen	9300776	TK	2005	D	12,950	417'04"	67'00"	39'09"
Nordic Helsinki	9361457	TK	2007	D	13,091	421'11"	66'11"	37'09"
(Spectator '07-'07)								
Nordic Mari	9422677	TK	2009	D	19,822	481'00"	77'10"	42'08"
(Clipper Mari '09-'14)								
Nordic Oslo	9300788	TK	2005	D	12,950	417'04"	67'00"	39'09"
(Sichem Oslo '05-'07)								
Nordic Stockholm	9328314	TK	2005	D	12,950	417'04"	67'00"	39'09"

IO-1 OCEAN CHALLENGE LTD., NICOSIA, CYPRUS
   FOLLOWING VESSELS UNDER CHARTER TO CANADIAN FOREST NAVIGATION LTD.

Bluewing	9230919	BC	2002	D	26,747	611'00"	77'09"	46'07"
Cinnamon	9239800	BC	2002	D	26,747	611'00"	77'09"	46'07"

IO-2 OCEANEX INC., MONTREAL, QUEBEC, CANADA *(oceanex.com)*

Oceanex Avalon	9315044	CO	2005	D	14,747	481'11"	85'00"	45'11"
Oceanex Connaigra	9649718	CO	2013	D	19,460	689'00"	97'01"	56'01"
Oceanex Sanderling	7603502	RR	1977	D	15,195	364'01"	88'05"	57'07
(Rauenfels '77-'80, Essen '80-'81, Kongsfjord '81-'83, Onno '83-'87, ASL Sanderling '87-'08)								

IO-3 OSM GROUP AS, KRISTIANSAND, NORWAY *(osm.no)*

Tromso	9435791	BC	2008	D	12,697	393'08"	67'00"	39'00"
(Gemi '08-'08, M.Y. Arctic '08-'11)								

Fleet Name Vessel Name	IMO #	Vessel Type	Year Built	Engine Type	Cargo Cap. or Gross*	Overall Length	Breadth	Depth
IP-1 **PARAKOU SHIPPING LTD., HONG KONG, CHINA** *(parakougroup.com)*								
FOLLOWING VESSELS UNDER CHARTER TO CANADIAN FOREST NAVIGATION LTD.								
Eider	9285938	BC	2004	D	37,249	655'10"	77'09"	50'02"
Emilie	9498236	BC	2010	D	29,800	610'03"	77'11"	47'11"
Gadwall	9358369	BC	2007	D	37,249	655'10"	77'09"	50'02"
Garganey	9358383	BC	2007	D	37,249	655'10"	77'09"	50'02"
Heloise	9498224	BC	2010	D	29,800	610'03"	77'11"	47'11"
Redhead	9285940	BC	2005	D	37,249	655'10"	77'09"	50'02"
Whistler	9358371	BC	2007	D	37,249	655'10"	77'09"	50'02"
Wigeon	9358395	BC	2007	D	37,249	655'10"	77'09"	50'02"
IP-2 **PETER DOHLE SCHIFFAHRTS, HAMBURG, GERMANY** *(doehle.de)*								
Diana	9370082	GC	2007	D	13,450	453'00"	68'11"	36'01"
IP-3 **POLISH STEAMSHIP CO., SZCZECIN, POLAND** *(polsteam.com)*								
Drawsko	9393450	BC	2010	D	30,000	623'04"	77'11"	47'11"
Ina	9521875	BC	2012	D	16,630	492'00"	77'05"	41'00"
Irma	9180396	BC	2000	D	34,946	655'10"	77'05"	50'02"
Iryda	9180384	BC	1999	D	34,946	655'10"	77'05"	50'02"
Isa	9180358	BC	1999	D	34,946	655'10"	77'05"	50'02"
Isadora	9180372	BC	1999	D	34,946	655'10"	77'05"	50'02"
Isolda	9180360	BC	1999	D	34,946	655'10"	77'05"	50'02"
Juno	9422378	BC	2011	D	30,000	623'04"	77'11"	47'11"
Lubie	9441984	BC	2011	D	30,000	623'04"	77'11"	47'11"
Mamry	9496264	BC	2012	D	30,000	623'04"	77'11"	47'11"
Miedwie	9393448	BC	2010	D	30,000	623'04"	77'11"	47'11"
Nogat	9154268	BC	1999	D	17,064	488'10"	75'06"	39'08"
Olza	9521837	BC	2012	D	16,630	492'00"	77'05"	41'00"
Orla	9154270	BC	1999	D	17,064	488'10"	75'06"	39'08"
Pilica	9154282	BC	1999	D	17,064	488'10"	75'06"	39'08"
Prosna	9521849	BC	2012	D	16,630	492'00"	77'05"	41'00"
Raba	9521825	BC	2012	D	16,630	492'00"	77'05"	41'00"
Regalica	9521758	BC	2011	D	16,630	492'00"	77'05"	41'00"
Resko	9393462	BC	2010	D	30,000	623'04"	77'11"	47'11"
Skawa	9521863	BC	2012	D	16,630	492'00"	77'05"	41'00"

HR Maria anchored in the St. Marys River. (Roger LeLievre)

Fleet Name / Vessel Name	IMO #	Vessel Type	Year Built	Engine Type	Cargo Cap. or Gross*	Overall Length	Breadth	Depth
Solina	9496252	BC	2012	D	30,000	623' 04"	77' 11"	47' 11"
Wicko	9393474	BC	2010	D	20,603	623' 04"	77' 11"	47' 11"
Ziemia Cieszynska	8418758	BC	1993	D	26,264	591' 02"	75' 09"	45' 07"
(Ziemia Cieszynska '93-'93, Lake Carling '93-'03)								
Ziemia Lodzka	8418746	BC	1992	D	26,264	591' 02"	75' 09"	45' 07"
(Ziemia Lodzka '92-'93, Lake Champlain '93-'03)								

IP-4   POT SCHEEPVAART BV, DELFZIJL, NETHERLANDS *(pot-scheepvaart.nl)*
FOLLOWING VESSELS UNDER CHARTER TO WAGENBORG SHIPPING

Kwintebank	9234288	GC	2002	D	8,664	433' 10"	52' 01"	31' 08"
Varnebank	9213739	GC	2000	D	8,664	433' 10"	52' 01"	31' 08"
Vikingbank	9604184	GC	2012	D	11,850	468' 00"	51' 09"	35' 04"

IR-1   REDERIET STENERSEN AS, BERGEN, NORWAY *(stenersen.com)*

Sten Aurora	9318565	TK	2008	D	16,613	472' 07"	75' 06"	40' 08"
Sten Bergen	9407988	TK	20098	D	16,611	472' 11"	76' 01"	40' 08"
Sten Suomi	9378723	TK	2008	D	16,611	472' 11"	76' 01"	40' 08"

IR-2   REEDEREI ECKHOFF & CO. GMBH, JORK, GERMANY *(reederei-eckhoff.de)*

Onego Ponza	9245263	GC	2002	D	9,900	455' 07"	52' 01"	35' 07"
(Sider Ponza '02-'02, Sider Monique '02-'03, Sider Ponza '03-'09)								

IR-3   REEDEREI GERD GORKE GMBH & CO., HOLLERN-TWIELENFLETH, GERMANY

BBC Hawaii	9358010	TK	2006	D	12,706	452' 11"	70' 01"	30' 01"
(Beluga Evaluation '06-'11, Nicola '11-'11)								

IR-4   REEDEREI KARL SCHLUTER GMBH & CO., RENDSBURG, GERMANY
FOLLOWING VESSEL UNDER CHARTER TO FEDNAV LTD.

Federal Mattawa	9315537	GC	2005	D	18,825	606' 11"	77' 09"	46' 03"

IR-5   REEDEREI NORD GMBH, HAMBURG, GERMANY *(reederei-nord.com)*

Nordisle	9457828	TK	2009	D	12,810	393' 08"	66' 11"	39' 00")
(Rio Daintree '09-'09)								
Nordport	9404144	TK	2008	D	13,132	421' 11"	67' 00"	37' 09")
(E R Elbe '08-'08)								

IR-6   RIGEL SCHIFFAHRTS GMBH, BREMEN, GERMANY *(rigel-hb.com)*

Amur Star	9480368	TK	2010	D	13,073	421' 11"	66' 11"	37' 09"

Nilufer Sultan at Montreal, assisted by the tug Océan Intrepide. (Ron Beaupré)

Puffin on the hook off downtown Detroit, Mich. (Mike Nicholls)

Fleet Name / Vessel Name	IMO #	Vessel Type	Year Built	Engine Type	Cargo Cap. or Gross*	Overall Length	Breadth	Depth
Colorado Star	9527609	TK	2010	D	13,073	421'11"	66'11"	37'09"
Ganges Star	9496692	TK	2010	D	13,073	421'11"	66'11"	37'09"
Isarstern	9105140	TK	1995	D	17,078	528'03"	75'06"	38'05"
Kongo Star	9508823	TK	2010	D	13,073	421'11"	66'11"	37'09"
Shannon Star	9503926	TK	2010	D	13,073	421'11"	66'11"	37'09"

IS-1 SARGEANT MARINE INC., BOCA RATON, FLORIDA, USA (sargeant.net)

Asphalt Carrier	9293545	TK	2010	D	9,230	356'00"	61'00"	34'09"

IS-2 SCAN-TRANS SHIPPING, NAESTVED, DENMARK (www.scan-trans.com)

Oslo Bulk 6	9589968	BC	2011	D	8,053	355'00"	59'09"	29'06"

IS-3 SCHULTE & BURNS GMBH & CO., PAPENBURG, GERMANY

Tiwala	9376775	GC	2008	D	5,484	350'04"	49'10"	21'08"

(Emstransporter '08-'08)

IS-4 SE SHIPPING, SINGAPORE, SINGAPORE (seshipping.com)

SE Potentia	9431472	BC	2009	D	12,840	454'05"	68'11"	36'01"

(Brattingsborg '09-'09)

IS-5 SEAFARERS SHIPPING INC., MANILA, PHILIPPINES

AS Omaria	9363819	TK	2008	D	19,992	447'05"	77'09"	43'10"

(Bow Omaria '08-'11)

IS-6 SEASTAR CHARTERING LTD., ATHENS, GREECE
FOLLOWING VESSELS UNDER CHARTER TO CANADIAN FOREST NAVIGATION CO. LTD.

Apollon	9146821	BC	1996	D	30,855	606'11"	77'05"	48'11"

(Spring Laker '96-'06)

IS-7 SERROMAH SHIPPING BV, ROTTERDAM, NETHERLANDS (serromahshipping.com)

Oriental Protea	9330381	TK	2005	D	14,246	440'02"	67'03"	38'01"
Shamrock Jupiter	9416082	TK	2009	D	19,998	481'00"	77'09"	42'08"

IS-8 SHANGHAI DIHENG SHIPPING CO., SHANGHAI, CHINA

Han Xin	9125889	BC	1996	D	7,713	352'02"	62'04"	34'09"

(Svenja '96-'06, Atlant Svenja '06-'12)

IS-9 SLOMAN NEOTUN SHIFFAHRTS, BREMEN, GERMANY (sloman-neptun.com)

Sloman Dispatcher	9620657	HL	2012	D	12,634	453'01"	68'11"	36'01"
Sloman Hera	9466714	TK	2012	D	16,427	476'02"	75'06"	41'00"
Sloman Herakles	9466726	TK	2012	D	16,427	476'02"	75'06"	41'00"
Sloman Hermes	9466738	TK	2012	D	16,427	476'02"	75'06"	41'00"

IS-10 SPLIETHOFF'S BEVRACHTINGSKANTOOR B.V., AMSTERDAM, NETHERLANDS (spliethoff.com)

Apollogracht	9014896	HL	1991	D	12,200	423'03"	62'00"	38'01"
Elandsgracht	9081332	HL	1995	D	15,593	452'09"	74'10"	42'06"
Flevogracht	9509956	HL	2012	D	12,500	447'10"	62'00"	38'03"
Floragracht	9509968	HL	2011	D	12,178	447'10"	62'00"	38'03"
Florijngracht	9428413	HL	2010	D	12,178	447'10"	62'00"	38'03"
Fortunagracht	9507609	HL	2012	D	12,178	447'10"	62'00"	38'03"
Merwedegracht	9571519	HL	2011	D	11,759	466'02"	62'00"	38'03"
Muntgracht	9571545	HL	2012	D	12,500	464'11"	62'00"	38'03"

IS-11 SUNSHIP SCHIFFAHRTSKONTOR KG, EMDEN, GERMANY (sunship.de)

Copenhagen	9457115	BC	2011	D	5,627	354'11"	54'06"	28'03"
Lake Ontario	9283538	BC	2004	D	27,000	606'11"	77'09"	46'03"

(Federal Manitou '04-'11)
FOLLOWING VESSELS UNDER CHARTER TO FEDNAV LTD.

Federal Miramichi	9315549	BC	2004	D	27,000	606'11"	77'09"	46'03"

IT-1 TARBIT TANKERS B.V., DORDRECHT, NETHERLANDS (tarbittankers.nl)

Stella Polaris	9187057	TK	1999	D	8,000	387'02"	55'09"	34'05"

IT-2 TECHNOMAR SHIPPING INC., ATHENS, GREECE

Sea Racer	9214252	BC	2000	D	18,320	485'07"	74'10"	40'00"

(Changi Hope '00-'08, Sea Grace '08-'09)

U

Fleet Name / Vessel Name	IMO #	Vessel Type	Year Built	Engine Type	Cargo Cap. or Gross*	Overall Length	Breadth	Depth
IT-3	**THODE JOHS SHIPPING CO, HAMBURG, GERMANY** *(johs-thode.de)*							
CL Hanse Gate	9283540	BC	2004	D	27,000	606' 11"	77' 09"	46' 03"
(Federal Matane '04-'11)								
IT-4	**TRANSATLANTIC, GOTHENBURG, SWEDEN** *(rabt.se)*							
TransHawk	9248552	BC	2005	D	16,740	467' 06"	72' 02"	39' 04"
(Sandon '05-'08)								
IT-5	**TRANSAL DENIZCILIK TICARET, ISTANBUL, TURKEY** *(www.transal.com.tr)*							
Ruby-T	9457878	TK	2010	D	21,224	541' 01"	75' 02"	42' 00"
IU-1	**UNI-TANKERS A/S, MIDDELFART, DENMARK** *(unitankers.com)*							
Fionia Swan	9328974	TK	2005	D	15,602	485' 07"	70' 10"	37' 01"
Selandia Swan	9371787	TK	2008	D	17,998	438' 11"	73' 06"	41' 04"
IU-2	**UNICORN TANKERS INTERNATIONAL LTD, LONDON, UNITED KINGDOM**							
Kowie	9382504	TK	2010	D	16,885	472' 05"	75' 06"	41' 00"
IU-3	**UTKILEN AS, BERGEN, NORWAY** *(utkilen.no)*							
Susana S	9406714	TK	2009	D	12,862	539' 02"	76' 01"	42' 00"

Federal Katsura upbound in the St. Lawrence Seaway. (Ronald Dole)

Fleet Name Vessel Name	IMO #	Vessel Type	Year Built	Engine Type	Cargo Cap. or Gross*	Overall Length	Breadth	Depth
IV-1 VBG DENIZCILIK SANAYI VE TICARET AS, ISTANBUL, TURKEY (vbgshipping.com)								
Nilufer Sultan	9410131	TK	2008	D	19,999	530' 04"	73' 06"	42' 00"
IW-1 W. BOCKSTIEGEL REEDEREI KG, EMDEN, GERMANY (reederei-bockstiegel.de)								
BBC Campana	9291963	GC	2003	D	12,782	453' 00"	68' 11"	24' 07"
BBC Colorado	9435117	GC	2004	D	12,750	454' 05"	68' 11"	36' 01"
BBC Delaware	9357212	GC	2004	D	12,782	453' 00"	68' 11"	24' 07"
BBC Florida	9433286	GC	2009	D	12,792	444' 05"	68' 11"	36' 01"
BBC Louisiana	9435105	GC	2008	D	12,750	454' 05"	68' 11"	36' 01"
BBC Maine	9357200	GC	2007	D	12,792	444' 05"	68' 11"	36' 01"
BBC Oregon	9501265	GC	2010	D	12,750	454' 05"	68' 11"	36' 01"
BBC Plata	9291975	GC	2005	D	12,750	454' 05"	68' 11"	36' 01"
Industrial Sailor	9501253	GC	2010	D	12,750	454' 05"	68' 11"	36' 01"
(BBC Barbuda '10-'10, **BBC Arizona** '10-'14)								
IW-2 WAGENBORG SHIPPING BV, DELFZIJL, NETHERLANDS (wagenborg.com)								
Adriaticborg	9546497	GC	2011	D	17,294	469' 02"	70' 06"	43' 08"
Africaborg	9365661	GC	2007	D	17,294	469' 02"	70' 06"	43' 08"
(Africaborg '07-'08, Tianshan '08-'09)								

Fleet Name Vessel Name	IMO #	Vessel Type	Year Built	Engine Type	Cargo Cap. or Gross*	Overall Length	Breadth	Depth
Alamosborg	9466348	GC	2011	D	17,294	469' 02"	70' 06"	43' 08"
Alaskaborg	9466374	GC	2012	D	17,294	469' 02"	70' 06"	43' 08"
Albanyborg	9466300	GC	2010	D	17,294	469' 02"	70' 06"	43' 08"
Amazoneborg	9333541	GC	2007	D	17,294	469' 02"	70' 06"	43' 08"
Americaborg	9365659	GC	2007	D	17,294	469' 02"	70' 06"	43' 08"
Amstelborg	9333527	GC	2006	D	17,294	469' 02"	70' 06"	43' 08"
Aragonborg	9466312	GC	2011	D	17,294	469' 02"	70' 06"	43' 08"
Arneborg	9333539	GC	2006	D	17,294	469' 02"	70' 06"	43' 08"
Arubaborg	9466295	GC	2010	D	17,294	469' 02"	70' 06"	43' 08"
Atlanticborg	9466350	GC	2012	D	17,294	469' 02"	70' 06"	43' 08"
Australiaborg	9397171	GC	2007	D	17,294	469' 02"	70' 06"	43' 08"
Avonborg (Archerborg '12-'12)	9466362	GC	2012	D	17,294	469' 02"	70' 06"	43' 08"
Beatrix (Fivelborg '09-'09)	9419280	GC	2009	D	14,603	507' 03"	56' 05"	37' 11"
Diezeborg (Diezeborg '00-'01, MSC Marmara '01-'03)	9225586	GC	2000	D	8,867	437' 08"	52' 00"	32' 02"
Dintelborg (Dintelborg '00-'01, MSC Dardanelles '01-'04)	9163685	GC	1999	D	8,867	437' 07"	52' 00"	32' 02"
Dongeborg	9163697	GC	1999	D	8,867	437' 08"	52' 00"	32' 02"
Ebroborg	9463451	GC	2010	D	10,750	452' 03"	52' 01"	36' 01"
Edenborg	9463449	GC	2010	D	10,750	452' 03"	52' 01"	36' 01"
Eeborg	9568328	GC	2012	D	12,004	474' 03"	52' 01"	36' 07"
Eemsborg	9225586	GC	2009	D	10,750	452' 03"	52' 01"	36' 01"
Elbeborg	9568249	GC	2011	D	12,004	474' 03"	52' 01"	36' 07"
Erieborg	9463437	GC	2009	D	10,750	452' 03"	52' 01"	36' 01"

Fleet Name / Vessel Name	IMO #	Vessel Type	Year Built	Engine Type	Cargo Cap. or Gross*	Overall Length	Breadth	Depth
Exeborg	9650482	GC	2011	D	12,004	474' 03"	52' 01"	36' 07"
Finnborg	9419321	GC	2011	D	14,603	507' 03"	56' 05"	37' 11"
Fivelborg	9419307	GC	2010	D	14,603	507' 03"	56' 05"	37' 11"
Flevoborg	9419292	GC	2010	D	14,603	507' 03"	56' 05"	37' 11"
Fraserborg	9419319	GC	2011	D	14,603	507' 03"	56' 05"	37' 11"
Fuldaborg	9559092	GC	2012	D	14,603	507' 03"	56' 05"	37' 11"
Kasteelborg	9155937	GC	1998	D	9,150	427' 01"	52' 01"	33' 06"
Keizersborg	9102904	GC	1996	D	9,150	427' 01"	52' 01"	33' 06"
Koningsborg	9155925	GC	1999	D	9,150	427' 01"	52' 01"	33' 06"
Maineborg	9228980	GC	2001	D	9,141	441' 05"	54' 02"	32' 02"
Medemborg	9142514	GC	1997	D	9,141	441' 05"	54' 02"	32' 02"
(Arion '97-'03)								
Merweborg	9142552	GC	1997	D	9,141	441' 05"	54' 02"	32' 02"
Metsaborg	9243801	GC	2002	D	9,141	441' 05"	54' 02"	32' 02"
Mississippiborg	9207508	GC	2000	D	9,141	441' 05"	54' 02"	32' 02"
Missouriborg	9228978	GC	2000	D	9,141	441' 05"	54' 02"	32' 02"
Moezelborg	9180839	GC	1999	D	9,141	441' 05"	54' 02"	32' 02"
Nassauborg	9248564	GC	2006	D	16,740	467' 03"	72' 06"	42' 00"
Reestborg	9592563	GC	2013	D	23,249	556' 11"	66' 11"	37' 11"
Reggeborg	9592575	GC	2014	D	23,249	556' 11"	66' 11"	37' 11"
Vaasaborg	9196242	GC	1999	D	8,664	433' 10"	52' 01"	31' 08"
Vancouverborg	9213741	GC	2001	D	9,857	433' 10"	52' 01"	31' 08"
Victoriaborg	9234276	GC	2001	D	9,857	433' 10"	52' 01"	31' 08"
Virginiaborg	9234290	GC	2001	D	9,857	433' 10"	52' 01"	31' 08"
Vlieborg	9554781	GC	2012	D	11,850	468' 00"	52' 01"	35' 04"
Vlistborg	9160346	GC	1999	D	8,664	433' 10"	52' 01"	31' 08"

Polish-flagged Regalica in the St. Marys River, May 2014. *(Roger LeLievre)*

Volgaborg	9631072	GC	2013	D	11,850	468' 00"	51' 09"	35' 04"
Voorneborg	9179373	GC	1999	D	8,664	433' 10"	52' 01"	31' 08"

At press time, Wagenborg Shipping also had the following vessels under charter. Please consult their respective fleets for details: **Kwintebank, Marietje Deborah, Marietje Marsilla, Varnebank, Vikingbank.**

IW-3   WIJNNE & BARENDS' CARGADOORS, DELFZIJL, NETHERLANDS *(wijnnebarends.com)*

Morgenstond I	9320506	GC	2006	D	12,000	469' 00"	62' 00"	35' 11"

*(Morgenstond I '06-'06, Beluga Locomotion '06-'08, Kent Locomotion '08-'08, Beluga Locomotion '08-'09, Morgenstond I '09-'10, **Kent Sunrise** '10-'12, Morgenstond I '12-'12, Clipper Athena '12-'14)*

Fleet Name Vessel Name	IMO #	Vessel Type	Year Built	Engine Type	Cargo Cap. or Gross*	Overall Length	Breadth	Depth
IY-1 **YARDIMCI SHIPPING GROUP, ISTANBUL, TURKEY** (www.yardimci.gen.tr)								
Ayane	9395991	TK	2010	D	16,745	472' 07"	75' 06"	40' 08"
CT Dublin	9395989	TK	2008	D	16,745	472' 07"	75' 06"	40' 08"
Elevit	9466609	TK	2012	D	16,745	472' 07"	75' 06"	40' 08"
IY-2 **YILMAR SHIPPING & TRADING LTD., ISTANBUL, TURKEY** (yilmar.com)								
YM Saturn	9362138	TK	2007	D	16,000	485' 07"	70' 10"	37' 01"
IZ-1 **ZEALAND SHIPPING BV, ALMERE, NETHERLANDS** (zealand-shipping.nl)								
Zealand Beatrix	9507087	GC	2010	D	13,089	441' 11"	67' 03"	36' 01"
Zealand Delilah	9507075	GC	2011	D	13,089	441' 11"	67' 03"	36' 01"
Zealand Juliana	9655951	GC	2012	D	16,736	500' 04"	73' 10"	35' 05"

Fortunagracht, part of a Cleveland-Europe express service inaugurated in 2014, in the Welland Canal. (Jeff Cameron)

GREAT LAKES MARITIME ACADEMY

Chart your course as a Merchant Marine Officer aboard the ships of the world. The Academy offers an exciting Bachelor's degree program which includes three semesters at sea and 100% job placement.

Marine Museums

William A. Irvin freighter museum at Duluth, Minn. (Glenn Blaszkiewicz)

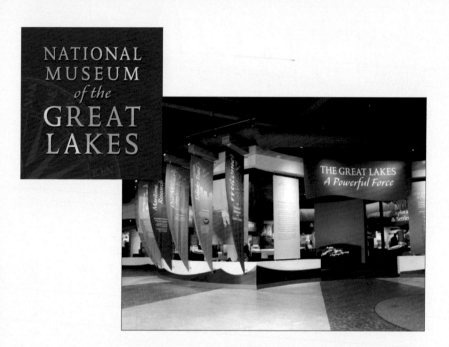

Museum Name / Vessel Name	Vessel Type	Year Built	Engine Type	Cargo Cap. or Gross*	Overall Length	Breadth	Depth
MU-1 BUFFALO AND ERIE COUNTY NAVAL & MILITARY PARK, BUFFALO, NY (buffalonavalpark.org)							
Croaker	MU	1944	D	1,526*	311' 07"	27' 02"	33' 09"
Former U. S. Navy Gato-class submarine IXSS-246; open to the public at Buffalo, NY							
Little Rock	MU	1945	T	10,670*	610' 01"	66' 04"	25' 00"
Former U. S. Navy Cleveland / Little Rock-class guided missile cruiser; open to the public at Buffalo, NY							
The Sullivans	MU	1943	T	2,500*	376' 06"	39' 08"	22' 08"
Former U. S. Navy Fletcher-class destroyer; open to the public at Buffalo, NY (Launched as USS Putnam)							
MU-2 CITY OF KEWAUNEE, KEWAUNEE, WI (cityofkewaunee.org)							
Ludington	MU	1943	D	249*	115' 00"	26' 00"	13' 08"
Built: Jakobson Shipyard, Oyster Bay, NY; former U.S. Army Corps of Engineers tug is open to the public as a marine museum at Kewaunee, WI (Major Wilbur F. Browder [LT-4] '43-'47)							
MU-3 DOOR COUNTY MARITIME MUSEUM & LIGHTHOUSE PRESERVATION SOCIETY INC., STURGEON BAY, WI (dcmm.org)							
John Purves	TB/MU	1919	D	436*	150' 00"	27' 06"	16' 08"
Built: Bethlehem Steel Co., Elizabeth, NJ; former Roen/Andrie Inc. tug has been refurbished as a museum display at Sturgeon Bay, WI (Butterfield '19-'42, LT-145 '42-'57)							
MU-4 DULUTH ENTERTAINMENT CONVENTION CENTER, DULUTH, MN (decc.org/william-a-irvin)							
William A. Irvin	MU	1938	T	14,050	610' 09"	60' 00"	32' 06"
Built: American Shipbuilding Co., Lorain, OH; former United States Steel Corp. bulk carrier last operated Dec. 16, 1978; open to the public at Duluth, MN							
MU-5 ERIE MARITIME MUSEUM, ERIE, PA (flagshipniagara.org)							
Niagara	MU/2B	1988	W	295*	198' 00"	32' 00"	10' 06"
Reconstruction of Oliver Hazard Perry's U. S. Navy brigantine from the War of 1812							
MU-6 FRIENDS OF THE NORISLE, MANITOWANING, ON (www.norisle.com)							
Norisle	MU	1946	R	1,668*	215' 09"	36' 03"	16' 00"
Built: Collingwood Shipyards, Collingwood, ON; former Ontario Northland Transportation Commission passenger vessel last operated in 1974; closed to the public while options for her future are considered							
MU-7 GREAT LAKES NAVAL MEMORIAL & MUSEUM, MUSKEGON, MI (silversidesmuseum.org)							
McLane	MU	1927	D	289*	125' 00"	24' 00"	12' 06"
Built: American Brown Boveri Electric Co.,Camden, NJ; former U.S. Coast Guard Buck & A Quarter class medium endurance cutter; on display at Muskegon, MI (USCGC McLane [WMEC-146] '27-'70, Manatra II '70-'93)							
Silversides	MU	1941	D/V	1,526*	311' 08"	27' 03"	33' 09"
Built: Mare Island Naval Yard, Vallejo, CA; former U.S. Navy Albacore (Gato) class submarine AGSS-236; open to the public at Muskegon, MI							
MU-8 GREAT LAKES SCIENCE CENTER, CLEVELAND, OH (greatscience.com)							
William G. Mather {2}	MU	1925	T	13,950	618' 00"	62' 00"	32' 00"
Built: Great Lakes Engineering Works, Ecorse, MI; former Cleveland-Cliffs Steamship Co. bulk carrier last operated Dec. 21, 1980; open to the public at Cleveland, OH, as part of the Great Lakes Science Center							
MU-9 H. LEE WHITE MARINE MUSEUM, OSWEGO, NY (hleewhitemarinemuseum.com)							
LT-5	MU	1943	D	305*	115' 00"	28' 00"	14' 00"
Built: Jakobson Shipyard, Oyster Bay, NY; former U.S. Army Corps of Engineers tug last operated in 1989; open to the public at Oswego, NY (Major Elisha K. Henson '43-'47, U.S. Army LT-5 '47-'47, Nash '47-'95)							
MU-10 HMCS HAIDA NATIONAL HISTORICAL SITE, HAMILTON, ON (hmcshaida.com)							
Haida	MU	1943	T	2,744*	377' 00"	37' 06"	15' 02"
Former Royal Canadian Navy Tribal class destroyer G-63 / DDE-215; open to the public at Hamilton, ON							
MU-11 ICEBREAKER MACKINAW MARITIME MUSEUM INC., MACKINAW CITY, MI (themackinaw.org)							
Mackinaw [WAGB-83]	MU	1944	D	5,252*	290' 00"	74' 00"	29' 00"
Built: Toledo Shipbuilding Co., Toledo, OH; former U.S. Coast Guard icebreaker was decommissioned in 2006; open to the public at Mackinaw City, MI (Launched as USCGC Manitowoc [WAG-83])							
MU-12 LAKE COUNTY HISTORICAL SOCIETY, TWO HARBORS, MN (lakecountyhistoricalsociety.org)							
Edna G.	MU	1896	R	154*	102' 00"	23' 00"	14' 06"
Built: Cleveland Shipbuilding Co., Cleveland, OH; former Duluth, Missabe & Iron Range Railroad tug last operated in 1981; open to the public at Two Harbors, MN							

MU-13 LE SAULT DE SAINTE MARIE HISTORIC SITES INC., SAULT STE. MARIE, MI *(saulthistoricsites.com)*
Valley Camp {2}   MU   1917   R   12,000   550′ 00″   58′ 00″   31′ 00″
   Built: American Shipbuilding Co., Lorain, OH; former Hanna Mining Co./Wilson Marine Transit Co./Republic
   Steel Corp. bulk carrier last operated in 1966; open to the public at Sault Ste. Marie, MI (Louis W. Hill '17-'55)

MU-14 MARINE MUSEUM OF THE GREAT LAKES AT KINGSTON, KINGSTON, ON *(marmuseum.ca)*
Alexander Henry   MU   1959   D   1,674*   210′ 00″   44′ 00″   17′ 09″
   Built: Port Arthur Shipbuilding Co., Port Arthur, ON; former Canadian Coast Guard icebreaker was retired in
   1985; open to the public at Kingston, ON

MU-15 MICHIGAN MARITIME MUSEUM, SOUTH HAVEN, MI *(michiganmaritimemuseum.org)*
Friends Good Will   TV/ES   2004   D/W   54*   56′ 05″   17′ 00″   11′ 03

MU-16 MUSÉE MARITIME DU QUÉBEC, L' ISLET, QC *(mmq.qc.ca)*
Ernest Lapoint   MU   1941   R   1,179*   185′ 00″   36′ 00″   22′ 06″
   Built: Davie Shipbuilding Co., Lauzon, QC; former Canadian Coast Guard icebreaker; open to the public at L'Islet, QC

MU-17 MUSEUM SHIP COL. JAMES M. SCHOONMAKER, TOLEDO, OH *(inlandseas.org)*
   OPERATED BY THE NATIONAL MUSEUM OF THE GREAT LAKES
Col. James M. Schoonmaker   MU   1911   T   15,000   617′ 00″   64′ 00″   33′ 01″
   Built: Great Lakes Engineering Works, Ecorse, MI; former Shenango Furnace Co./Republic Steel Co./Cleveland-
   Cliffs Steamship Co. bulk carrier last operated in 1980; open to the public at Toledo, OH, under the auspices of the
   Great Lakes Historical Society (Col. James M. Schoonmaker 1911-'69, Willis B. Boyer '69-2011)

MU-18 PORT HURON MUSEUM, PORT HURON, MI *(phmuseum.org)*
Huron   MU   1920   D   392*   96′ 05″   24′ 00″   10′ 00″
   Built: Charles L. Seabury Co., Morris Heights, NY; former U.S. Coast Guard lightship WLV-526 was retired
   Aug. 20, 1970; open to the public at Port Huron, MI (Lightship 103 – Relief [WAL-526] '20-'36)

MU-19 ROBERT AND SARA KLINGLER, MARINE CITY, MI *(uscgcbramble.com)*
Bramble   MU   1944   DE   1,025*   180′ 00″   37′ 00″   17′ 04″
   Built: Zenith Dredge Co., Duluth, MN; former U.S. Coast Guard buoy tender/icebreaker was retired in 2003
   (USCGC Bramble [WLB-392] '44-'03)

MU-20 SAGINAW VALLEY NAVAL SHIP MUSEUM, BAY CITY, MI *(ussedson.org)*
Edson [DD-946]   MU   1958   D   418′ 03″   45′ 03″
   Built: Bath Iron Works, Bath, ME; Forrest Sherman-class destroyer was decommissioned in '88; from '89-'04 on
   display at the Intrepid Sea, Air and Space Museum, New York City. Declared a U.S. National Historic Landmark
   in '90; Open as a marine museum at Bay City, MI

MU-21 S.S. CITY OF MILWAUKEE – NATIONAL HISTORIC LANDMARK, MANISTEE, MI *(carferry.com)*
Acacia   MU   1944   DE   1,025*   180′ 00″   37′ 00″   17′ 04″
   Built: Marine Iron and Shipbuilding Corp., Duluth, MN; former U.S. Coast Guard bouy tender/icebreaker
   was decommissioned in '06; (Launched as USCGC Thistle [WAGL-406])
City of Milwaukee   MU   1931   R   26 cars   360′ 00″   56′ 03″   21′ 06″
   Built: Manitowoc Shipbuilding Co., Manitowoc, WI; train ferry sailed for the Grand Trunk Railroad '31-'78
   and the Ann Arbor Railroad '78-'81; open to the public at Manistee, MI

MU-22 S.S. COLUMBIA PROJECT, NEW YORK, NY *(sscolumbia.org)*
Columbia {2}   5077333   PA   1902   R   968*   216′ 00″   60′ 00″   13′ 06″
   Built: Detroit Dry Dock Co, Wyandotte, MI; former Detroit to Bob-Lo Island passenger steamer last operated
   Sept. 2, 1991; towed to drydock at Toledo, Ohio, in 2014 for refurbishment before relocation to the East Coast

MU-23 S.S. KEEWATIN MARINE MUSEUM, PORT McNICOLL, ON *(sskeewatin.com)*
Keewatin {2}   MU   1907   Q   3,856*   346′ 00″   43′ 08″   26′ 06″
   Built: Fairfield Shipbuilding and Engineering Co. Ltd., Govan, Scotland; former Canadian Pacific Railway Co.
   passenger vessel last operated Nov. 29, 1965; served as a marine museum since 1967 in Douglas, MI, and now
   Port McNicoll, ON; Operated by the non-profit group Friends of the Keewatin

MU-24 S.S. METEOR WHALEBACK SHIP MUSEUM, SUPERIOR, WI *(superiorpublicmuseums.org)*
Meteor {2}   MU   1896   R   40,100   380′ 00″   45′ 00″   26′ 00″
   Built: American Steel Barge Co., Superior, WI; former ore carrier/auto carrier/tanker is the last vessel of
   whaleback design surviving on the Great Lakes; Cleveland Tankers vessel last operated in 1969;
   open to the public at Superior, WI (Frank Rockefeller 1896-'28, South Park '1928-'43)

MU-25 S.S. MILWAUKEE CLIPPER PRESERVATION INC., MUSKEGON, MI *(milwaukeeclipper.com)*
Milwaukee Clipper   MU   1904   Q   4,272   361′ 00″   45′ 00″   28′ 00″
   Built: American Shipbuilding Co., Cleveland, OH; rebuilt in '40 at Manitowoc Shipbuilding Co., Manitowoc,
   WI; former Wisconsin & Michigan Steamship Co. passenger/auto carrier last operated in 1970; undergoing
   restoration at Muskegon, MI; open to the public on weekends (Juniata '04-'41)

117

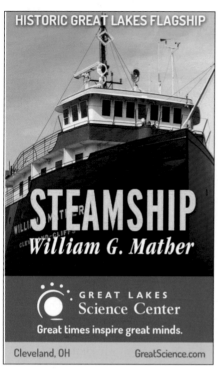
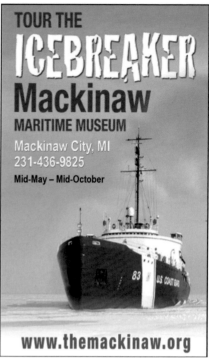
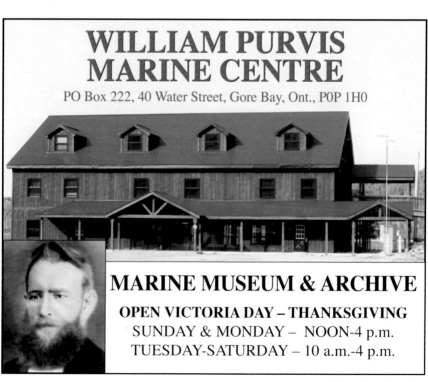

MU-26 ST. MARYS RIVER MARINE CENTRE, SAULT STE. MARIE, ON (norgoma.org)

Norgoma	MU	1950	D	1,477*	188'00"	37'06"	22'06"

Built: Collingwood Shipyards, Collingwood, ON; former Ontario Northland Transportation Commission passenger vessel last operated in 1974; open to the public at Sault Ste. Marie, ON

MU-27 USS COD SUBMARINE MEMORIAL, CLEVELAND, OH (usscod.org)

Cod	MU	1943	D/V	1,525*	311'08"	27'02"	33'09"

Built: Electric Boat Co., Groton, CT; former U.S. Navy Albacore (Gato) class submarine IXSS-224 open to the public at Cleveland, OH

MU-28 USS LST 393 VETERANS MUSEUM, MUSKEGON, MI (lst393.org)

LST-393	MU	1942	D	2,100	328'00"	50'00"	25'00"

Built: Newport News Shipbuilding and Dry Dock Co., Newport News, VA; former U.S. Navy/Wisconsin & Michigan Steamship Co. vessel last operated July 31, 1973; open to the public at Muskegon, MI
(USS LST-393 '42-'47, Highway 16 '47-'99)

MU-29 WISCONSIN MARITIME MUSEUM, MANITOWOC, WI (wisconsinmaritime.org)

Cobia	MU	1944	D/V	1,500*	311'09"	27'03"	33'09"

Built: Electric Boat Co., Groton, CT; former U. S. Navy Gato class submarine AGSS-245 is open to the public at Manitowoc, WI

Museum Ship Stack Markings

Museum Ship
City of Milwaukee
Manistee, MI

Museum Ship Col.
James M. Schoonmaker
Toledo, OH

Museum Ship
Keewatin
Port McNicoll, ON

Museum Ship
Alexander Henry
Kingston, ON

Museum Ship
HMCS Haida
Hamilton, ON

Museum Ships
USS Little Rock
USS The Sullivans
Buffalo, N.Y.

Museum Ship
Meteor
Superior, WI

Museum Ship
Milwaukee Clipper
Muskegon, MI

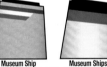
Museum Ships
Norgoma (Sault Ste. Marie, ON)
Norisle (Manitowaning, ON)

Museum Ship
Valley Camp
Sault Ste. Marie, MI

Museum Ship
William A. Irvin
Duluth, MN

Museum Ship
William G. Mather
Cleveland, OH

Museum Ship
USCG Mackinaw
Mackinaw City, MI

Museum Tug
John Purves
Sturgeon Bay, WI

Museum Tug
Edna G.
Two Harbors, MN

Information can change without notice. Call ahead to verify location and hours.

ANTIQUE BOAT MUSEUM, 750 MARY ST., CLAYTON, NY – (315) 686-4104: A large collection of freshwater boats and engines. Annual show is the first weekend of August. Seasonal. *(abm.org)*

ASHTABULA MARINE & U.S. COAST GUARD MEMORIAL MUSEUM, 1071 WALNUT BLVD., ASHTABULA, OH – (440) 964-6847: Housed in the 1898-built former lighthouse keeper's residence, the museum includes models, paintings, artifacts, photos, the world's only working scale model of a Hullett ore unloading machine and the pilothouse from the steamer *Thomas Walters*. Seasonal. *(ashtabulamarinemuseum.org)*

CANAL PARK MARINE MUSEUM, ALONGSIDE THE SHIP CANAL, DULUTH, MN – (218) 727-2497: Museum provides displays, historic artifacts and programs that explain the roles of Duluth and Superior in Great Lakes shipping as well as the job of the U.S. Army Corps of Engineers in maintaining the nation's waterways. Many excellent models and other artifacts are on display. Open all year. *(lsmma.com)*

DOOR COUNTY MARITIME MUSEUM & LIGHTHOUSE PRESERVATION SOCIETY INC., 120 N. MADISON AVE., STURGEON BAY, WI – (920) 743-5958: Many excellent models help portray the role shipbuilding has played in the Door Peninsula. Open all year. *(dcmm.org)*

DOSSIN GREAT LAKES MUSEUM, 100 THE STRAND, BELLE ISLE, DETROIT, MI – (313) 852-4051: Models, interpretive displays, the smoking room from the 1912 passenger steamer *City of Detroit III*, an anchor from the *Edmund Fitzgerald* and the pilothouse from the steamer *William Clay Ford* are on display. *(detroithistorical.org/main/dossin)*

ELGIN MILITARY MUSEUM, ST. THOMAS, ON – (519) 633-7641. The museum has obtained *HMCS Ojibwa*, a Cold War Oberon-class submarine, and she is open to the public at Port Burwell, Ont. *(projectojibwa.ca)*

ERIE MARITIME MUSEUM, 150 E. FRONT ST., ERIE, PA – (814) 452-2744. Displays depict the Battle of Lake Erie and more. Check ahead to see if the U.S. Brig *Niagara* is in port. Open all year. flagshipniagara.org)

Sault Ste. Marie's Valley Camp museum ship got a paint job in 2014. (Roger LeLievre)

FAIRPORT HARBOR MUSEUM, 129 SECOND ST., FAIRPORT, OH – (440) 354-4825: Located in the Fairport Lighthouse, displays include the pilothouse from the *Frontenac* and the mainmast of the first *USS Michigan*. Seasonal. *(fairportharborlighthouse.org)*

NATIONAL MUSEUM OF THE GREAT LAKES, TOLEDO, OHIO – (419) 214-5000: Exhibits include artifacts, impressive ship models, an interpretive film, hands-on activities for kids, a maritime park and the restored 1911-steamboat *Col. James M. Schoonmaker*. *(inlandseas.org)*

GREAT LAKES SHIPWRECK MUSEUM, WHITEFISH POINT, MI – (906) 635-1742 or (800)-635-1742: Lighthouse and shipwreck artifacts, a shipwreck video theater, the restored lighthouse keeper's quarters and an *Edmund Fitzgerald* display that includes the ship's bell. Seasonal. *(shipwreckmuseum.com)*

LE SAULT DE SAINTE MARIE HISTORIC SITES INC., 501 E. WATER ST., SAULT STE. MARIE, MI – (906) 632-3658: The 1917-built steamer *Valley Camp* is the centerpiece of this museum. The ship's three cargo holds house artifacts, models, aquariums, photos and other memorabilia, as well as a tribute to the *Edmund Fitzgerald* that includes the ill-fated vessel's lifeboats. Seasonal. *(thevalleycamp.com)*

LOWER LAKES MARINE HISTORICAL SOCIETY, 66 ERIE ST., BUFFALO, NY – (716) 849-0914: Exhibits explore local maritime history. Open all year, Thursday and Sunday only. *(llmhs.org)*

MARITIME MUSEUM OF SANDUSKY, 125 MEIGS ST., SANDUSKY, OHIO – (419) 624-0274: Exhibits explore local maritime history. Open all year. *(sanduskymaritime.org)*

MARQUETTE MARITIME MUSEUM, EAST RIDGE & LAKESHORE BLVD., MARQUETTE, MI – (906) 226-2006: Museum re-creates the offices of the first commercial fishing and passenger freight companies. Displays also include photos, models and artifacts. Seasonal. *(mqtmaritimemuseum.com)*

MICHIGAN MARITIME MUSEUM, 260 DYCKMAN AVE., SOUTH HAVEN, MI – (269) 637-8078: Exhibits dedicated to the U.S. Lifesaving Service and Coast Guard. Displays tell the story of different kinds of boats and their uses on the lakes. The tall ship *Friends Good Will* operates during the summer. Open all year. *(michiganmaritimemuseum.org)*

MUSKOKA BOAT AND HERITAGE CENTRE, GRAVENHURST, ON – (705) 687-2115: Visiting this museum, which includes many models of the early steamships to serve the area, is the perfect complement to a trip on the vintage *RMS Segwun*, moored adjacent. *(realmuskoka.com/muskoka-boat-and-heritage-centre)*

PORT COLBORNE HISTORICAL AND MARINE MUSEUM, 280 KING ST., PORT COLBORNE, ON – (905) 834-7604: Wheelhouse from the steam tug *Yvonne Dupre Jr.*, an anchor from the *Raleigh* and a lifeboat from the steamer *Hochelaga* are among the museum's displays. Seasonal.

U.S. ARMY CORPS OF ENGINEERS MUSEUM, SOO LOCKS VISITOR CENTER, SAULT STE. MARIE, MI – (906) 632-7020: Exhibits include a working model of the Soo Locks, historic photos and a 25-minute film. Free; open May-November. Check at the Visitor Center information desk for a list of vessels expected at the locks.

WELLAND CANAL VISITOR CENTRE, AT LOCK 3, THOROLD, ON – (905) 984-8880: Museum traces the development of the Welland Canal. Museum and adjacent gift shop open year 'round. Observation deck open during the navigation season. Check at the information desk for vessels expected at Lock 3.

WILLIAM PURVIS MARINE CENTRE, 40 WATER ST., GORE BAY, ON – Marine museum and archive. Open Victoria Day-Thanksgiving (Canadian).

WISCONSIN MARITIME MUSEUM, 75 MARITIME DRIVE, MANITOWOC, WI – (866) 724-2356: Displays explore the history of area shipbuilding and also honor submariners and submarines built in Manitowoc. One of the massive engines of the Straits of Mackinac trainferry *Chief Wawatam* is impressively on display. The World War II sub *Cobia* is adjacent to the museum and open for tours. Open all year. *(wisconsinmaritime.org)*

Icebreaker-museum Mackinaw, Mackinaw City, Mich. (Brian Jaeshke)

Aerial view of the National Museum of the Great Lakes at Toledo, Ohio, and its signature display, the 1911-vintage Col. James M. Schoonmaker. (Paul C. LaMarre III)

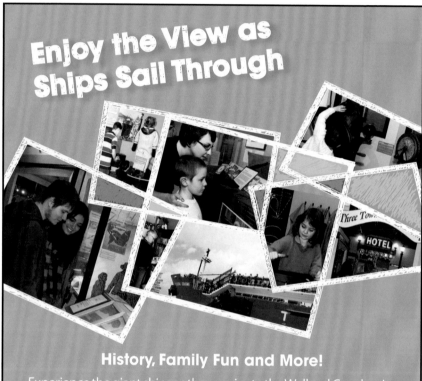

Enjoy the View as Ships Sail Through

History, Family Fun and More!

Experience the giant ships as they navigate the Welland Canal, enjoy a picnic in our outdoor Discovery Park and take in some local history in the museum. A great day for all ages! Admission is by Donation.

St. Catharines MUSEUM

CITY OF ST. CATHARINES

Follow us:

 @StCMuseum

St. Catharines Museum & Welland Canals Centre
1932 Welland Canals Parkway, St. Catharines, ON
museum@stcatharines.ca or 1-800-305-5134
stcatharines.ca

Stacks and Flags

G.A. Tomlinson displays the herald of the now-defunct Columbia Transportation Co., circa the 1960s. *(Paul C. LaMarre Jr.)*

COLORS OF THE GREAT LAKES

Abaco Marine Towing
Clayton, NY

Algoma Central Corp.
St. Catharines, ON

Algoma Central Corp.
St. Catharines, ON

American Steamship Co.
Williamsville, NY

Andrie Inc.
Muskegon, MI

Andrie Specialized
Norton Shores, MI

ArcelorMittal Mines Canada
Port Cartier, QC

Arnold Transit Co.
Mackinac Island, MI

Basic Marine Inc.
Escanaba, MI

Bay City Boat Lines
Bay City, MI

Beaver Island Boat Co.
Charlevoix, MI

Blue Heron Co.
Tobermory, ON

Buffalo Dept. of Public Works
Buffalo, N.Y.

Busch Marine Inc.
Carrollton, MI

Calumet River Fleeting
Chicago, IL

Canada Steamship Lines
Montreal, QC

Canada Steamship Lines
Montreal, QC

Canadian Coast Guard
Ottawa, ON

Canadian Wheat Board Algoma Central – Mgr
Winnipeg, MN

Causley Marine Contracting LLC
Bay City, MI

Central Marine Logistics Inc. Operator for ArcelorMittal
Griffith, IN

Chicago Fire Dept.
Chicago, IL

Cleveland Fire Dept.
Cleveland, OH

Columbia Yacht Club
Chicago, IL

Croisières AML Inc.
Québec, QC

Dean Construction Co.
Belle River, ON

Detroit City Fire Dept.
Detroit, MI

Diamond Jack's River Tours
Detroit, MI

Duc D'Orleans Cruise Boat
Corunna, ON

Durocher Marine
Cheboygan, MI

Eastern Upper Peninsula Transportation Authority
Sault Ste. Marie, MI

Erie Sand & Gravel
Erie, PA

Essroc Canada Inc. Algoma Central – Mgr
North York, ON

Fincanteri Marine Group Bay Shipbuilding Co.
Sturgeon, Bay, WI

Fraser Shipyards Inc.
Superior, WI

Gaelic Tugboat Co.
Detroit, MI

Gallagher Marine Construction Co. Inc.
Escanaba, MI

Gananoque Boat Line
Gananoque, ON

Geo. Gradel Co.
Toledo, OH

Goodtime Cruise Line
Cleveland, OH

Grand Portage / Isle Royale Trans. Line
Superior, WI

Gravel & Lake Service
Thunder Bay, ON

Great Lakes Dock & Materials
Muskegon, MI

Great Lakes Fleet Inc. Key Lakes Inc.– Mgr.
Duluth, MN

Great Lakes & International Towing & Salvage
Burlington, ON

Great Lakes Maritime Academy
Traverse City, MI

Great Lakes Science Center
Ann Arbor, MI

Great Lakes Towing Co.
Cleveland, OH

AND SEAWAY SMOKESTACKS

Groupe C.T.M.A.
Cap-aux-Meules, QC

Groupe Desgagnés Inc.
Québec City, QC

Groupe Desgagnés Inc.
Québec City, QC

Groupe Desgagnés Inc.
Québec City, QC

Haimark Line
Denver, CO

Hamilton Port Authority
Hamilton, ON

Heritage Marine
Two Harbors, MN

Horne Transportation
Wolfe Island, ON

Inland Lakes Management
Alpena, MI

**Interlake Steamship Co.
Lakes Shipping Co.**
Richfield, OH

J.W. Westcott Co.
Detroit, MI

Kindra Lake Towing
Chicago, IL

The King Company
Holland, MI

Lafarge Canada Inc.
Montreal, QC

Lafarge North America Inc.
Southfield, MI

Lake Erie Island Cruises
Sandusky, OH

**Lake Michigan Carferry
Service Inc.**
Ludington, MI

Le Groupe Océan Inc.
Québec, QC

**Lower Lakes Towing
Lower Lakes Transportation**
Port Dover, ON / Williamsville, NY

Luedtke Engineering
Frankfort, MI

MCM Marine Inc.
Sault Ste. Marie, MI

MacDonald Marine Ltd.
Goderich, ON

**Madeline Island
Ferry Line Inc.**
LaPointe, WI

Malcolm Marine
St. Clair, MI

Lake Erie Island Cruises

Lake Michigan Carferry

Manitou Island Transit
Leland, MI

Marine Tech LLC
Duluth, MN

Mariposa Cruise Line
Toronto, ON

**McAsphalt Marine
Transportation**
Scarborough, ON

McKeil Marine Ltd.
Hamilton, ON

McKeil Marine Ltd.
Hamilton, ON

McNally International
Hamilton, ON

Midwest Maritime Corp.
Milwaukee, WI

Miller Boat Line
Put-in-Bay, OH

Ministry of Transportation
Downsview, ON

Montreal Port Authority
Montreal, QC

M/V Zeus LC
Chesapeake City, MD

**Muskoka Steamship
& Historical Society**
Gravenhurst, ON

Nadro Marine Services
Port Dover, ON

**New York State Marine
Highway Transportation**
Troy, NY

**Owen Sound
Transportation Co. Ltd.**
Owen Sound, ON

Pearl Seas Cruises LLC.
Guilford, CT

Pere Marquette Shipping
Ludington, MI

**Port City Steamship
Port City Tug Inc.**
Muskegon, MI

Purvis Marine Ltd.
Sault Ste. Marie, ON

Roen Salvage Co.
Sturgeon Bay, WI

Ryba Marine Construction
Cheboygan, MI

Selvick Marine Towing Corp.
Sturgeon Bay, WI

Shoreline Sightseeing Co.
Chicago, IL

129

Société des Traversiers Du Québec
Québec, QC

Soo Locks Boat Tours
Sault Ste. Marie, MI

St. James Marine Co.
Beaver Island, MI

St. Lawrence Cruise Lines Inc.
Kingston, ON

St. Lawrence Seaway Development Corp.
Massena, NY

St. Lawrence Seaway Management Corp.
Cornwall, ON

St. Marys Cement Group
Toronto, ON

Sterling Fuels Ltd.
Hamilton, ON

Thousand Islands & Seaway Cruises
Brockville, ON

Thunder Bay Tug Services Ltd.
Thunder Bay, ON

Thunder Bay Tug Services Ltd.
Thunder Bay, ON

Toronto Drydock Ltd.
Toronto, ON

Toronto Port Authority
Toronto, ON

United States Army Corps of Engineers
Chicago, IL

United States Coast Guard 9th Coast Guard District
Cleveland, OH

United States National Park Service
Houghton, MI

U.S. Oil Div. U.S. Venture Inc.
Appleton, WI

Upper Lakes Towing Co.
Escanaba, MI

SALTWATER FLEETS ON THE SEAWAY

ABC Maritime
Nyon, Switzerland

Ace Tankers CV
Amsterdam, Netherlands

Alliance Tankers
Hamilton, Bermuda

Ardmore Shipping Ltd.
Cork, Ireland

Armador Gemi Isletmeciligi Ticaret Ltd.
Istanbul, Turkey

ARA Group
Werkendam, Netherlands

Atlantska Plovidba
Dubrovnik, Croatia

Bergesen Worldwide Ltd.
Oslo, Norway

Bernhard Schulte Group
Hamburg, Germany

BigLift Shipping
Amsterdam, Netherlands

Blystad Tankers Inc.
Oslo, Norway

Briese Schiffahrts GMBH & Co. KG
Leer, Germany

Canadian Forest Navigation Co. Ltd.
Montreal, QC, Canada

Chemfleet Shipping
Istanbul, Turkey

Chemikalien Seetransport
Hamburg, Germany

Chemnav Inc.
Athens, Greece

Clipper Group AS
Copenhagen, Denmark

Coastal Shipping Ltd. (Div. Woodward Group)
Goose Bay, NL, Canada

Columbia Shipmanagement
Hamburg, Germany

Conti Reederei Management
Munich, Germany

Cosco Southern Asphalt Shipping Co.
Guangzhou, China

Danser Van Gent
Delfzijl, Netherlands

Duzgit Gemi Insa Sanayi
Istanbul, Turkey

Eastern Pacific Shipping
Singapore

Eitzen Chemical ASA
Oslo, Norway

Elbe Shipping GMBH
Drochtersen, Germany

Enzian Ship Management
Zürich, Switzerland

Fednav International Ltd.
Montreal, QC, Canada

Fednav International Ltd.
Montreal, QC, Canada

Finbeta
Savona, Italy

Flinter Shipping
Barendrecht, Netherlands

Freese Reederei Group
Stade, Germany

Freese Shipping
Stade, Germany

Hansa Heavy Lift GMBH
Bremen, Germany

Harren & Partner Schiffahrts GMBH
Bremen, Germany

Hartman Seatrade
Urk, Netherlands

Herning Shipping AS
Herning, Denmark

Intersee Schiffahrts-Gesellschaft MbH & Co.
Haren-Ems, Germany

Intership Navigation Co.
Limassol, Cyprus

Jo Tankers
Spijkenisse, Netherlands

Johann M.K. Blumenthal GMBH & Co.
Hamburg, Germany

Jumbo Shipping Co. SA
Rotterdam, Netherlands

Kallianis Bros Shipping
Athens, Greece

Knutsen O.A.S. Shipping
Haugesund, Norway

Lauranne Shipping BV
Ghent, Netherlands

Liamare Shipping BV
Maartensdijk, Netherlands

Lithuanian Shipping Co.
Klaipeda, Lithuania

Lloyd Fonds Singapore
Singapore, Singapore

Marida Tankers Inc.
Norwalk, CT, USA

Mastermind Shipmanagement Ltd.
Limassol, Cyprus

Mega Chemical Tankers Ltd.
Singapore, Singapore

Mineralien Schiffahrt Spedition
Schnaittenbach, Germany

Navigation Maritime Bulgare Ltd.
Varna, Bulgaria

Neste Shipping OY
Espoo, Finland

Nicholas G. Moundreas Shipping
Piraeus, Greece

Nordana Shipping Co.
Copenhagen, Denmark

Nordic Tankers A/S
Copenhagen, Denmark

Oceanex Inc.
Montreal, QC, Canada

OSM Group AS
Kristiansand, Norway

Parakou Shipping Ltd.
Hong Kong, China

Peter Dohle Schiffahrts
Hamburg, Germany

Polish Steamship Co.
Szczecin, Poland

Pot Scheepvaart BV
Delfzijl, Netherlands

Rederiet Stenersen AS
Bergen, Norway

Reederei Eckhoff and Co. GMBH
Jork, Germany

Reederei Nord GMBH
Hamburg, Germany

Rigel Schiffahrts GMBH
Bremen, Germany

Sargeant Marine Inc.
Boca Raton, FL, USA

Scan-Trans Shipping
Naestved, Denmark

SE Shipping
Singapore, Singapore

Sloman Neotun Shiffahrts
Bremen, Germany

Spliethoff's
Amsterdam, Netherlands

Tarbit Tankers B.V.
Dordrecht, Netherlands

TB Marine Shipmanagement GMBH & Co.
Hamburg, Germany

Thode Johs Shipping Co
Hamburg, Germany

Transal Denizcilik Tickaret
Istanbul, Turkey

Transatlantic
Gothenburg, Sweden

Utkilen AS
Bergen, Norway

Uni-Tankers A/S
Middlefart, Denmark

W. Bockstiegel Reederei KG
Emden, Germany

Wagenborg Shipping
Delfzijl, Netherlands

Yardimci Shipping Group
Istanbul, Turkey

Yilmar Shipping & Trading Ltd.
Istanbul, Turkey

Zealand Shipping BV
Almere, Netherlands

FLAGS OF REGISTRY

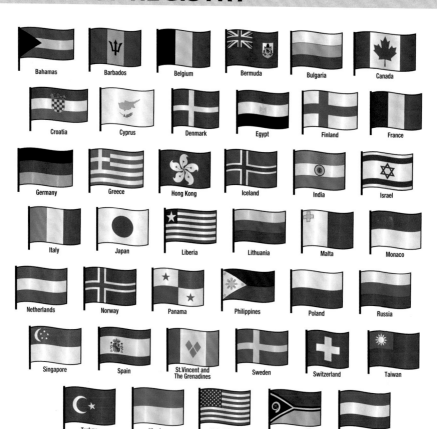

Bahamas — Barbados — Belgium — Bermuda — Bulgaria — Canada

Croatia — Cyprus — Denmark — Egypt — Finland — France

Germany — Greece — Hong Kong — Iceland — India — Israel

Italy — Japan — Liberia — Lithuania — Malta — Monaco

Netherlands — Norway — Panama — Philippines — Poland — Russia

Singapore — Spain — St.Vincent and The Grenadines — Sweden — Switzerland — Taiwan

Turkey — Ukraine — United States — Vanuatu — Yugoslavia

Algoma Central Corp.
St. Catherines, ON

American Steamship Co.
Williamsville, NY

Andrie Inc.
Muskegon, MI

ArcelorMittal Central Marine Logistics
Griffith, IN

Canada Steamship Lines Inc. (CSL)
Montreal, QC

Canadian Coast Guard
Ottawa, ON

Canadian Forest Navigation Co. Ltd.
Montreal, QC

Fednav Ltd.
Montreal, QC

Flinter Shipping
Barendrecht, Netherlands

Gaelic Tugboat Co.
Detroit, MI

Great Lakes Fleet Inc. Key Lakes Inc. - Mgr.
Duluth, MN

Great Lakes Maritime Academy
Traverse City, MI

Great Lakes Towing Co.
Cleveland, OH

Groupe Desgagnés Inc.
Québec, QC

Inland Lakes Management Inc.
Alpena, MI

Interlake Steamship Co Lakes Shipping Co.
Richfield, OH

J.W. Westcott Co.
Detroit, MI

LaFarge Canada Inc.
Montreal, QC

Lake Michigan Carferry Service Inc.
Ludington, MI

Le Groupe Océan Inc.
Québec, QC

Lower Lakes Towing Ltd. Lower Lakes Transportation Co.
Port Dover, ON / Williamsville, NY

McAsphalt Marine Transportation Ltd.
Scarborough, ON

McKeil Marine Ltd.
Hamilton, ON

Owen Sound Transportation Co. Ltd.
Owen Sound, ON

Pere Marquette Shipping Co.
Ludington, MI

Polish Steamship Co.
Szczecin, Poland

Purvis Marine Ltd.
Sault Ste. Marie, ON

St.Lawrence Seaway Development Corp.
Massena, NY

St.Lawrence Seaway Management Corp.
Cornwall, ON

U.S. Army Corps of Engineers
Cincinnatti, OH

U.S. Coast Guard
Cleveland, OH

Wagenborg Shipping
Delfzijl, Netherlands

Other Flags of Note

Dangerous Cargo On Board

Pilot On Board

Diver Down

DONT GIVE UP THE SHIP
Commodore Perry War of 1812 flag, often flown by lake vessels

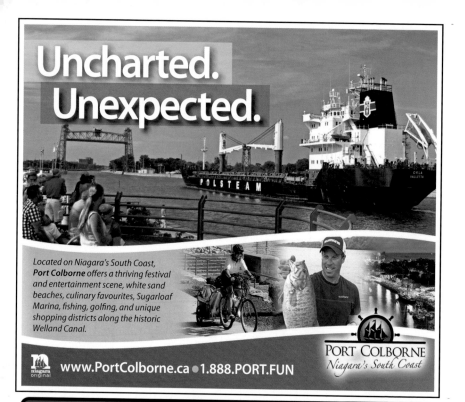

134

Extra Tonnage

- **Ports**
- **Cargoes**
- **Locks**
- **Canals**

USCG Hollyhock working with aids to navigation as Paul R. Tregurtha passes by. (Steve Jowett)

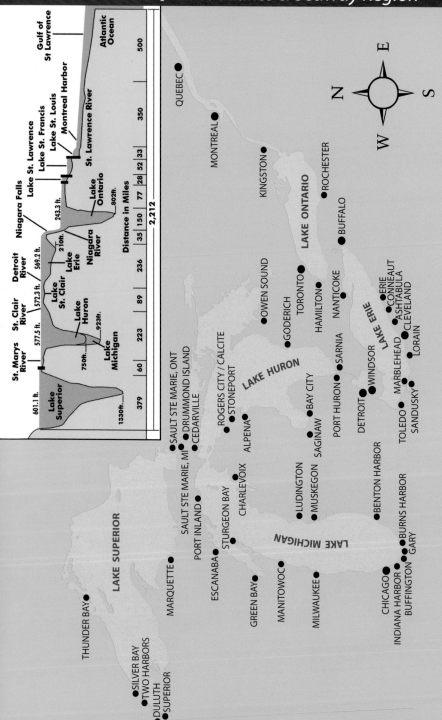

Distance in Miles

St. Marys River		St. Clair River	Detroit River	Niagara Falls	Lake St. Lawrence					Montreal Harbor	
379	60	89	223	236	35	150	77	28	52	33	350	500

601.1 ft. — Lake Superior — 1330 m.

577.5 ft. — Lake Huron — 750 m. — Lake Michigan — 923 m.

572.3 ft. — Lake St. Clair

569.2 ft. — Lake Erie — 210 m.

243.3 ft. — Niagara River — 802 ft.

Lake Ontario

Gulf of St Lawrence

Atlantic Ocean

St. Lawrence River

Lake St. Francis

Lake St. Louis

2,212

N E W S

LAKE SUPERIOR

THUNDER BAY
SILVER BAY
TWO HARBORS
DULUTH
SUPERIOR
MARQUETTE
ESCANABA
GREEN BAY
MANITOWOC
MILWAUKEE
CHICAGO
INDIANA HARBOR
BUFFINGTON
GARY
BURNS HARBOR
BENTON HARBOR
MUSKEGON
LUDINGTON
CHARLEVOIX
STURGEON BAY
PORT INLAND
SAULT STE MARIE, MI
SAULT STE MARIE, ONT
DRUMMOND ISLAND
CEDARVILLE
ROGERS CITY / CALCITE
STONEPORT
ALPENA

LAKE MICHIGAN

LAKE HURON

OWEN SOUND
GODERICH
TORONTO
HAMILTON
NANTICOKE
SARNIA
PORT HURON
DETROIT
WINDSOR
MARBLEHEAD
TOLEDO
SANDUSKY
LORAIN
CLEVELAND
ASHTABULA
CONNEAUT
ERIE
BUFFALO
ROCHESTER
KINGSTON
MONTREAL
QUEBEC
SAGINAW
BAY CITY

LAKE ERIE

LAKE ONTARIO

Taconite ore is loaded for delivery to lower lakes steel mills at Duluth, Two Harbors, Taconite Harbor and Silver Bay, Minn., as well as Superior, Wis., and Escanaba, Mich. Limestone-loading ports are Port Inland, Cedarville, Drummond Island, Calcite, Rogers City and Stoneport, Mich., and Marblehead, Ohio. Coal ports are Superior, Wis., S. Chicago, Ill., and the Ohio ports of Toledo, Sandusky, Ashtabula and Conneaut. Petroleum is loaded aboard vessels at Sarnia, Ont., and E. Chicago, Ind. Grain export ports include Duluth, Minn.; Milwaukee and Superior, Wis.; and the Ontario ports of Thunder Bay, Sarnia and Owen Sound.

The primary U.S. iron ore and limestone receiving ports are Cleveland and Chicago, as well as Gary, Burns Harbor and Indiana Harbor, Ind.; Detroit and Toledo; as well as Lorain, Ashtabula and Conneaut, Ohio. Nanticoke, Hamilton, and Sault Ste. Marie, Ont., are major ore-receiving ports in Canada. Coal is carried by self-unloaders to power plants in the U.S. and Canada. Most grain loaded on the lakes is destined for export via the St. Lawrence Seaway. Cement from Alpena and Charlevoix, Mich., is delivered to terminals from Lake Superior to Lake Ontario. Tankers bring petroleum products to cities as diverse in size as Cleveland, as well as Cheboygan, Detroit, Escanaba and Muskegon, Mich. Self-unloaders carry limestone, coal, road salt and sand to cities throughout the region.

Indiana Harbor loading coal at the SMET dock in Superior, Wis. (Chris Mazzella)

AVERAGE RUNNING TIMES

Times listed are for downbound passages. Reverse for upbound times. Times vary with speed / weather / traffic.

LAKE SUPERIOR
Duluth/Superior – Soo Locks .... 24 hrs
Marquette or Thunder Bay – Soo Locks .... 12 hrs

ST. MARYS RIVER
Soo Locks – DeTour, Mich. .... 6 hrs
DeTour – Port Huron .... 19 hrs

LAKE HURON
DeTour – Mackinac Bridge .... 2 hrs
DeTour – Port Huron .... 19 hrs
Harbor Beach – Port Huron .... 4 hrs

LAKE MICHIGAN
Gray's Reef Light – Gary, Ind. .... 22 hrs

LAKE ERIE
Detroit River Light – Toledo .... 1.75 hrs
Detroit River Light – Southeast Shoal .... 3 hrs
Southeast Shoal – Long Point .... 9 hrs
Long Point – CIP 15 (Welland Canal) .... 7 hrs
Detroit River Light – Port Colborne piers
(Welland Canal) .... 19 hrs

LAKE ONTARIO
Welland Canal (Port Weller) – Hamilton .... 2 hrs
Welland Canal (Port Weller) – Cape Vincent, N.Y.
(call-in points at Newcastle, mid-lake and
Sodus Point) .... 12 hrs

AGRICULTURAL PRODUCTS – Wheat, grain, soybeans, canola, flax and oats are shipped on the Great Lakes. Some is used domestically, but most is shipped to international markets overseas.

BUNKER C – A special grade of heavy fuel oil, also known as No. 6 fuel.

CEMENT CLINKER – A material, made by heating ground limestone and clay, that is ground up to a fine powder to produce cement.

CLINKER – The incombustible residue that remains after the combustion of coal.

COAL – Both eastern (high sulfur, used in industry) and western (low sulfur, burned at power plants) coal are shipped aboard Great Lakes vessels.

COKE – A byproduct of blended coals baked in ovens until mostly pure carbon is left. Coke is used to generate the high heat necessary to make steel in blast furnaces.

COKE BREEZE – Byproduct of coke production.

DOLOMITE – Rock similar to limestone but somewhat harder and heavier.

FLUXSTONE – Taconite pellets premixed with limestone, so no limestone needs to be added to the mix in a blast furnace.

IRON FINES – Fines (ore less than 6mm in diameter) are created as a result of mining, crushing and processing the larger pieces of ore. See **SINTER**.

LIMESTONE – Common sedimentary rock consisting mostly of calcium carbonate used as a building stone and in the manufacture of lime, carbon dioxide and cement.

MILL SCALE – Byproduct of the shaping of iron and steel.

PETROLEUM COKE – Petroleum coke (petcoke) is the ultimate bottom end of oil refining – the parts of crude oil that will not vaporize in the refining process. It is mostly used as fuel (sometimes blended with coal) in power plants.

PIG IRON – Crude iron that is the direct product of the blast furnace and is refined to produce steel, wrought iron or ingot iron.

POTASH – A compound used for fertilizer.

SALT – Most salt shipped on the Great Lakes is used on roads and highways during the winter to melt ice.

SINTER – Broken taconite pellets, a.k.a. taconite pellet chips and fines. Small, but still useful in the blast furnace.

SLAG – Byproduct of the steelmaking process is used in the production of concrete and as seal coat cover, a base for paving, septic drain fields and railroad ballast.

TACONITE – A low-grade iron ore, containing about 27 percent iron and 51 percent silica, found as a hard rock formation in the Lake Superior region. It is pelletized for shipment to steel mills (see below).

TRAP ROCK – Rock, usually ground fairly fine, for use as foundations and roads or walkways. It is mined near Bruce Mines, Ont., and loaded there.

Why taconite pellets?

The high-grade iron ore (around 60 percent pure) that was mined on the ranges around Lake Superior was mostly exhausted in the tremendous mining efforts of World War II and in the early 1950s. There was still plenty of iron ore in the ground, but it was about 20-30 percent iron. To mine and ship all that ore in its natural form would have been expensive, so engineers developed the taconite pelletization process to increase the iron content of the product coming off the ranges headed for the steel mills. Pellets have a number of positive attributes. Their iron content (and the content of other elements) can be precisely controlled so the steel mills know exactly what they are getting. Pellets are relatively moisture free compared with raw iron ore, so they are less prone to freeze in rail cars, storage piles or dock pockets. This means the pellets can be shipped for a much longer

Taconite pellets being loaded into a laker.

season than natural iron ore, so companies need fewer rail cars and ships to carry the same amount of pellets, thus saving money on labor and infrasructure. Pellets are also uniform in size, shape and mass, making them very easy to handle on conveyor belt systems, which makes for speedy, precise ship loading and unloading using a shipboard self-unloading system, again cutting down on costs.

A self-unloader's system of belts carries the cargo from the hold, across the boom and onto the dock.

Vessels transiting the St. Clair River, Lake St. Clair and the Detroit River are under the jurisdiction of Sarnia Traffic and must radio their positions at predetermined locations. Call-in points (bold type on map) are not the same for upbound and downbound traffic. Average running times between call-in points are below. *

UPBOUND	Buoys 1&2	Black River	Stag Isl.	Salt Dock	X-32	Crib Light	Grassy Isl.
Detroit River Lt.	8:10	7:50	7:20	6:00	4:20	4:00	1:35
Grassy Island	6:45	6:25	5:55	4:35	2:55	2:35	
St. Clair Crib	4:10	3:50	3:20	2:00	0:25		
Light X-32	3:50	3:30	3:00	1:35			
Salt Dock	2:10	1:50	1:20				
Stag Isl. Upper	0:50	0:35					
Black River	0:20						

DOWNBOUND	Det. River	Grassy Isl.	Belle Isl.	Crib Light	Light 23	Salt Dock	Black River	7&8
30 min. above buoys 11 & 12	9:05	7:35	6:25	5:10	3:55	3:10	1:20	0:40
Buoys 7 & 8	8:15	6:55	5:45	4:30	3:15	2:30	0:40	
Black River	7:45	6:15	5:05	3:50	2:35	1:50		
Salt Dock	5:55	4:25	3:15	2:00	0:45			
Light 23	5:10	3:40	2:30	1:10				
St. Clair Crib	3:55	2:25	1:10					
USCG Belle Isle	2:40	1:10						
Grassy Isl.	1:30							

* Times can change if vessels stop for fuel or are delayed by other traffic.

BUOYS 11 & 12
DOWNBOUND ONLY

BUOYS 7 & 8
DOWNBOUND ONLY

BUOYS 1 & 2
UPBOUND ONLY

LAKE HURON

PORT HURON

SARNIA

IMPERIAL FUEL DOCK

BLACK RIVER

STAG ISLAND UPPER
UPBOUND ONLY

SHELL FUEL DOCK

ST. CLAIR

ST. CLAIR EDISON POWER PLANT RECOR POINT

MARINE CITY

SALT DOCK

ALGONAC

HARSENS ISLAND

LIGHT 23
DOWNBOUND ONLY

X(RAY) 32
UPBOUND ONLY

ST. CLAIR CRIB LIGHT

LAKE ST. CLAIR

USCG BELLE ISLE
DOWNBOUND ONLY

J.W. WESTCOTT MAILBOAT

DETROIT

WINDSOR

MISTERSKY FUEL

ROUGE RIVER

STERLING FUEL

GRASSY ISLAND

FIGHTING ISLAND

GROSSE ILE

LIVINGSTONE CHANNEL

AMHERSTBURG CHANNEL

DETROIT RIVER LIGHT

N
W   E
S

POINT PELEE

PELEE PASSAGE

MONROE

LAKE ERIE

PELEE ISLAND

SOUTHEAST SHOAL

TOLEDO

The **St. Marys River** flows out of the southeast corner of Lake Superior in a southeasterly direction to Lake Huron. Vessels transiting the St. Marys River system are under the jurisdiction of Soo Traffic, part of the U.S. Coast Guard at Sault Ste. Marie, Mich., and must radio their positions on VHF Ch. 12 (156.600 MHz) at predetermined locations. Vessels in the vicinity of the Soo Locks fall under the jurisdiction of the lockmaster, who must be contacted on VHF Ch. 14 (156.700 MHz) for lock assignments.

Call-in points (bold type on map) are not the same for upbound and downbound traffic. Approximate running times between call-in points are at left; times may vary due to other traffic and weather. Because of their size, 1,000-footers take more time to transit than smaller vessels.

Arrival times at the Soo Locks are available at the Information Center located in the locks park. Upbound vessels must make a pre-call to Soo Traffic one hour before entering the river at DeTour, and downbound traffic is required to make a one-hour pre-call above Ile Parisienne.

** Upbound traffic passes Neebish Island on the east side. Downbound traffic passes the island to the west, through the Rock Cut, a channel dynamited out of solid rock in the early 1900s.

UPBOUND	J'ct. Buoy	Nine Mile	Miss. Point	Clear Locks	Gros Cap
DeTour	1:35	3:35	4:20	5:50	7:25
Junction Buoy		1:50	2:45	4:15	5:50
Nine Mile Point			0:55	2:25	4:00
Mission Point*				1:30	3:05
Clear of Locks					1:35

DOWNBOUND	Gros Cap	Big Point	Clear Locks	Nine Mile	J'ct Buoy	DeTour
Ile Parisienne	0:45	1:55	3:25	4:20	6:20	8:00
Gros Cap		1:10	2:40	3:35	5:35	7:15
Big Point*			1:30	2:25	4:25	6:05
Clear of Locks				0:55	2:55	4:35
Nine Mile Point					2:00	3:40
Junction Buoy						1:40

* Lockmaster only

WHITEFISH BAY

ILE PARISIENNE
DOWNBOUND ONLY

CANADA

GROS CAP
UPBOUND ONLY

WEST PIER
EAST PIER
SAULT STE MARIE, ON
MISSION POINT
SUGAR ISLAND
SOO LOCKS
BIG POINT
SAULT STE MARIE, MI

U.S.A.

LAKE GEORGE

NINE MILE POINT

LAKE NICOLET

STRIBLING POINT

BARBEAU
NEEBISH ISLAND**
ROCK CUT

JOHNSON POINT

WINTER POINT

MUNUSCONG LAKE

ST. JOSEPH ISLAND

MUD LAKE JUNCTION BUOY

LIME ISLAND

RABER

DRUMMOND ISLAND

DETOUR VILLAGE

DETOUR
REEF LIGHT

LAKE HURON

N W E S

The Soo Locks at Sault Ste. Marie, Mich., on the St. Marys River, overcome a 21-foot difference in water levels between Lake Superior and lakes Huron, Michigan and Erie.

Under the jurisdiction of the U.S. Army Corps of Engineers, the locks operate on gravity, as do all locks in the St. Lawrence Seaway system. No pumps are used to empty or fill the lock chambers; valves are opened, and water is allowed to seek its own level. All traffic passes through the locks toll-free.

Traffic is dispatched by radio to the appropriate lock according to size, other vessels in the locks area and the time the captain first calls in to the lockmaster. All vessels longer than 730 feet and/or wider than 76 feet are restricted by size to the Poe, or second, lock. A vessel is under engine and thruster control at all times, with crews ready to drop mooring lines over bollards on the lock wall to stop its movement.

As soon as the vessel is in position, engines are stopped and mooring lines made fast. If the vessel is being lowered, valves at the lower end of the lock chamber are opened to allow the water inside to flow out. If the vessel is being raised, valves at the upper end of the chamber are opened to allow water to enter. When the water reaches the desired level, the valves are closed, the protective boom is raised, the gates are opened, and the vessel leaves the lock.

The first canal on the American side was built from 1853-55. That canal was destroyed in 1888 by workers making way for newer, bigger locks.

MacArthur Lock

Named after World War II Gen. Douglas MacArthur, the MacArthur Lock is 800 feet long (243.8 meters) between inner gates, 80 feet wide (24.4 meters) and 31 feet deep (9.4 meters) over the sills. The lock was built in 1942-43 and opened to traffic on July 11, 1943. Vessel size is limited to 730 feet long (222.5 meters) by 76 feet wide (23 meters).

Poe Lock

The Poe Lock is 1,200 feet long (365.8 meters), 110 feet wide (33.5 meters) and has a depth over the sills of 32 feet (9.8 meters). Named after Col. Orlando M. Poe, it was built in the years 1961-68. The lock's vessel size limit is 1,100 feet long (335.3 meters) by 105 feet wide (32 meters).

Davis and Sabin locks

Dating from the first two decades of the 20th century, these two locks are no longer used. Work began in 2009 to replace them with one new Poe-sized lock, at an estimated cost of more than $500 million. However the project remains stalled due to lack of funding.

Canadian Lock

The Canadian Lock at Sault Ste. Marie, Ont., has its origin in a canal constructed from 1887-95. The present lock, operated by Parks Canada, is used by pleasure craft, tugs and tour boats.

About the Soo Locks ...

The Empire State Building is 1,250 feet tall. The largest vessel using the Soo Locks is 1,014 feet long. This vessel, the American-flagged *Paul R. Tregurtha*, carried 3,219,646 net tons of cargo through the locks during the 1998 season.

There are about 140 major freighters, barges and tankers engaged almost exclusively in the Great Lakes and Seaway trade. That number is augmented by a variety of saltwater vessels, or "salties," that enter the system during the season.

The Great Lakes shipping season runs from late March to late December. In the spring and fall, a small fleet of icebreakers operated by the U.S. and Canadian coast guards and commercial tugs helps keep navigation channels open.

A vessel traveling from the Atlantic Ocean to Lake Superior through the St. Lawrence Seaway and the Soo Locks rises nearly 600 feet. The first lift, a total of 224 feet, is provided by the seven St. Lawrence Seaway locks that begin at Montreal. The Welland Canal, connecting Lake Erie and Lake Ontario and bypassing Niagara Falls, raises vessels an additional 326 feet. The Soo Locks complete the process.

One short blast of a vessel's whistle while in the lock means "cast off lines."

A red-and-white flag flying from a vessel's mast indicates a pilot is on board. Saltwater vessels pick up pilots at various points in their voyage.

During 1953, 128 million tons of freight moved through the locks. This amazing record stands.

The St. Marys River, running 80 miles (128.7 km) from Isle Parisienne at its north end to DeTour Reef Light at its south end, connects Lake Superior with Lake Huron. It includes two engineering marvels – the Soo Locks at Sault Ste. Marie and the West Neebish Cut at Barbeau, Mich., a channel dynamited out of solid rock that allows traffic to pass to the west side of Neebish Island.

LOCKS & CANALS / *Welland Canal*

The 28-mile (44 km) Welland Canal is the fourth version of a waterway link between Lake Ontario and Lake Erie, first built in 1829. The present canal was completed in 1932, deepened in the 1950s as part of the Seaway project and further straightened in 1973. Today its eight locks, all Canadian, lift ships 326 feet (100 meters) over the Niagara Escarpment.

Each of the seven Welland Canal locks has an average lift of 46.5 feet (14.2 meters). All locks (except Lock 8) are 859 feet (261.8 meters) long, 80 feet (24.4 meters) wide and 30 feet (9.1 meters) deep. Lock 8 measures 1,380 feet (420.6 m) long.

The largest vessel that may transit the canal is 740 feet (225.5 meters) long, 78 feet (23.8 meters) wide and 26.5 feet (8.08 meters) in draft. **Locks 1, 2** and **3** are at Port Weller and St. Catharines, Ont., on the Lake Ontario end of the waterway. At Lock 3, the Welland Canal Viewing Center and Museum also houses an information desk (which posts a list of vessels expected at the lock), a gift shop and restaurant.

At Thorold, **Locks 4, 5** and **6**, twinned to help speed passage of vessels, are controlled with an elaborate interlocking system for safety. These locks (positioned end to end, they resemble a short flight of stairs) have an aggregate lift of 139.5 feet (42.5 meters). Just south of locks **4, 5** and **6** is Lock 7. **Lock 8**, seven miles (11.2 km) upstream at Port Colborne, completes the process, making the final adjustment to Lake Erie's level.

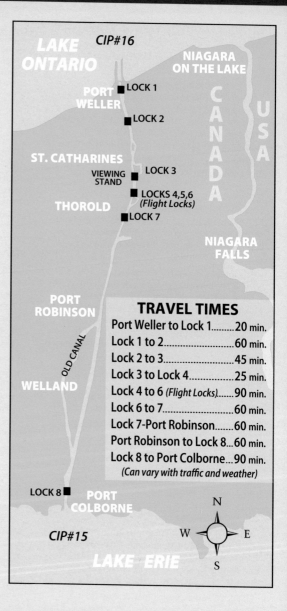

TRAVEL TIMES

Port Weller to Lock 1	20 min.
Lock 1 to 2	60 min.
Lock 2 to 3	45 min.
Lock 3 to Lock 4	25 min.
Lock 4 to 6 *(Flight Locks)*	90 min.
Lock 6 to 7	60 min.
Lock 7-Port Robinson	60 min.
Port Robinson to Lock 8	60 min.
Lock 8 to Port Colborne	90 min.

(Can vary with traffic and weather)

In 1973, a new channel was constructed to replace the section of the old canal that bisected the city of Welland. The Welland Bypass eliminated long delays for navigation, road and rail traffic. Two tunnels allow auto and train traffic to pass beneath the canal.

The average passage time for the canal is 8-11 hours, with the majority of the time spent transiting Locks 4-7. All vessel traffic though the Welland Canal is regulated by a control center, Seaway Welland, which also remotely operates the locks and the traffic bridges over the canal. Vessels passing through the Welland Canal and St. Lawrence Seaway must carry a qualified pilot at all times.

Frontenac in the MacArthur Lock at Sault Ste. Marie, Mich. (Roger LeLievre)

Grain carrier Manitoba exiting the Welland Canal at Port Colborne, Ont., with one of the canal's picturesque bridges astern. (Matt Miner)

143

ST LAMBERT

MONTREAL

ST LAMBERT
LOCK

CÔTE STE
CATHERINE LOCK

LAKE ST. LOUIS

BEAUHARNOIS
CANAL

BEAUHARNOIS
LOCKS

LAKE ST. FRANCOIS

CORNWALL

SNELL LOCK

EISENHOWER LOCK

LONG SAULT

INGLESIDE

MASSENA

CANADA

MORRISBURG

IROQUOIS

IROQUOIS LOCK

OGDENSBURG

PRESCOTT

U.S.A.

OTTAWA

BROCKVILLE

ALEXANDRIA BAY

CAPE VINCENT

KINGSTON

LAKE ONTARIO

Mamry enters the Seaway near Montreal. *(Ron Beaupré)*

SEAWAY – LOCK LIFTS

St. Lambert Lock	15 ft.
Côte Ste. Catherine Lock	30 ft.
Lower Beauharnois Lock	41 ft.
Upper Beauharnois Lock	41 ft.
Snell Lock	45 ft
Eisenhower Lock	38 ft.
Iroquois Lock	1 ft.

N E S W

The St. Lawrence Seaway is a waterway extending some 2,038 miles (3,701.4 km) from the Atlantic Ocean to the head of the Great Lakes at Duluth, Minn., including Montreal harbor and the Welland Canal. More specifically, it is a system of locks and canals (U.S. and Canadian), built between 1954 and 1958 at a cost of $474 million and opened in 1959, that allows vessels to pass from Montreal to the Welland Canal at the western end of Lake Ontario. For the Montreal-Lake Ontario section, the average transit time is 24 hours upbound and 22 hours downbound. The difference is mainly due to the current in the St. Lawrence River. The vessel size limit within this system is 740 feet (225.6 meters) long, 78 feet (23.8 meters) wide and 26 feet (7.9 meters) draft. It takes 8-10 days for a ship to go from Lake Superior to the Atlantic Ocean.

LOCK DIMENSIONS

Length...................766 feet (233.5 meters)
Width.............................80 feet (24 meters
Depth .... 30 feet (9.1 meters)

Closest to the ocean is the **St. Lambert Lock**, which lifts ships some 15 feet (4.6 meters) from Montreal harbor to the level of the Laprairie Basin,

through which the channel sweeps in a great arc 8.5 miles (13.7 km) long to the second lock. The **Côte Ste. Catherine Lock**, like the other six St. Lawrence Seaway locks, is built to the dimensions shown in the table above. The Côte Ste. Catherine lifts ships from the level of the Laprairie Basin 30 feet (9.1 meters) to the level of Lake Saint-Louis, bypassing the Lachine Rapids. Beyond it, the channel runs 7.5 miles (12.1 km) before reaching Lake Saint-Louis.

The **Lower Beauharnois Lock**, bypassing the Beauharnois Power House, lifts ships 41 feet (12.5 meters) and sends them through a short canal to the **Upper Beauharnois Lock**, where they are lifted 41 feet (12.5 meters) to reach the Beauharnois Canal. After a 13-mile (20.9 km) trip in the canal and a 30-mile (48.3 km) passage through Lake Saint Francis, vessels reach the U.S. border and the **Snell Lock**, which has a lift of 45 feet (13.7 meters) and empties into the 10-mile (16.1 km) Wiley-Dondero Canal.

After passing through the Wiley-Dondero, ships are raised another 38 feet (11.6 meters) by the **Dwight D. Eisenhower Lock**, after which they enter Lake St. Lawrence, the pool upon which nearby power-generating stations draw for their turbines located a mile to the north.

At the western end of Lake St. Lawrence, the **Iroquois Lock** allows ships to bypass the Iroquois Control Dam. The lift here is only about 1 foot (0.3 meters). Once in the waters west of Iroquois, the channel meanders through the Thousand Islands to Lake Ontario, the Welland Canal, and beyond.

Ferry C.T.M.A. Voyageur, based at Cap-aux-Meules, QC. (Delphis Duhamel)

With an inexpensive VHF scanner, boatwatchers can tune to ship-to-ship and ship-to-shore traffic using the following frequency guide.

Calling/distress only	Ch. 16 – 156.800 MHz	Calling/distress only
Commercial vessels only	Ch. 06 – 156.300 MHz	Working channel
Commercial vessels only	Ch. 08 – 156.400 MHz	Working channel
DeTour Reef – Lake St. Clair Light	Ch. 11 – 156.550 MHz	Sarnia Traffic - Sect. 1
Long Point Light – Lake St. Clair Light	Ch. 12 – 156.600 MHz	Sarnia Traffic - Sect. 2
Montreal – Mid-Lake St. Francis	Ch. 14 – 156.700 MHz	Seaway Beauharnois – Sect. 1
Mid-Lake St. Francis – Bradford Island	Ch. 12 – 156.600 MHz	Seaway Eisenhower – Sect. 2
Bradford Island – Crossover Island	Ch. 11 – 156.550 MHz	Seaway Iroquois – Sect. 3
Crossover Island-Cape Vincent	Ch. 13 – 156.650 MHz	Seaway Clayton – Sect. 4 St. Lawrence River portion
Cape Vincent – Mid-Lake Ontario	Ch. 12 – 156.600 MHz	Seaway Sodus – Sect. 4 Lake Ontario portion
Seaway Pilot Office – Cape Vincent	Ch. 14 – 156.700 MHz	Pilotage traffic
Mid-Lake Ontario – Welland Canal	Ch. 11 – 156.550 MHz	Seaway Newcastle – Sect. 5
Welland Canal	Ch. 14 – 156.700 MHz	Seaway Welland – Sect. 6
Welland Canal to Long Point Light	Ch. 11 – 156.550 MHz	Seaway Long Point – Sect. 7
Montreal Traffic	Ch. 10 – 156.500 MHz	Vessel traffic
Soo Traffic	Ch. 12 – 156.600 MHz	Vessel control, Sault Ste. Marie,
Lockmaster, Soo Locks	Ch. 14 – 156.700 MHz	Soo Lockmaster (WUE-21)
Coast Guard traffic	Ch. 21 – 157.050 MHz	United States Coast Guard
Coast Guard traffic	Ch. 22 – 157.100 MHz	United States Coast Guard
U.S. mailboat, Detroit, MI	Ch. 10 – 156.500 MHz	Mailboat *J. W. Westcott II*

Hear vessel traffic online at broadcastify.com – click on the 'Listen' button

The following prerecorded messages help track vessel arrivals and departures

Boatwatcher's Hotline	(218) 722-6489	Superior, Duluth, Two Harbors, Taconite Harbor and Silver Bay
CSX coal docks/Torco dock	(419) 697-2304	Toledo, Ohio, vessel information
Eisenhower Lock	(315) 769-2422	Eisenhower Lock vessel traffic
Michigan Limestone dock	(989) 734-2117	Calcite, Mich., vessel information
Michigan Limestone dock	(906) 484-2201	Press 1 – Cedarville passages
Presque Isle Corp.	(989) 595-6611	Stoneport vessel information ext. 7
Seaway Vessel Locator	(450) 672-4115	
Soo Traffic	(906) 635-3224	Previous day – St. Marys River
Soo Traffic – hotline	(906) 253-9290	Soo Locks traffic information
Superior Midwest Energy	(715) 395-3559	Superior, Wis., vessel information
Thunder Bay Port Authority	(807) 345-1256	Thunder Bay, Ont., vessel information
Vantage Point, Boatnerd HQ	(810) 985-9057	St. Clair River traffic
Welland Canal tape	(905) 688-6462	Welland Canal traffic

MEANINGS OF BOAT WHISTLES

1 SHORT: I intend to leave you on my port side (answered by same if agreed upon).

2 SHORT: I intend to leave you on my starboard side (answered by same if agreed upon). (Passing arrangements may be agreed upon by radio. If so, no whistle signal is required.)

1 PROLONGED: Vessel leaving dock.

3 SHORT: Operating astern propulsion.

1 PROLONGED, SOUNDED AT INTERVALS OF NOT MORE THAN 2 MINUTES: Vessel moving in restricted visibility.

1 SHORT, 1 PROLONGED, 1 SHORT: Vessel at anchor in restricted visibility (optional). May be accompanied by the ringing of a bell on the forward part of the ship and a gong on the aft end.

3 PROLONGED & 2 SHORT: Salute (formal).

1 PROLONGED & 2 SHORT: Salute (commonly used).

3 PROLONGED & 1 SHORT: International Shipmasters' Association member salute.

5 OR MORE SHORT BLASTS SOUNDED RAPIDLY: Danger.

Cruising

Segwun stirs memories as she waits at her Gravenhurst, Ont., dock. (Roger LeLievre)

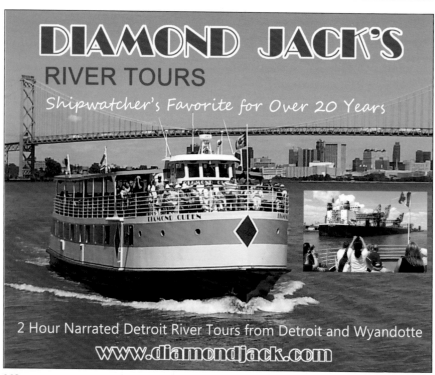

German liner Hamburg in the Welland Canal in 2014. *(John C. Knecht)*

Who's on deck
Familiar names and a spruced-up newcomer

This season will see the return of two passenger vessels that cruised the Great Lakes and St. Lawrence Seaway last year, plus the introduction of a new vessel that came inland more than a decade ago under another name. As expected, *Hamburg* and *Pearl Mist* are both coming back this summer, the former with mostly European tourists and the latter catering more to passengers from this hemisphere.

The 105-stateroom *Saint Laurent* is the new kid on the block. She may be familiar to shipwatchers as the former *Cape May Light*, which came inland in 2001 under the ownership of American Classic Voyages Co. That company went out of business after the Sept. 11, 2001 attacks in the U.S. crippled the travel industry and economy. *Cape May Light* was eventually operated as *Sea Voyager* but remained largely unused aside from a charter to the U.S. government to house aid workers after the 2010 Haiti earthquake. Now, after undergoing a $3.5 million refurbishment, she's ready to put her best face forward in 2015, sailing under the banner of well-known U.S. travel and cruise operator Haimark. Her itineraries include a 10-day "French Canadian Maritimes and North Atlantic" cruise, "Historic Coastal New England" 13-day trips, and "Historic St. Lawrence River to America's Five Great Lakes" cruises, which offer voyages on the St. Lawrence River from Montreal to Chicago. It is expected the vessel's operators will cater mostly to the North American market. She will retreat to saltwater during the winter.

Drawing of Saint Laurent.

Pearl Mist in 2014.

And don't forget about regulars Blount Small Ship Adventures and St. Lawrence Cruise Lines, offering the kind of small-ship travel some customers prefer.

One vessel familiar in Great Lakes ports, the *Yorktown*, won't be back. She was sold at auction in 2014 and was renamed *Americana* by her new, Nevada-based owner, and is currently laid up.

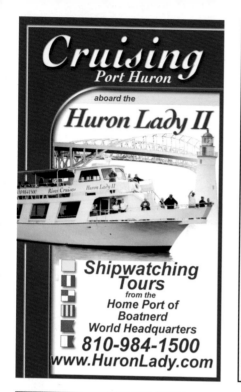

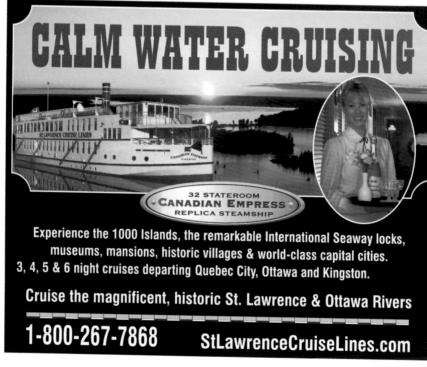

Classic cruise

If your idea of the perfect passenger ship is more classic than current, then Canada's historic steamer *Segwun* just may be the perfect ride

The vessel, built in 1887, offers excursions in season from the picturesque wharf at Gravenhurst, in Ontario's Muskoka Lakes region, operated by the non-profit Muskoka Steamship & Historical Society.

The *Know Your Ships* crew took the ship's annual, day-long, 100-mile trip in late July, which began with a scenic cruise on Lake Muskoka, past the Millionaire's Row of homes and cottages, before sailing up the Indian River to the Port Carling Locks. One of the best parts of the cruise was watching the *Segwun*'s coal-fueled,

Artist's rendition of the restored Segwun.

hand-fired reciprocating steam engine pumping away. Another highlight was hearing the ship's melodious steam whistle, which the captain was happy to blow. And *Segwun*'s gleaming woodwork and two dining rooms served as a glorious reminder of the heyday of steamboat travel of years gone by.

Measuring 125 feet and carrying 97 passengers, the *Segwun* was built in Glasgow, Scotland, and assembled at Gravenhurst. The ship was originally a paddlewheel steamer named *Nipissing II*, transporting passengers, mail and freight to cottages, resorts and homes along the Muskoka Lakes. By 1914, *Nipissing II* was withdrawn from service. Ten years later, in 1924, following World War I, work began to rebuild the superstructure of the vessel, and twin-propeller engines were ordered from Scotland. In 1925, the ship was given her current name. In Ojibwa, it means "springtime." By 1958, with mail delivery taking more land routes, *Segwun* made her last trip and was decommissioned. In 1962, she was converted into a floating maritime museum at Gravenhurst Wharf and thus escaped deconstruction. Work began in 1973, with help from steamship enthusiasts of the Muskoka Steamship & Historical Society and the Ontario Road Builders, and the *Segwun* was officially relaunched in 1974. After further restoration, *Segwun* began her current career in 1981.

Each summer she attracts thousands of tourists to Muskoka, enabling passengers to see the area as it should be seen, by water. If you go, don't miss the Muskoka Boat and Heritage Centre nearby, with its detailed ship models, maritime artifacts and other displays exploring the history of this beautiful area. It's a little off the beaten path but well worth the trip. – *Roger LeLievre*

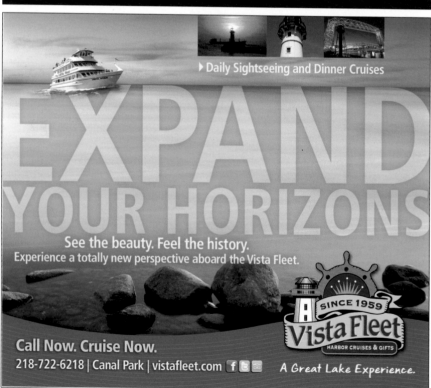

INTRODUCING

LUXURY COASTAL EXPEDITIONS

Aboard the All-New MS Saint Laurent

AMERICA'S FIVE GREAT LAKES • CANADIAN MARITIMES • NEW ENGLAND • PANAMA CANAL
CENTRAL & SOUTH AMERICA

CLIFF ROCK BAR & GRILLE

EXPANSIVE OUTDOOR VENUES

OWNER'S SUITE

MODERN STATEROOMS & SUITES

SHEARWATER DINING ROOM

ELEGANT DINING OPTIONS

Reserve your space now.
Call 855 424 6275 or visit haimarkline.com

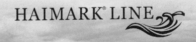

HAIMARK® LINE

Great White Fleet

JOHN HENRY
Foreword by the Right Honourable Paul Martin, PC, CC

Great White Fleet

Celebrating
CANADA STEAMSHIP LINES
Passenger Ships

In 'Great White Fleet: Celebrating Canada Steamship Lines Passenger Ships,' the first book devoted exclusively to the huge fleet of passenger steamers once operated by C.S.L. on the Great Lakes and St. Lawrence River, journalist and author John Henry traces their history from the creation of this great enterprise in 1913, when it inherited more than 50 passenger vessels from predecessor companies, until the last of these splendid ships were retired in 1965.

Hardcover 8 ½" x 11 3/8" – 142 pages, 120 illustrations
$30. Available from online booksellers

Historic Gallery

Parker Evans entering the Eisenhower Lock. (Matt Miner Collection)

Launch day for Scott Misener, Port Weller Dry Docks, Ltd., 1954. (Skip Gillham Collection)

Upper Lakes Shipping Ltd.'s Canadian Leader, shown in 2008, was scrapped in 2010. (Wade P. Streeter)

*Armco (now American Valor)
in Oglebay Norton colors, May
2004.* (Roger LeLievre)

*Cleveland Cliffs' Pontiac, upbound at dusk in
the St. Marys River, 1978.* (Roger LeLievre)

Cadillac and tug Idaho at Cleveland, date unknown. (Peter B. Worden Collection)

Martha Hindman at anchor in the 1970s near the Soo Locks. (Roger LeLievre)

Eastland's end

July 24 marks the 100th anniversary of the worst tragedy in Great Lakes history. Even though the vessel was just 20 feet from the dock, 844 people were lost when she rolled over in 1915.

Built in 1902 by the Jenks Ship Building Company of Port Huron, Mich., the *Eastland* was owned by the St. Joseph and Chicago Steamship Co. On the date of the disaster, she and two other Great Lakes passenger steamers, *Theodore Roosevelt* and *Petoskey*, had been chartered to take employees from the Western Electric Co. in Illinois to a picnic in Michigan City, Ind.

It is believed a rush of passengers to the side of the steamer farthest from the dock made the *Eastland* unstable, causing her to tip over. The huge loss of life occurred despite the fast response by the crew of a nearby vessel that came alongside the hull to allow those stranded on the capsized *Eastland* to leap to safety. Ironically, it was safety that may have been responsible for the accident. In 1915, the new federal Seamen's Act had been passed because of the *Titanic* disaster. This required retrofitting of a complete set of lifeboats on the *Eastland* and many other passenger vessels. This additional weight on an upper deck may have made the *Eastland* more dangerous and worsened a preexisting problem of being top-heavy.

Following the disaster, the *Eastland* was raised, salvaged and sold to the U.S. Navy. After modifications, she was designated as a gunboat and renamed *USS Wilmette*. She was used primarily as a training vessel on the Great Lakes and was scrapped following World War II.

Eastland at Cleveland in happier times. *(Peter B. Worden Collection)*

Georgian Bay from Detroit's Ambassador Bridge, 1980. (Jeff Mast)

Edward L. Ryerson at Milwaukee, Wis., for repairs in April 1997. (Andy LaBorde)

Sir Denys Lowson, Port Weller piers. *(Jeff Cameron Collection)*

Goofing off on the J.E. Upson (inset) in the 1940s or '50s. *(Tom Manse Collection)*

Hand-tinted image of the bulk carrier E.W. Oglebay of 1896 at Mission Point in Sault Ste. Marie, Mich. *(A.E. Young Photo / Tom Manse Collection)*

Montrose in the Detroit River after a collision in 1962. (UPI photo, Tom Manse Collection)

Upper Lakes Shipping's Pathfinder (later Goderich) and the passenger ship Keewatin in the Soo Locks in the mid-1960s. The dirt channel between the two vessels would soon become the site of the second Poe Lock. *(Tom Manse Collection)*

Benson Ford departs Duluth, Minn., sometime after 1924. (Tom Manse Collection)

HISTORIC

 **American Can of Canada**
Marathon, ON

 **Escanaba Towing Co.**
Escanaba, MI

 **Federal Motorships Corp.**
Buffalo, N.Y.

 **Great Lakes Steamship Co.**
Cleveland, OH

 **Inland Lines Ltd.**
Winnipeg, MB

 **J.E. Russell Co. Ltd.**
Toronto, ON

 **Lakehead Transportation Co.**
Winnipeg, MB

 **Lehigh Valley Transit Co.**
Allentown, PA

 Menominee Transit Co.
Cleveland, OH

 **Montreal Transportation Co.**
Montreal, QC

 **Northern Michigan Transit Company**

 **Northwest Steamships Ltd.**
Toronto, ON

 **Ocean Lines Ltd.**
(Canada SS Lines, Mgr.)
Hamilton, BWI

 **Redland Steamhip Co.**
Chicago, IL

 Rutland Lake Michigan Transit Co.
Chicago, IL

 Saginaw Dock and Terminal Co.
Saginaw, MI

 **Sinclair Refining Co.**
New York, NY

 **Western Transit Co.**
Buffalo, NY

 Coastal Canada Marine Ltd.
Toronto, ON

 Enerchem Transport Inc.
Toronto, ON

 Incan Ships Ltd.
Thunder Bay, ON

 A.B. McLean & Sons
Sault Ste. Marie, ON

 North American Towing
Duluth, MN

 Pioneer Shipping Ltd.
Montreal, QC

Smokestacks of the Kinsman Marine Transit (left), Bethlehem Steel and Republic Steel companies, all of Cleveland, Ohio. All images circa the 1970s. (Roger LeLievre)

166

Responsive?
You Bet!

Interlake Steamship has a long tradition of being responsive to its customers and meeting their cargo delivery challenges. Our knowledgeable and accommodating marketing personnel, together with experienced and conscientious vessel crews, will work with you to deliver your cargo where, when and how you want it. Interlake's versatile and reliable nine-vessel self-unloading fleet, with cargo capacities ranging from 17,000 to 68,000 gross tons, is ready to fulfill your Great Lakes transportation needs.

Experience our commitment to superior customer service. Put the responsive Interlake team to work for you.

INTERLAKE STEAMSHIP
On the Great Lakes since 1913

The Interlake Steamship Company
7300 Engle Road
Middleburg Heights, Ohio 44130

Phone: 440-260-6900 • 800-327-3855
FAX: 440-260-6945

Email: boconnor@interlake-steamship.com
Website: www.interlakesteamship.com

vessel Index

Manistee upbound at the Detroit River Light.
(Wade P. Streeter)

Vessel Name	Fleet #	Vessel Name	Fleet #	Vessel Name	Fleet #	Vessel Name	Fleet #
BBC Fuji	IB-8	Blain M	M-12	Buxton II	K-5	Caribou Isle	C-3
BBC Greenland	IB-8	Block, Joseph L.	C-6			Carina	A-1
BBC Hawaii	IR-3	Blough, Roger	G-14			Carlee Emily	K-2
BBC Houston	IB-8	Bluebill	IN-1			Carleton, George N.	G-11
BBC Jade	IB-8	Blue Dog	S-11	C.T.M.A. Vacancier	C-25	Carl M.	M-14
BBC Kibo	IB-8	Blue Heron	U-9	C.T.M.A. Voyageur	C-25	Carol Ann	K-5
BBC Kwiatkowski	IB-8	Blue Heron V	B-9	Cadillac	S-22	Carrick, John J.	M-11
BBC Louisiana	IW-1	Blue Phoenix I	IB-6	California	G-15	Carrol C. 1	M-12
BBC Maine	IW-1	Bluewing	IO-1	Callaway, Cason J.	G-14	Catherine-Legardeur	S-12
BBC Mississippi	IB-8	BMI-192	B-3	Callie M.	M-8	Cavalier Maxim	C-23
BBC Oregon	IW-1	BMI-FDD-1	B-3	Calumet	L-15	Cedarglen	C-2
BBC Plata	IW-1	BMT 3	B-15	Cameron O	S-5	Celebrezze,	
BBC Rhine	IE-3	Boatman No. 3	M-12	Camille-Marcoux	S-12	Anthony J.	C-17
BBC Rushmore	IB-8	Boatman No. 6	M-12	Canadian	M-14	Celine	IE-5
BBC Scandinavia	IB-8	Bogdan	IN-2	Canadian Argosy	M-14	Cemba	C-5
BBC Steinhoeft	IE-3	Boland, John J.	A-6	Canadian Empress	S-18	CGB-12001	U-3
BBC Sweden	IB-8	Bold World	IB-2	Canadian Jubilee	D-2	CGB-12002	U-3
BBC Switzerland	IB-8	Bonnie B III	M-12	Cantankerus	E-6	Challenge	G-18
BBC Volga	IB-8	Boothe Sr., Ken	A-6	Cape Brulé	E-4	Champion	C-7, D-10
BBC Xingang	IB-8	Bowditch	A-1	Cape Challion	C-3	Channel Cat	M-17
Beatrix	IW-2	Bowes, Bobby	D-2	Cape Commodore	C-3	Charlevoix	C-9, L-10
Beaver	A-12	Boyd, David	G-20	Cape Crow	E-4	Charlie E.	M-7
Beaver Delta II	M-14	Bramble	MU-19	Cape Discovery	C-3	Charlotte C	IC-2
Beaver Gamma	M-14	Brant	IN-1	Cape Dundas	C-3	Charlotte Theresa	IH-7
Beaver Islander	B-7	Breaker	N-4	Cape Egmont	IC-8	Chem Hydra	IA-2
Beaver State	M-1	Brentholmen	IA-3	Cape Hearne	C-3	Chem Norma	IA-2
Becker, Edith M.	S-1	Bright Star	S-11	Cape Lambton	C-3	Chemtrans Elbe	IC-4
Bee Jay	G-4	Bristol Bay	U-3	Cape Mercy	C-3	Chemtrans Havel	IC-4
Bell 1, Marilyn	T-12	Brochu	A-10	Cape Providence	C-3	Chemtrans Mabuhay	IC-4
Ben	IL-4	Brown, Prentiss	S-2	Cape Rescue	C-3	Cheraw	U-2
Bessie B	W-9	Brutus I	T-12	Cape Storm	C-3	Chestnut	IN-1
Betsiamites	L-11	Buckley	K-4	Caporal Kaeble V	C-3	Chi-Cheemaun	O-9
Beverly M 1	M-12	Buckthorn	U-3	Cap Streeter	S-11	Chicago Elite	S-15
Bide-A-Wee	S-13	Buffalo	A-6	Capt. Keith	M-5	Chicago's Classic Lady	C-12
Billmaier, D.L.	U-2	Bunyan, Paul	U-2	Capt. Shepler	S-8	Chicago's First Lady	C-12
Birchglen	C-2	Burns Harbor	A-6	Captain George	W-3	Chicago's Leading Lady	C-12
Biscayne Bay	U-3	Busch, Edwin C.	B-15	Carey, Emmett J.	O-8	Chicago's Little Lady	C-12
Black, Martha L.	C-3	Busch, Gregory J.	B-15	Cargo Carrier I	M-14	Chief Shingwauk	R-3
Blacky	IN-1	Busse, Fred A.	L-12	Cargo Master	M-14	Chippewa	A-12

C

Lee A. Tregurtha and Philip R. Clarke pass in a hazy Mackinac Straits. (Logan Vasicek)

Vessel Name	Fleet #
Lake Guardian	U-4
Lake Ontario	IS-11
Lakes Contender	A-6
Lambert Spirit	M-12
Lapointe, Ernest	MU-16
La Prairie	L-11
Larsholmen	IA-3
La Salle	S-22
Latham, William H.	N-4
Latimer, Radcliffe R.	A-2
Laud, Sam	A-6
Laurentian	G-13
Le Cageux	Q-1
Leitch, John D.	A-2
Leona B.	M-20
Leonard M.	M-12
Le Phil D.	L-11
Le Voyageur	S-13
Liamare	IL-2
Lime Island	B-2
Limnos	C-3
Linda Jean	N-8
Linnea	W-6
Linnhurst	G-2
Lita	IJ-2
Little Rock	MU-1
Lois M.	M-12
Lokholmen	IA-3
Lomer-Gouin	S-12
Louie S.	R-4
Louisiana	G-15
LS Christine	IL-1
LS Jacoba	IL-1
LST-393	MU-28
LT-5	MU-9
Lubie	IP-3
Lucien-L.	S-12
Ludington	MU-2
Luebbert	II-3
Luedtke, Alan K.	L-16
Luedtke, Chris E.	L-16
Luedtke, Erich R.	L-16
Luedtke, Karl E.	L-16
Luedtke, Kurt R.	L-16
Luedtke, Paul L.	L-16
Lugano	IM-3
Lyulin	IN-2

M

Vessel Name	Fleet #
Macassa Bay	W-8
Maccoa	IN-1
MacKay, Tony	M-12
Mackenzie, Wm. Lyon	T-10
Mackinac Express	A-12
Mackinac Islander	A-12
Mackinaw (WAGB-83)	MU-11
Mackinaw (WLBB-30)	U-3
Madeline	M-3
Madison	M-1

Vessel Name	Fleet #
Maemi	IK-4
Maggie Girl	M-14
Maid of the Mist IV	M-4
Maid of the Mist VI	M-4
Maid of the Mist VII	M-4
Maineborg	IW-2
Maine	G-15
Mainland	IB-4
Maisonneuve	M-26
Malden	P-8
Mamry	IP-3
Manatra	U-7
Mandarin	IN-1
Manistee	L-15
Manitoba	L-14
Manitou Isle	M-6
Manitoulin	L-14
Manitou	M-5, T-14
Manitowoc	L-15, U-2
Maple City	T-12
Mapleglen	C-2
Maple Grove	O-1
Margot	N-6
Marida Melissa	IM-1
Marida Mulberry	IM-1
Marietje Deborah	ID-2
Marietje Marsilla	ID-2
Marissa Rose	D-3
Market, Wm.	M-21
Marlyn	S-11
Marquette	C-13, S-22
Martin, Rt. Hon. Paul J.	C-2
Mary Ellen I	L-9
Marysville	G-1
Massachusetts	G-15
Mather, William G.	MU-8
Matt Allen	K-5
McBride, Sam	C-14
McCarthy Jr., Walter J.	A-6
McCauley	U-2
McKee, Bradshaw	S-2
McKee Sons	L-7
McKeil, Evans	M-12
McKeil, Tim	M-12
McLane	MU-7
McLeod, Norman	M-11
McQueen, F.R.	M-14
MCT Breithorn	IM-5
MCT Monte Rosa	IM-5
MCT Stockhorn	IM-5
Medemborg	IW-2
Mega	L-11
Mehmet A	IC-3
Menasha	M-15
Menier Consol	T-9
Merweborg	IW-2
Merwedegracht	IS-10
Mesabi Miner	I-5
Meteor	MU-24
Metis	E-8
Metsaborg	IW-2
Michigan	U-8

Vessel Name	Fleet #
Michipicoten	L-14
Middle Channel	C-7
Miedwie	IP-3
Mighty Jake	G-7
Mighty Jessie	G-7
Mighty Jimmy	G-7
Mighty John III	G-7
Milwaukee Clipper	MU-25
Milwaukee	G-15
Miners Castle	P-2
Minnesota	G-15
Miseford	T-5
Mishe Mokwa	M-6
Misner, H.H.	G-17
Miss Edna	K-5
Mississagi	L-14
Mississippiborg	IW-2
Mississippi	G-15
Miss Kim Simpson	T-13
Miss Laura	M-8
Miss Libby	D-9
Miss Midland	M-19
Miss Munising	M-27
Missouriborg	IW-2
Missouri	G-15
Miss Superior	P-2
Mister Joe	M-14
Mist of Avalon	L-13
Mitiq	N-9
MM Newfoundland	M-12
Mobile Bay	U-3
Moby Dick	G-7
Moezelborg	IW-2
Mohawk	M-1
Molly M. 1	N-1
Moore, Olive L.	L-15
Morgan	K-4
Morgenstond I	IW-3
Morholmen	IA-3
Morrish, Thomas R.	R-6
Morro Bay	U-3
Motti	L-11
Mottler	IN-1
Mrs. C.	C-21
MSM Douro	IM-4
Munson, John G.	G-14
Muntgracht	IS-10
Muskie	G-19
Mystic Blue	M-31, S-15

Vessel Name	Fleet #
Nancy Anne	D-10
Nancy J.	H-4
Nassauborg	IW-2
Nathan S	C-1
Nautica Queen	N-2
Neah Bay	U-3
Nebraska	G-15
Neebish Islander II	E-1
Neeskay	U-10
Nels J.	H-4

Vessel Name	Fleet #
Nelson, Gaylord	W-10
Neptune III	D-2
New Beginnings	T-13
New Jersey	G-15
New York	G-15
Niagara Guardian	H-5
Niagara	MU-5
Niagara Prince	B-8
Niagara Queen II	O-7
Niagara Spirit	M-12
Niagara Thunder	H-5
Niagara Wonder	H-5
Nichevo II	M-3
Nickelena	B-3
Nicolet	U-2
Niki S	C-1
Nilufer Sultan	IV-1
Nipigon Osprey	O-6
No. 55	M-1
No. 56	M-1
Noble, Robert	W-5
Nogat	IP-3
Nokomis	S-13
Nordic Copenhagen	IN-8
Nordic Helsinki	IN-8
Nordic Mari	IN-8
Nordic Oslo	IN-8
Nordic Stockholm	IN-8
Nordik Express	G-21
Nordisle	IR-5
Nordport	IR-5
Norgoma	MU-26
Norisle	MU-6
North Carolina	G-15
North Channel	C-7
North Contender	IE-2
North Dakota	G-15
Northern Lighter	A-14
Northern Spirit I	M-9
North Fighter	IE-2
North Star	C-8
Northwestern	G-16
Noyes, Hack	W-10
Nunavut Spirit	M-12

Vessel Name	Fleet #
Oakglen	C-2
Oberstar, Hon. James L.	I-5
Obsession III	C-24
Ocean Crescent	II-1
Océan A. Simard	L-11
Océan Abys	L-11
Océan Arctique	L-11
Océan Basques	L-11
Océan Bertrand Jeansonne	L-11
Océan Bravo	L-11
Océan Charlie	L-11
Océan Cote-Nord	L-11
Océan Delta	L-11
Océan Echo II	L-11

175

Vessel Name	Fleet #	Vessel Name	Fleet #	Vessel Name	Fleet #	Vessel Name	Fleet #
Océan Express	L-11	Onego Bora	IM-4	Patricia D	G-3	Prairieland	G-7
Océan Foxtrot	L-11	Onego Ponza	IR-2	Paula M.	M-14	Presque Isle	G-14
Océan Georgie Bain	L-11	Ongiara	C-14	Pearl Mist	P-4	Pride of Michigan	U-7
Océan Golf	L-11	Ontamich	B-10	Pelee Islander	M-25	Pride	W-7
Océan Guide	L-11	Ontario Explorer	O-6	Peninsula	G-11	Primrose	M-12
Océan Henry Bain	L-11	Oriental Protea	IS-7	Pennsylvania	G-15	Princess Wenonah	B-4
Océan Hercule	L-11	Oriole	M-9	Perelik	IN-2	Private Robertson VC	C-3
Océan Intrepide	L-11	Orla	IP-3	Pere Marquette 41	P-1	Prosna	IP-3
Océan Jupiter	L-11	Orsula	IA-8	Performance	S-19	Provmar Terminal	S-23
Océan K. Rusby	L-11	Osborne, F.M.	O-8	Pete, C. West	B-1	Puffin	IH-3
Océan Lima	L-11	Oshawa	M-14	Peter-Fraser	S-12	Purcell, Robert W.	A-8
Océan Pierre Julien	L-11	Oslo Bulk 6	IS-2	Peter Ronna	IB-8	Purple Gem	IB-4
Océan Raymond Lemay	L-11	Osogovo	IN-2	Petite Forte	S-21	Purves, John	MU-3
Océan Ross Gaudreault	L-11	Oste	IC-4	Pictured Rocks	P-2	Purvis, W. I. Scott	P-8
Océan Sept-Iles	L-11	Ostrander, G.L.	L-2	Pierson, Robert S.	L-14	Purvis, W.J. Isaac	P-8
Océan Serge Genois	L-11	Ottawa	A-12	Pilica	IP-3	Purvis, W.J. Ivan	P-8
Océan Stevns	L-11	Ouilmette	W-6	Pineglen	C-2	Put-in-Bay	M-21
Océan Traverse Nord	L-11	Outer Island	E-5	Pioneerland	G-7		
Océan Tundra	L-11	Ovation	I-1	Pioneer Princess	T-11		
Océan Yvan Desgagnés	L-11			Pioneer Queen	T-11		
Oceanex Avalon	IO-2			Pitts Carillon	G-3	**Q**	
Oceanex Connaigra	IO-2	**P**		Pitts No. 3	G-3	Qamutik	N-9
Oceanex Sanderling	IO-2	Pacific Dawn	IH-4	Playfair	T-8	Quinte Loyalist	M-25
Odyssey II	S-15	Pacific Huron	IF-5	PML 2501	P-8		
Ohio	G-15	Paddy Miles	H-7	PML 357	P-8		
Ojibway	L-14, S-14	Palabora	IH-3	PML 9000	P-8	**R**	
Oklahoma	G-15	Palau	IH-3	PML Alton	P-8	Raba	IP-3
Old Mission	K-4	Palembang	IH-3	PML Ironmaster	P-8	Racine	U-2
Olza	IP-3	Palmerton	IH-3	PML Tucci	P-8	Radisson, Pierre	C-3
Omni-Atlas	L-11	Panagia	IH-3	PML Tucker	P-8	Radisson	S-12, S-22
Omni-Richelieu	L-11	Pangani	IH-3	Pochard S	IA-7	Radium Yellowknife	T-9
		Panthera	IH-3	Point Valour	T-5	Ramira	IA-4
		Papoose III	K-6	Point Viking	C-20	Randolph, Curtis	D-4
		Pathfinder	I-5, T-8	Port City Princess	P-5	Ranger III	U-6
						Rebecca Lynn	A-8

Pineglen passes Port Huron, Mich. / Sarnia, Ont. (Steve Jowett)

Vessel Name	Fleet #	Vessel Name	Fleet #	Vessel Name	Fleet #	Vessel Name	Fleet #
Redhead	IP-1	Sacré Bleu	S-8	Selvick, Sharon M.	S-5	Sichem Onomichi	IE-2
Red Witch	T-2	Saginaw	L-14	Selvick, William C.	S-5	Sichem Paris	IE-2
Reestborg	IW-2	Saint Laurent	H-1	SE Potentia	IS-4	Silversides	MU-7
Regalica	IP-3	Salarium	C-2	Serena	II-3	Simcoe Islander	C-22
Reggeborg	IW-2	Salvage Monarch	T-9	Service Boat No. 1	L-11	Simonsen	U-2
Reliance	P-8	Salvor	M-12	Service Boat No. 2	L-11	Sioux	M-1
Rennie, Thomas	C-14	Sandpiper	H-3	Service Boat No. 4	L-11	Sir Henry	IH-5
Resko	IP-3	Sandra Mary	M-14	Seymour, Wilf	M-12	Sjard	IB-8
Rest, William	T-12	Sapphire	IF-3	Shamrock	J-3	Skawa	IP-3
Rhode Island	G-15	Sarah B.	G-12	Shamrock Jupiter	IS-7	Skyline Queen	M-16
Richter, Arni J.	W-5	Sarah No. 1	D-9	Shannon	G-1	Sloman Dispatcher	IS-9
Ridgway, Benjamin	H-7	Schlaeger, Victor L.	C-11	Shannon Star	IR-6	Sloman Hera	IS-9
Rio Dauphin	IC-8	Schoening, Herman	II-3	Sharon M I	M-12	Sloman Herakles	IS-9
Risley, Samuel	C-3	Schoonmaker,		Shenehon	G-13	Sloman Hermes	IS-9
River Queen	Q-2	Col. James M.	MU-17	Sherwin, John	I-5	Smith, Dean R.	M-8
Robert John	G-11	Schulte, Edzard	IB-3	Shipsands	T-13	Smith, F.C.G.	C-3
Robert W.	T-5	Schulte, Elisabeth	IB-3	Shirley Ann	C-8	Smith Jr., L.L.	U-11
Robin Lynn	S-7	Schulte, Elisalex	IB-3	Shirley Irene	K-2	Sofia	II-3
Robinson Bay	S-19	Schulte, Everhard	IB-3	Shoreline (The)	S-9	Solina	IP-3
Rochelle Kaye	R-6	Schwartz, H.J.	U-2	Shoreline II	S-11	Songa Challenge	IB-7
Rocket	P-8	SCL Bern	IE-5	Shoveler	IN-1	Songa Diamond	IB-7
Roman, Stephen B.	E-8	Sea Bear	S-3	Showboat	M-9	Songa Eagle	IB-7
Rosalee D.	T-5	Sea Eagle II	S-21	Sichem Beijing	IE-2	Songa Emerald	IB-7
Rosemary	M-9	Sea Fox II	T-4	Sichem Challenge	IE-2	Songa Falcon	IL-5
Roter Sand	E-2	Seahound	N-1	Sichem Contester	IE-2	Songa Jade	IB-7
Rouble, J.R.	D-9	Sea Hunter III	G-9	Sichem Defiance	IE-2	Songa Opal	IB-7
Ruby-T	IT-5	Sea Prince II	R-3	Sichem Dubai	IE-2	Songa Peace	IB-7
Ruddy	IN-1	Sea Racer	IT-2	Sichem Edinburgh	IE-2	Songa Ruby	IB-7
Ryerson, Edward L.	C-6	Seaway Supplier	S-4	Sichem Hiroshima	IE-2	Songa Sapphire	IB-7
		Segwun	M-29	Sichem Hong Kong	IE-2	Songa Topaz	IB-7
		Selandia Swan	IU-1	Sichem Melbourne	IE-2	Soulanges	E-4
		Selvick, Bonnie G.	R-1	Sichem Montreal	IE-2	South Bass	M-21
S		Selvick, John M.	C-1	Sichem Mumbai	IE-2	South Carolina	G-15
S/VM 86	M-12	Selvick, Kimberly	C-1	Sichem New York	IE-2	South Channel	C-7
Sabina	IE-5						

Vessel Name	Fleet #	Vessel Name	Fleet #	Vessel Name	Fleet #	Vessel Name	Fleet #
Spartan	A-8, L-5	Strandja	IN-2	Thunder Cape	C-3	Vancouverborg	IW-2
Spartan II	A-8	Sturgeon	G-19	Timberland	G-7	VanEnkevort, Joyce L.	V-1
Speer, Edgar B.	G-14	Sugar Islander II	E-1	Timesaver II	D-9	Varnebank	IP-4
Spence, John	M-12	Sullivan, Denis	D-7	Timmy A.	R-4	Veler	U-2
Spencer, Sarah	T-3	Sullivans (The)	MU-1	Tina Theresa	IH-7	Vermont	G-15
Spirit of Buffalo	B-14	Sundaisy E	IE-4	Titan	E-9	Versluis, James J.	C-10
Spirit of Chicago	S-15	Sundew	J-2	Tiwala	IS-3	Viateur's Spirit	M-12
Spring	IN-5	Superior	G-15	Tobias	M-12	Victoriaborg	IW-2
Spruceglen	C-2	Susana S	IU-3	Torrent	IN-1	Victoria	II-3
Spuds	R-4	Susan L	S-5	Townsend, Paul H.	I-2	Victorian Princess	V-2
St. Clair	A-6	Susan Michelle	D-1	Tracer	IB-5	Victorious	M-11
St. John, J.S	E-7	Sweezy, R.O.	H-9	Tracy	C-3	Victory	L-15
St. Lawrence II	B-11	Sykes, Wilfred	C-6	Tramper	IB-5	Vigilant I	N-1
St. Marys Cement	S-21			TransHawk	IT-4	Vikingbank	IP-4
St. Marys Cement II	S-21			Transporter	IB-5	Viking I	V-3
St. Marys Challenger	S-2	**T**		Tregurtha, Lee A.	I-5	Virginiaborg	IW-2
St. Marys Conquest	S-2			Tregurtha, Paul R.	I-5	Virginia	G-15
Stacey Dawn	C-21	Tanker II	J-3	Trillum	C-14	Vista King	M-22
Stanyer, D.L.	M-14	Tanner	K-4	Tromso	IO-3	Vista Queen	V-4
Star of Chicago	S-11	Taukamaim	L-10	Tufty	IN-1	Vista Star	V-4
State of Michigan	G-16	Tecumseh	L-14	Tundra	IN-1	Vitosha	IN-2
STC 2004	B-15	Tecumseh II	P-8	Twolan, W.N.	B-12	Vlieborg	IW-2
Ste. Claire	M-10	Tenacious	R-6			Vlistborg	IW-2
Ste. Claire V (The)	A-7	Terry D	C-1	**U-V**		VM/S Hercules	S-20
Steelhead	M-17	Texas	G-15			VM/S Maisonneuve	S-20
Stella Borealis	C-18	Thompson, Joseph H.	U-12	Umiak I	IF-2	VM/S St. Lambert	S-20
Stella Polaris	IT-1	Thompson Jr.,		Umiavut	N-9	Volgaborg	IW-2
Stellaprima	IJ-4	Joseph H.	U-12	Uncle Sam 7	U-1	Voorneborg	IW-2
Sten Aurora	IR-1	Thorco Arctic	IM-2	Undaunted	P-1	Voyageur II	G-9
Sten Bergen	IR-1	Thousand Islander	G-5	Vaasaborg	IW-2	Voyageur	M-22, S-11
Sten Suomi	IR-1	Thousand Islander II	G-5	Vac	N-1		
Sterling Energy	S-23	Thousand Islander III	G-5	Vachon	A-10	**W**	
Stormont	M-12	Thousand Islander IV	G-5	Vale	IL-4		
Straits Express	A-12	Thousand Islander V	G-5	Valerie B.	D-10	Walpole Islander	W-1
Straits of Mackinac II	A-12	Three Rivers	IF-5	Valley Camp	MU-13	Warner, Coloma L.	W-4
		Thunder Bay	C-2				

Cason J. Callaway unloading at Buffington, Ind.. (Gary L. Clark)

Vessel Name	Fleet #	Vessel Name	Fleet #	Vessel Name	Fleet #	Vessel Name	Fleet #
Warner, William L.	W-4	Westcott II, J.W.	J-1	Windy	T-1	Yankee Clipper	V-5
Warner Provider	W-4	Whalen, J.F.	M-14	Winter	IN-5	YM Saturn	IY-2
Washington	G-15, W-5	Wheatley, Christopher	C-11	Wisconsin	G-15, L-6	Yulia	IM-6
Wayward Princess	N-3	Whistler	IP-1	Wolfe Islander III	M-25	Zealand Beatrix	IZ-1
Welcome (The)	S-8	Whitby	M-14	Wolf River	G-11	Zealand Delilah	IZ-1
Welland	D-1	White, H. Lee	A-6	Wyandot	S-8	Zealand Juliana	IZ-1
Wendella	W-6	Whitefish Bay (tug)	U-2	Wyatt M.	M-12	Zeus	M-30, IF-4
Wendella LTD	W-6	Whitefish Bay	C-2	Wyoming	G-15	Zhuang Yuan Ao	IC-11
Wendy Anne	S-17	Wicko	IP-3			Ziemia Cieszynska	IP-3
Wenonah II	M-29	Wigeon	IP-1			Ziemia Lodzka	IP-3
Wenonah	N-7	Willmac	M-14				
Weser	IC-4	Windmill Point	T-12				

X-Y-Z

Yankcanuck	P-8

Experience the Marine Art of Paul C. LaMarre Jr.

www.greatlakesmarineart.com

DATE	NAME	LOCATION / DETAILS

Every year, *Know Your Ships* gets hundreds of photos from readers who hope to see their shots in the next edition. Obviously, there isn't room for

them all. So we've created a gallery of some of these photos on our website. Please visit and enjoy these additional submissions. We also have more than 30 *KYS* videos on the site, as well as historic photo galleries, a tug gallery, a gallery of past cover images, historic stacks and more.

Please visit knowyourships.com

ADVERTISER INDEX *Thank you!*

The information in this book, *current as of March 1, 2015, was obtained from the U.S. Army Corps of Engineers, the U.S. Coast Guard, the Lake Carriers' Association, Lloyd's Register of Shipping, NOAA, Transport Canada, The St. Lawrence Seaway Authority, Internet Ships Register, Shipfax, Tugfax, BoatNerd.com and individual vessel owners / operators.*